Parents in Positive Control

E. Robbins Kimball M.D.

Sea Grape
Press
box 4122
Boca Raton, FL 33429

Published by: Sea Grape Press
box 4122
Boca Raton, FL 33429

Copyright © 1987 E. Robbins Kimball M.D.

Library of Congress Catalog Card Number: 87-091723

All rights reserved. No part of this book may be reproduced or transmitted in any form or by any means, electronic or mechanical, including photocopying, recording or by any information storage and retrieval system, without the written permission of E. Robbins Kimball or Sea Grape Press, except where permitted by law.

Printed in the United States of America

ISBN: 0-9619113-0-1

"Not to conform, not to destroy, but to want to and know how to transform and fulfill."

Nathan Pusey

DEDICATION

To the late Dr. Clifford Grulee for encouragement, Dr. Douglas Buchanan for inspiration, Dr. Herbert Philipsborn for advice, and Alicia my wife for 46 years of patience; also my children, grandchildren and thousands of little patients.

To the Evanston Infant Welfare for financial support and the Dee Fund of the Evanston Hospital for paying for the work of the summer research fellows, namely: Catherine Wilcox, Cynthia Godshalk, Lindsay Wilson, Barbara Bennett, Richard Lussky, Bruce Massel, Mary Ellen Quinlan, Letitia Carlson and Jeffrey McKeever. They prepared the data for the Vogelbach computer at Northwestern University.

To James Mitchell and Leon Zuckerman and the people in the Research Laboratory of the Evanston Hospital. To Gail Blair for her generous art work. To David C. Kimball for criticism and polish and to his brilliant wife Mary Doyle-Kimball for editing. I give my hearty thanks to the above and to many I haven't mentioned who had a part.

CONTENTS

Preface   i

PART I
COMPARTMENTATION

I   JOHNNY WON'T SLEEP AT NIGHT 1
II   WHAT IS COMPARTMENTATION 3
      Definition: 3;   Concept: 3
III   THE WONDER AND GLORY OF CREATION 5
IV   THE PLAYPEN IS ONLY THE FIRST STEP 10
      How to begin compartmentation: 10
V   YOUR CHILD'S CRIB 12
VI   GATES 16
      Gated Room 16;   Strategic Gates: 17
      The Gated Porch: 18;   Fenced Yard: 19
VII   TETHERING 21
      On The Leash 23
VIII   COMPARTMENTATION & NURSERY SCHOOLS 25
IX   HOW TO RECOMPARTMENTIZE 29
      The Three Phases Of Crying 29
X   CASE HISTORIES OF SKIP AND BUZZIE 33
      Power Without Brakes 45
XI   WHAT COMPARTMENTATION CAN DO FOR YOUR CHILD 50
      The Compartmentized Appear to Learn Faster 51
      More Sure of Themselves 52;   More Assertive 52
      The Compartmentized have fewer accidents 53
      They Become Better Students 53
      A Chart To Record Growth and Performance 54
XII   A CLOSER LOOK AT OVERACHIEVEMENT 61
XIII   WHAT CAN COMPARTMENTATION DO FOR PARENTS? 64
      Gives You More Self Esteem 64
      Makes Mothers More Productive 64
      Makes You A Stronger Parent 65;   Makes A Better Marriage 66
      The Golf Widow 66;   Improves Your Sex Life 69

PART II
SUBSTITUTIONS FOR COMPARTMENTATION

XIV   BREAST-FEEDING 73
      Nursing 73;   One Physician's Approach to Breast-feeding 74
      The Value of Breast-feeding 77;   Prenatal Preparations 81
      Hand Expression 82 ; Breast Anatomy and Physiology 86
      The Mind of the Mother 87 Technique of Breast-feeding 88
      First Day of Nursing 89;   Need for Water 93;   Rooming In 93
      Second Day of Nursing 95;   Third Day of Nursing 96
      Excessive Engorgement 97;   The Let Down Reflex 98
      The Fourth Day of Nursing 99;   Failure to Suckle 100
      Failure to Nurse Because of Asphyxia & Concussion   101
      Sore Nipples   102;   Small White Spots on the Nipples   107

XIV	BREAST-FEEDING...................................CONTINUED	
	Jaundice 107; Going Home from the Hospital 108	
	Household Help 109; Fluctuations in the Amount of Breast Milk 111	
	No Schedule, Please 112; The Danger Weeks 113	
	Importance of Fathers: In Breast-feeding 115	
	How Much Should I Socialize While Breast-feeding? 117	
	La Leche League 118; Excessive Flow of Milk 120	
	Caesarian and Breast-feeding 121; Delayed Milk 121	
	Overfeeding of Breast Milk 122	
	How to Increase Your Breast Milk 122	
	Colic 123; The Treatment of Colic 124	
	Nursing Away from Home 126	
	Nursing During Menstruation 127; Refusal of One Breast 127	
	Pulling Away from the Breast 127; Sabotage 128	
	Pumping and Storage of Milk 129	
	The Human Milk Bank 129; The Premature Baby 133	
	Burping 133; How Much Should a Baby Sleep? 134	
	Diarrhea 134; Constipation in the Breast-fed 135	
	Diet of the Mother 135; Breast-feeding Twins and Triplets 135	
	Nipples Burn and Breasts Ache 136; Lumps in the Breast 137	
	Breast Abscess and Plugged Duct 137	
	Controversy in Treatment of Breast Abscess 139	
	Illness in the Mother & Baby Requiring Weaning 141	
	If You Don't Give Solids at Six Months He'll Steal 142	
	Occasional Bottle? 143; Oral Contraceptives & Breast-feeding 144	
	Breast-feeding While Taking Medicine 144	
	Pregnancy and Breast-feeding 144	
	Should I Wean When Pregnant? 145	
	Allergic to Breast Milk 145	
	Breast Milk Too Rich or Too Weak? 145	
	Breast-feeding an Adopted Child 145	
	Adoption Agencies and Breast-feeding 146	
	The Lactator 146; Breast-feeding and Silicone Implants 147	
	How to Prevent Spoiling 147	
	Is the Enjoyment of Breast-feeding Sexual 149	
	Working and Breast-feeding 150; Weaning 151	
	Prolonged Breast-feeding for Allergic Families 153	
XV	VARIATIONS ON A THEME: COMPARTMENTATION	157
	Nurseries 157; No-Man's Land 157; Nannies 158	
XVI	TOYS	159
	Kinds of Toys Do Three- & Four-Year Olds Need 160	
XVII	JEALOUSY	162
XVIII	SOME COMMON QUESTIONS & OBJECTIONS CONCERNING COMPARTMENTATION	165
XIX	TOILET TRAINING	171
XX	THE SINGLE PARENT & COMPARTMENTATION	173
XXI	DAY CARE CENTERS	179
XXII	CAN COMPARTMENTATION BE OVERDONE	186
XXIII	FURTHER OBSERVATIONS OF MOTHERS	188
XXIV	AFFECTION, AUTHORITY, AND APPROVAL	190
EPILOGUE		192

Preface

The human's ability to reason probably begins at eight with an abstract ethical sense and improves as he or she reaches adulthood. In some people it continues into old age. This ability to reason has tremendous variability. We don't know how much is inherited and how much comes from the environment. As parents, perhaps it is better that we don't know, but that is little consolation.

The philosophies and theories of child rearing span a wide range. At one end is the concept of strict discipline; at the other, complete self demand. Should you as a parent tell your child what to do because you know what is best for him? Or should you let him do what he wants so as not to stifle his initiative? These extremes have been in conflict for a long time. The good work in growth and development started by Dr. Arnold Gesell in 1911 has gathered the extremes toward center. Even so, we do not know enough about how much to expect from children, especially the young ones.

Often we expect too much for whatever insecure reasons, and the child objects to the point where his objections become well-organized techniques of resistance and self-indulgent habits of disobedience. Or perhaps we give too much too soon and squelch the hunger and curiosity to learn.

At the other end of the spectrum, there are those who expect and give so little that the infant can lose all will to survive. Perhaps to perish, or another to discover an inner strength, or to be unprepared when confronted with society's great demands. There is no such thing as benign neglect.

The purpose of this book is to attempt to give parents, single or married, a blueprint for successfully dealing with their pre-school children. It outlines much of what to expect in each stage of growth and development. Appropriate vehicles of control are offered to channel children's energy into experiences which are positive for both mother and her offspring as well as balancing the dependent/independent feelings of this very sensitive parent and child relationship. The risk is too great to not recognize this balance and strive for a manageable solution. In your arms is the future.

My patients and their parents may recognize themselves in my many stereotyped examples. Their names and incidents have been altered to maintain doctor-patient confidentiality.

In general the pronoun *he* refers to both sexes.

E. Robbins Kimball M.D.
14750 Beach Boulevard, # 23
Jacksonville, FL 32250

PART I
COMPARTMENTATION
CHAPTER I
JOHNNIE WON'T SLEEP AT NIGHT

"Johnnie wakes up every night screaming. Gets us both up. One of us has to rock him back to sleep. Six months ago my wife took our year-old son to visit her folks in New York. She took Johnnie to her old pediatrician. He said Johnnie should be weaned. 'When the baby is one year old, that is enough breast-feeding!'"

"Johnnie has been waking up every night since he was weaned. The La Leche League recommends letting the baby decide when to stop breast-feeding. He slept beautifully all night long while breast-feeding."

"Getting up every night is driving us both crazy. I'm tired all the time. It's hard to function at the office. I can't take it anymore. We need something to make this kid sleep."

With little variation, I've heard this complaint every day for 42 years. I gave Johnnie my routine modified Gesell developmental test[1] while he sat

---

[1] Dr. Arnold Lucius Gesell (1880-1961) was to the pre-school child what the Frenchman Alfred Binet (1857-1911) was to the school child. Before the turn of the century, the French were struggling with organizing general public tax supported education. Most French children had been learning the three "R's" privately. The school organizers asked Binet what to teach at this age. Binet said he didn't know, but collected large groups of children of various school age and gave them a list of questions which became used worldwide as the Binet Test. It was the beginning of the I.Q. concept that was used widely for the soldiers in WWI.

In 1911 Gesell began the same type of testing of infants and toddlers in an orphanage in Minnesota.

In the 1920's Dr. Milton C. Winternitz, Dean of Yale University School of Medicine, raised many millions of dollars and created the Institute of Human Relations with Gesell as the chief researcher in child development. Gesell wrote prolifically and documented his observations with motion pictures. The Gesell Development Scale is used worldwide - with and without modifications. Physicians and scientists, standing on Gesell's shoulders, are still serving the public and doing research at Yale at what is now called The Gesell Institute of Child Development.

My modification of the Gesell tests is the chart entitled: *A Chart to Record Growth and Performance*. There are examples of a typical chart on pages 58-60. They are four-page forms with the front cover giving the family and immunization records. Order from the publisher in hundred unit quantities. They are printed in two inks for easy use. Ask your doctor to order some and chart your child's progress. An instructional video will soon be available and is recommended for professional use. See order form on back page.

When I refer to the Gesell test, I mean my modification which is on his mother's lap. At eighteen months he did not pile three blocks. He did not put the blocks into the cup which they usually do when one year old. He knew that the red pill was under the cup, but was "afraid" to pick up the cup to get the pill (an eleven month test). In short Johnnie showed the typical non-adaptability associated with not spending any time in a playpen or gated room.

His parents had given up the playpen on Johnnie's first birthday. "He had outgrown it," they said.

I explained that for Johnnie, having the run of their apartment all his waking hours was like being the president of two companies while one is on strike.

Johnnie can't sleep; he has nightmares. Most of the time, lower level corporate employees are not the ones who have trouble sleeping. It is usually the president of the company who can't sleep. For Johnnie the run of five rooms is too much for his 18 month old mind. He's too young to be president.

"Put him back in the playpen. Buy some gates. Make one room childproof and put a gate on the door. Let him cry five minutes in the playpen, pick him up, kiss him and put him in the gated room. Let him cry five more minutes, kiss him and put him back in the playpen. Shift him every five minutes. Do this at least ten times. After you have interrupted his crying every five minutes for one hour, let him out of the playpen. The next morning, and regularly thereafter, put him back in, but interrupt his crying every five minutes for ten times. By the fourth day he will play either in the playpen or the gated room for two to four hours a day," -- this is the prescription I gave Johnnie's parents.

I saw Johnnie a month later. Johnnie was now 19 months old. He piled four blocks which is on a par with the Gesell test for 21 months. In 30 days Johnnie had adjusted to his new routine and his behavior had gone from ten months to 21 months.

Johnnie's father summed it up this way: "As soon as he was back in the playpen he slept the night. It's remarkable that such a simple solution works so well."

---

explained in Chapter XI.

CHAPTER II
WHAT IS COMPARTMENTATION?

Definition:

In the *Random House Dictionary of the English Language* compartmentation is the subdivision of the hull of a ship into water tight compartments. The more widely used word compartmentalize often refers to categories as well as compartments, therefore compartmentation, as I use it connotes a thoroughness in the separation of the pre-school child world from the adult world for half his or her waking hours. The practice of compartmentation involves keeping your child in a safe environment (crib, playpen, gated room, gated areas and/or fenced yard or tethering) for two to four hours a day.

Concept:

The concept of compartmentation is not new in nature. It begins with the creation of life. After the sperm unites with the ovum, the fertilized egg burrows into the wall of the uterus where it is compartmentized from the rest of the body until it weighs about seven pounds.

When human babies are born they need more prolonged protection than any other animal. Babies are cradled in their mother's arms to protect them from their new environment. This is a type of compartmentation. Everybody knows that touching and rocking is an absolute necessity to normal growth and development. While mother rests, she puts her baby in a safe place -- a crib, playpen or some other form of compartmentation. Unlike many newborn animals, human babies cannot protect themselves. Mothers have to protect them from all dangers for a long time. When mothers are not holding their babies, they are compartmentizing them away from dangers. After babies have learned to walk, they are even more likely to destroy themselves because they have developed power without brakes or steering.

In the dwellings of primitive peoples, there are fewer things that are valuable or dangerous to small children. Without electricity, books, and other adult valuables, there are few "no, nos" for the toddler. There is less frustration when the child is young. The parents in these primitive cultures do not understand why more civilized parents spank their toddlers. Those who compartmentize don't have to spank. Primitive cultures have strapped the infants on to the backs of mothers and carried them everywhere. This is a form of compartmentation, similar in effect to the pouch of the kangaroo.

After animals were domesticated and the wheel was invented, life became more complicated. Yet great-great-grandmother had other hands to help her. Usually there was an aunt or grandmother living with her in her household. Help was inexpensive and easily found. These mothers used playpens, gates and fenced yards without thinking about compartmentation as such. They had fewer conveniences and fewer dangers for small children.

Now young people set up housekeeping independently with many conveniences and all kinds of dangers. Mother's helpers are too expensive for most modern young couples. Compartmentation is a necessity. Today household accidents are the greatest cause for hospital visits in children. The two-year-old does not understand that a bottle of aspirin is different from candy. He or she also does not understand that climbing his or her grandfather's floor to ceiling bookcases is different from climbing the slides in the park. Children do not understand the modern world of electricity and chemicals.

Children have the ability to move around and get into trouble when they are one year old. It is not until they are four that they can stop at verbal commands and suppress their insatiable curiosity.

At four the electricity is traveling from one neuron to another in the child's brain sufficiently for the child to be aware of, but still not fully understand, the concept of "mine and thine."

The function of the pre-schooler's mind is not unlike the college student inebriate, who knows and can remember but seems not to be able to suppress an action. The electricity passing through the "wires" (nerves) connecting his billions of "batteries" (neurons) gets stopped at the synapses (those delicate filamentous connections between the nerves) because they are bathed in alcohol. In children the synapses are fine; it is the wires that are uncovered and unfortunately some remain so until they are 25 years old. Pre-school children need to be deliberately separated from the modern adult world for part of their waking hours. Perhaps that is why a cynical father of four boys told me that his children should be kept in a barrel and fed through the bung until eight.

CHAPTER III

THE WONDER AND GLORY OF CREATION

"O Lord, our Lord, how excellent is thy name in all the earth: who hast set thy wonder and glory above the heavens." PSALMS 8:1

Wonder was found, wet with amniotic fluid and partially covered with fetal membranes in the middle of the barn floor, having been kicked through the boards of the box stall. Her mother Eva, had been a race horse and was the granddaughter of one of the greatest trotters of all time.

Our mother first saw Eva at the race track of a county fair. Eva trotted well as long as she remained calm, but the slightest excitement made her break and run. Then she had to be pulled down and slowed until she was trotting again. This happened with such increasing frequency, her owner became completely disgusted. But Eva's beautiful head, arched neck, and lively step appealed to mother, and it was not long before a sharp horse purchase was made at an insultingly low price, considering Eva's pedigree.

So Eva came home and was ridden by us children. Soon it was found that Eva had a long trot that covered much distance but required accurate posting for comfort. Then, with scarcely any urging, she broke into an easy run that was delightfully fast. Eva became dearly loved by all the family, and she seemed happy in her new home. She pulled the hayrake and the sleigh, but mostly she was ridden. She was always free. She was faster than any of the other horses and very cooperative when ridden by someone not afraid of her -- usually a member of the family. But in any strange situation she became excited and no one could reason with her. Then she could be controlled only by force. Often she threw her rider, unless he or she could demonstrate superiority. Friends were always amazed by Eva's docility when she was ridden by a member of the family. This trait in Eva persisted through two motherhoods and into her old age. This was Wonder's mother, who could never be controlled by gentleness, only by force.

Wonder's father was a thoroughbred who five years previously had been retired to stud after an inconspicuous career. He was even more spirited than Eva and he had a bad disposition. He once dragged his keeper around by biting his thigh, yet he was handsome as well as powerful.

Wonder lay in a puddle of amniotic fluid, holding her head high. breathing freely the cool, early spring air. Her mother stood back with her head in the farthermost corner of the stall. Having kicked her offspring through the wooden slats of the stall, she paid little attention to the children who were wiping Wonder dry. In a few minutes the filly stood, and it was then that she got her name. Mother came into the barn and beheld the stilt-legged bay, who was free from any white mark. As the filly walked shakily, mother exclaimed, "Wonder and glory of creation." Thus the first-born was called Wonder, and later, the second-born, was called Glory.

Wonder was led back into the stall with her mother, and an attempt was made to help Wonder suckle; but her mother squealed and kicked her away. Then two men held Eva and father spoke harshly to her, which had always worked before; but she reared and kicked so violently that we feared she might injure her foal. So Wonder was put in a stall by herself. The next day another attempt was made to have Wonder suckle, but her mother would not allow it.

Men, women and children from the neighboring farms came to see Wonder, and still another attempt was made to have Wonder get something to drink from her mother. But Eva still kicked her away. One man twisted Eva's upper lip to distract her; two men braced themselves on each side of Eva. Father held Wonder in his arms and guided the eager colt to her mother's udder. With a squeal, Eva threw herself on her back and flailed her legs. That settled it. No further attempts were made to induce Eva to nurse her baby. A formula of one-third evaporated milk, two thirds boiled water, and five percent sugar was mixed and put into an eight ounce nursing bottle with a lamb's nursing nipple. Wonder drank it and went to sleep.

Wonder grew and developed rapidly. When she was only two weeks old, we children made a small halter for her and led her around. Wonder always followed willingly. The humans fed her and were her friends; and the horses were not. Whenever she came near her mother and the other horses, they all wheeled and kicked her. Fortunately, she was quick enough not to get hurt and wise enough to stay away.

The children led Wonder at a walk and at a trot but were not allowed to gallop her for fear it might excite her too much. When Wonder was only a few weeks old she could be led easily. Then we noticed that she always avoided the puddles. The children laughed and exclaimed, "Wonder doesn't want to get her feet wet." Mother, a skilled lover of horses, attempted to lead Wonder through one of the larger puddles; but Wonder balked and reared to avoid getting her feet wet. After every rain, a deliberate attempt was made to lead Wonder through a puddle. She jumped or went around the small ones and balked completely at the big ones. We children spent much time trying to coax her out of this balky trait, but to no avail. She did not want to get her feet wet.

When we were in school, Wonder had to be turned out with the other horses. It was then that she seemed pitiful. She was a small spindly filly walking on long, spindly legs. She always kept her distance from the other horses. If she didn't they all, including her mother, rushed at her with ears lain back and teeth showing and wheeled and kicked.

Wonder's desire to be in the company of humans increased with age, long after she had outgrown the nursing bottle. The older she got, the more plaintive became her whinny to remain with the humans. The company of the other horses was her second choice, and she could not bear to be alone.

When I was home, I allowed her to have the run of the farm. We tried to teach her not to walk through the sprouting garden and to refrain from eating the tender corn shoots, but she did not understand such talk. Even the violent shouts and the dirt balls that were thrown caused only temporary obedience. As soon as our backs were turned, she went into the garden again. When we went to school, she was put in the pasture with the other horses. When we were out of school, we turned her loose and did what we could to keep her out of the garden.

During summer vacation, Wonder was out of the pasture more than she was in it. The attempts to save the crops were more emphatic in an effort to be successful and more frustrating because they failed. And when she was pastured by herself or with the other horses her whinny became even more unendurable. Finally we prevailed upon father and mother to let her loose for the summer. Wonder had won. Father said, "After all, we have planted more corn and vegetables than we can use. Let Wonder eat some of them." Throughout the summer she usually spent most of her time following one of us over the farm. She ate generously from the garden. She became a little queen. We took her into the kitchen and once into the living room, but mother discouraged this practice. Wonder became so intimate with us that when any of us playfully slapped her on the rump, instead of jumping like most colts do, she just turned her head slowly and looked. It made father wonder how she would respond to the riding crop when she was grown.

Wonder liked to tease. In the summer Wonder usually slept with the other horses in the pasture or barnyard. But after the fall frosts, it was too cold to sleep out of doors. Wonder was reluctant to go to bed in a stall in the barn before dark. Because of my homework I tried to get Wonder to bed before dark. I walked out to lead her to the barn; she walked in the opposite direction. I trotted and she trotted -- just ahead. I ran and she kept ahead of me. When I walked, she walked. I tried for ten minutes but I could not catch her. Usually when I was not trying to put her in the barn she followed me all over the farm.

I went into the house and began my homework. It became very dark and she was alone. I let her whinny for about fifteen minutes and then I went out to her. She ran to me immediately and nuzzled me affectionately. When I turned to walk to the barn, she followed meekly.

Like the humans who tease but don't like to be teased; Wonder did not like to be teased. Sometimes the younger children crowded her as she passed through the doorways in the house. They pulled her tail or pinched her flank. She lay back her ears in response; but that was all. Yet gradually she developed a dislike for boys, who were not members of the family. Whenever one visited the farm, she lay back her ears and bared her teeth. One day she chased a boy of eleven completely out of the yard.

The second summer she still roamed the farm and was every- one's pet. I had my appendix removed, and I spent my convalescence reading on the lawn. Wonder grazed on the lawn beside me. Once she lay down at my feet like a large dog, and I put my feet on her flank while she dozed.

The third summer she was bridled and carried my sister around on her back while one of us led her. She seemed to enjoy this and never was frightened unless someone tried to make her go through water.

By the fourth summer, Wonder weighed half a ton and could no longer be brought into the house. She spent most of her time in the pasture with the other horses whose company she now preferred. She was no longer afraid of them. On the contrary, they were afraid of her. Every kick and bite she had received in her youth, she now repaid doubly. Even Major, the big black gelding, ran from her. She had the speed and strength to handle them all, and she thoroughly enjoyed her new power.

Wonder still balked if she couldn't jump over or go around every puddle. Once she was ridden at a full gallop toward a wide brook. When she saw that she could not jump it, she slid on her haunches to a stop. In every other way, she turned out to be a very satisfactory horse. Wonder was finally sold to a great horse lover, a woman who didn't try to make her get her feet wet.

Glory was Eva's second colt. Like Wonder, she was born at night and found in the morning. She was a beautiful chestnut with three white stockings and a blaze. Wobbling on stilts, Glory was guided to her mother's udder while her mother was haltered and held. Eva squealed a little but submitted. Soon Glory suckled normally and ran daintily at her mother's side. Eva protected her from all dangers, including the jealousy of Wonder and the other horses.

Unlike Wonder, Glory preferred the company of her mother and the other horses. She was never brought into the house. She was never teased and never had to be driven out of the garden. Glory was handled gently from an early age. She grew and flourished. At the state fair that fall, she and her mother took first prize as the best mare and foal. When she was a few weeks old, she was haltered and led, but for only a short time. Unlike Wonder, she was never allowed to develop a technique of disobedience against her trainers. At the age of eighteen months Glory was saddled for the first time. Father, standing beside her, pointed to a loose girth. Glory jumped sideways and knocked me down while I was standing on the other side. Then she stood and trembled. When I picked myself up I patted her and she stopped trembling. There was no need for punishment, only care that she was not pushed to the point of learning how to resist.

At two, Glory was ridden, it was only after she had been fondled, leaned on, and lain on. Finally my sister, the lightest in the family, mounted while I led her around. It was such a gradual process that Glory never actually learned how to resist. From her quick responses and her spirit we knew she certainly had the hereditary background to resist.

Unlike Wonder, Glory was loved both by her mother and humans. Even though Wonder was not loved or suckled by her mother, she received and returned a great deal of love in the human family, considerably more than the average horse. Yet her sister, Glory, and her younger half-sister and half-brother would gallop through water and were not as arrogant with the other horses. Why the difference? Was it because Wonder was not suckled and never received her own mother's love? Our family had never had the experience of rearing a colt. It was also completely new to Eva.

An experienced horse breeder said that if Wonder had spent more time with the horses in the pasture, as Glory had, she would have learned not to object to puddles. Wonder would have followed the other horses through water without thinking about it. The free run of the farm necessitated her receiving many "no, nos",which she learned to resist. And the teasing spoiled some of the trainer-trainee relationships. She became so familiar with humans that she lost respect for them. In some areas, disobedience became habitual.

The adult horse has about the same lack of appreciation of "mine and thine" as that of the 18-month old human. The "high school horse" (the smart circus performer) seems to be about like a 20-month old human in thinking ability. The smart horse does not have, and never will have, enough neurons to act any older than the human toddler who babbles disconnected words. The billions of neurons that the human received before his mother was eight weeks pregnant do not function completely until the human is 25 years old. Then the neurons become functionally connected (myelination of the nerve fibers.) Thus the 20-month old infant has about the same functional intelligence as the smart grown up horse.

If the horse trainer tried to teach the horse "mine and thine" in the same way that the average parent tries to teach his toddler, the horse would develop techniques of resistance and habits of disobedience that would last a life time. The growth of intelligence in the human child is so explosive that he/she outgrows those protective techniques of resistance that he develops from inappropriate handling. Or does he/she remember them in the subconscious?

CHAPTER IV

THE PLAYPEN IS ONLY THE FIRST STEP

How to begin compartmentation:

Compartmentation begins with the playpen. Before your baby learns to cruise, put him or her into the playpen. If you put your child in the playpen after breakfast, when the stomach is full, his blood sugar is up, and he hasn't had free run then he won't cry. Don't even take time to wash the cereal off his face. You can do that better when he's in the playpen. If you put the child down on the floor, while you are rinsing the dishes, then he will cry when you put him in the playpen. Of course children prefer to explore the kitchen with you chasing them.

Children should spend about one-half of their waking hours in the playpen -- about four hours a day. Some parents find two hours a day sufficient. For another four hours you are feeding, bathing, changing, playing and chasing them while they crawl about the house. The rest of the time they are sleeping.

The playpen must be clean and empty to be effective. If it is messy and full of toys, the baby cannot move around and he or she will cry. If the playpen is empty you can then hand the baby one toy to concentrate on. When the baby is tired of the first toy, give him or her a second. When you give the child the third toy, remove the first. By the rotation of three or four toys you prolong your child's ability to concentrate. When presenting the new and taking away the discarded, simultaneously you make a smaller number of toys do. Also you increase the hunger to acquire.

Even though your baby accepts the playpen at first, do not overdo it. Let him get used to it gradually. If he is tired or sick, he will resent being left too long in any one place. At first, you should not keep your child in the playpen for more than one hour without interruption. Move him from the playpen to the highchair, to the crib. Cuddle him during the moves.

Move the playpen from room to room. Some babies are quiet only when you are in the same room. Move the playpen into a room where you can work. Put it near a window so that your child can look out or near a mirror where he can see another baby.

In fine weather move the playpen out of doors. Your young baby will be amused for an hour watching the leaves blow, the birds fly, and older children play. The location of the playpen has a lot to do with how your baby feels about staying in it. *It is also important to compartmentize at the same time every day.*

Pick a playpen that is big enough to allow your baby to practice rolling, crawling, and stepping. Choose a playpen that is sturdily built. The square playpens with wooden bars are best. Babies learn to climb the sides of the nylon mesh playpens.

Reinforce the bottom with a piece of plywood as soon as you buy it.

Your baby will not like the playpen when the floor sags, and they all do when the baby gets heavier. A playpen that folds easily, or one on wheels, is easy to move about the house. The crib-playpen is good for vacations and weekends away from home.

A waterproof pad to cover the floor is useful when your baby is small. It is important to be able to leave the baby's diaper off during the playpen time when he or she has a diaper rash.

As your baby grows older and more aggressive, she will cry to be taken out because she is bored. She is becoming more venturesome and wants to widen her horizons. So, you must have an alternate area in which to compartmentize your baby. You must child proof a room and put a gate on it. (The gated room is explained in detail in CHAPTER VI.) After she cries five minutes in the playpen, pick her up and kiss her and put her in the room with a gate. When she cries in the gated room for five minutes, kiss her and put her back in the playpen.

By moving your child back and forth, you can extend the period of compartmentation to the nearly ideal four hours a day. It is usually impossible and not worth trying to have the four hours all at once. Break up the time: two or three hours after breakfast, some indoors and some out. After the nap you can compartmentize for an hour or so. When your spouse comes home, he can take the baby out and play. A variety of experiences keeps a baby happy.

At the end of the day it is a good idea for one of you to take the baby while the other one is preparing dinner. Toddlers thrive on both extremes: Free run with parents chasing them and compartmentation in a playpen -- about four hours of each. Be consistent and persistent.

You can compartmentize, in even a one-room apartment, by tethering. Attach a screw and eye to the woodwork near the floor and tie a six to ten foot rope to it and to your child's belt.

If there are only two rooms in your apartment, you can put a gate between the rooms and make one of them child proof. The other room can contain all the adult gadgets, cooking facilities, books, study and writing materials.

It is unfortunate that the concept of compartmentation is not better understood by the architects who design housing facilities for students, interns, instructors, and other hard-working young couples who are just getting started. I know of many housing projects where no provision is made for the pre-school child inside or outside. It is like having a horse without a corral.

CHAPTER V
YOUR CHILD'S CRIB

"Move over" whispered Skip to his mother in the wee hours of the morning. When he had gone to his father's side of the bed, he had been ordered back to his own bed. Neither his mother or father liked their sleep being disturbed. Father especially felt tired the next day in his competitive activities. Mother also felt it, but endured it with more grace. Usually mother was too sleepy to resist. Also she enjoyed cuddling him. Once he was where he wanted to be Skip went to sleep immediately. He had a delightful smile in the morning.

Skip's bed was the usual six year crib.[1] It's sides measured 24 inches -- 20 inches above the mattress. At two years Skip could climb up the 20 inch side, swing his leg over the top and let himself down to the floor like a monkey. But he could not climb back into bed.

Skip's mother spoke to Buzzie's mother about her problem. Buzzie was also two years old. Buzzie's mother told her that when Buzzie was able to climb out of the six year crib, they bought a junior bed. It had low sides on it to keep Buzzie from rolling out of it in his sleep. Buzzie could climb in and out of the junior bed at will. When Buzzie came into their room at night his father ordered him back to bed. If he didn't obey his father carried him back. If he got out again, his father spanked him.

Buzzie became afraid to get out of bed. When he screamed out in the night from a bad dream his mother went in to him and cuddled him until he went back to sleep.

Some parents try tying the bedroom door shut. The child care books which recommend this technique say children fall asleep on the floor. Other mothers, who breast-feed their children, through the toddler age like to sleep with their children in bed with them. These are relaxed women who devoted their lives completely to their children. They are usually calm in temperament. Their husbands are also. One father, a lawyer however, told me that three small children, his wife, and two big dogs in even a king size bed was too much. He was so tired one morning that he argued on the wrong side of an important case.

Career women, or those heavily involved in community work have the same complaints -- they don't want their whole family sleeping in the master bedroom. Mothers who remain at home can sometimes go back to

---

[1] The six year-old's crib is built big enough and strong enough for a child to sleep in until the age of six. Unfortunately 90% of American children are moved out of the six-year crib when they can climb over the 24-inch side at about 2 years of age. They can get out of this crib, but they cannot get back into it. So they are moved into a "Junior bed" which is like a small twin bed which they can get in and out of at will. Frequently they are kept in the junior beds by spanking or threats of same.

bed if their children go to nursery school. Yet some of them have indicated that having any children in their beds is a sure way to ruin their sex lives.

When Skip's mother called me and told me that Skip was starting to get out of bed every night, I told her to have a carpenter come in and make an extension to the sides of the crib so that it measures 48 inches above the mattress. Most six year cribs have 24 inch sides that measure 20 inches above the mattress. An agile two year old can climb out. Some two year olds can climb out of the cribs with 48 inch sides. In children's hospitals the cribs are 48 inches high but they put a net over the top which is tied down so that the "monkey climbers" cannot get out, fall, and fracture their skulls. Unfortunately hospital beds are not available in the eighties for retail purchases. Also they are very expensive.

Have a carpenter make a 30 inch extension to the sides of the crib. Use wood 1/2" X 2" for the corners and 1/4" or 3/8" X 1 1/2" slats running horizontally for the sides and the ends. The slats should be no more than 2 1/2 inches apart so that the child cannot get his head stuck and choke.

Skip's father knew a fireman who, on his days off, did carpentry work. He made an extension so when the sides were pulled up they were 52" tall -- 48 inches above the mattress. (See diagram of THE BEAR CAGE.)

Two weeks later Skip's mother again found Skip in bed with her in the morning. He had learned how to climb over the 48" side without hurting himself.

"You forgot to put the lid on the crib," Skip's father told the carpenter.

After the crib was completed according to the diagram Skip did not want to go in it when his father was putting him to bed.

"You're a bear aren't you?"

"Yes," Skip said; he had recently visited the zoo.

"Bears get in their cages."

So Skip got into the BEAR CAGE.

Father turned out the light. Skip wanted a drink of water. Father went to the bathroom and got a glass of water but he didn't turn on the light.

Skip took only two swallows andthen wanted to tinkle.

"You just have!" but his father untied the side let it down and took him to the bathroom. He did nothing. Still in the dark father carried him back to bed and pulled up the side and tied it. Then Skip wanted another drink.

"You just had a drink!"

Patting him through the bars he began to rub his back while saying his prayers in unison with Skip.

While Skip lay on his stomach his father continued to rub his back gently. After a few moments he tiptoed out of the bedroom. Skip called out again saying that he had "to tinkle."

"You already have!"

His father sat on the floor and very gently again rubbed his back. Then in a soft monotone he told how "tired little boy blue got walking home from school. He thought that the path across the field would never end. Then there was the walk through the woods. Then another field with hay stacks in it. He slowly walked around the nearest stack. He never felt so tired. He found a soft place and sat down at the edge of the stack. He leaned back against the sweet smelling hay. He watched the white fluffy clouds pass blotting out the sun. Before he knew it he was asleep.

Before his father had finished this story Skip was asleep.

"Sweet dreams" father whispered gently. Then a few moments later he tiptoed out of the room.

Note how Skip's father handled, each individual disappointment to the child in going to bed, one at a time. He turned off the light. In the dark room he gave a drink of water. He even untied the side of the crib and took him to the bathroom in the dark. He took no steps backwards. The disappointment of separation came one at a time. He did not turn off the light and leave the room at the same time.

Compartmentation is not recommended to parents who have emotional problems which affect their decision making. These types of people need professional help with child rearing.

While our two sons were sleeping in the "bear cage", there was much criticism from friends and from a few professionals. Some thought it cruel. One neighbor, who had a noncompartmentized daughter told me that she thought that the bear cage was dangerous.

"There might be a fire and the child could not get out," she said.

In all the reports that I have read where small children had perished in a fire; smoke inhalation or the rapid spread of fire resulted in the entrapment rather than compartmentation. Usually the children had been left alone without sitters when the fire started. In the eighties such neglectful guardians are indicted for child abuse.

Several psychiatrists have criticized Dr. B.F. Skinner for keeping his second daughter in the "Skinner Box"[2] for sleeping and half her waking

---

[2] Dr. Burrhas Frederic Skinner, the prestigious professor of psychology at Harvard University, is the father of behavior modification. He designed and built the famous "Skinner box" for his daughter. It was glassed with shades, air conditioned, and had disposable paper sheets that could be changed by pressing a button. No diapers. She slept in "the box." Then for half her waking hours, she played in "the box" between being taken out for walks and play indoors and out. Despite much criticism his daughter and his friends children, who used "the box" grew up to be well adjusted adults.

Dr. Skinner believes, "More control instead of less control is necessary in child rearing. The 'free human spirit' is a myth that parents and teachers must discard before they can create a climate in which their children will overachieve. Parents and educators must learn more about growth to make intelligently controlled environments."

Dr. Skinner agrees with compartmentation, but modestly states that he has not kept longitudinal records.

hours during the day. She is now grown and the mother of three. Both she and her many friends have used the "Skinner Box" very successfully.

Of the techniques for compartmentation the "bear cage" has taken the brunt of the criticism. Probably it has been partly aesthetic.

One of my smart fathers of six used the bear cage for five of his younger children. He lashed a pipe to each corner of the usual six year crib so that the top of each pipe was 48 inches above the mattress. Then using chicken wire he made the cover. Despite its makeshift look it was very effective. Two became honor students and mothers, one a scientist who recently married. The two boys became lawyers. One of the daughters became a 100,000 dollar a year corporate executive after graduating from the Wharton School of Business. While this independent thinking father was using the "bear cage" made of chicken wire, he received much criticism similar to the criticism that was levied on my other patients using chicken wire to heighten the front porch railings and the back yard fences.

WARNING:

Many years ago two tragedies occurred by compartmentizing in the usual crib with 24 inch sides. One two-year old was tethered by a harness. He climbed out. Another got his head caught between the railing and the net tied over the top of the crib to keep him in. Both two-year olds literally hanged themselves. Eventually parents will not be able to buy cribs with sides that are only 24 inches high. Only cribs with 50 inch sides with lids, like in hospitals, will be available.

In compartmentizing it is important to have a crib that a toddler can not get out of, and the sides and lid high enough so that the child can walk around in it without bumping his head.

Another WARNING:

I don't like closed doors when using techniques of compartmentation. As a parent you should be able to see and hear your pre-school child at all times. Also no child should be allowed to cry for more than five minutes without trying to find out why he or she is crying.

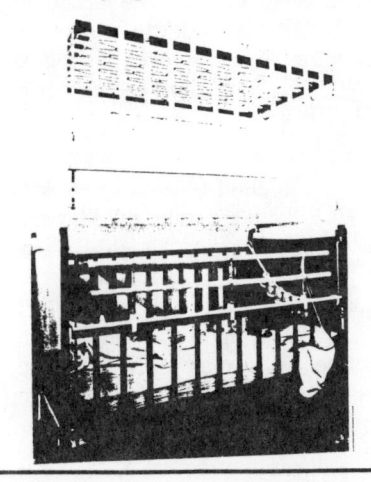

CHAPTER VI
GATES

Before your child becomes bored with the playpen and is old enough to climb out of it, prepare a gated playroom. Sit down with your spouse and decide which room you are going to make childproof. Choose a room that is bright and pleasant. It is nice if the child can look out a window. You must be able to see, hear, and talk to your child while he or she is in the gated room.

The room must be absolutely safe. Remove the standing lamps and insert plastic plugs into the electrical outlets. These can be purchased inexpensively at the hardware store. Chests of drawers must be removed, locked, or emptied of adult valuables. Some of my parents have put a bar right down through the handle of every drawer and then padlocked the bar. If you have chosen an upstairs room, make sure that the window screens are strong and fastened securely. Remove the chairs that your child could climb on and fall from or that may tip over.

The room must be childproof so that you don't have to put restrictions on your child while he is in it. Don't put your child in his playroom and then expect him *not* to open drawers. That is not compartmentation. You should never have to say *"no"* to your child while he is in the gated room.

When your child gets bored in the gated room, pick her up and kiss her and put her into the playpen. Move the playpen into the kitchen so that she is near you and you can talk to her while you do your work before you take her out of doors. It is much better to put the child into the playpen when she is tired of her room than to let her run loose. Going back into the playpen for a little while makes her appreciate the gated room. Don't put your playpen away just because the child spends more time in the gated room. If your child can climb over the gate, put another gate above it.

One very resourceful father installed a screen door at the entrance to one room. This is not as difficult as it sounds. The regular door can be taken off and the screen door substituted. When your children get bigger, the regular door can be put back on. Do not compartmentize your child behind a solid door. He or she would feel shut off from the world. Even a solid Dutch half-door is not as good as a gate or a screen door.

Remember that you only compartmentize a child for half his waking hours. During the other half he will learn that there are some rules he must observe. During this time he can learn about objects which can't be included in his playpen, gated room, or fenced yard. Constant crawling and running free, all over the house all his waking hours, where he is exposed to many more *"nos"* than he can understand; is like going to class all day long instead of experiencing a balance between the classroom, exercise, recreation and study. Just as an adult needs some time away from learning so does the child.

STRATEGIC GATES

When your child outgrows the gated room, you can expand the play area by using a multiple gate system. Or you can use strategic gates as a substitute for the gated room if you cannot childproof a whole room. A system of gates will enable you to compartmentize longer.

The play area might include the child's bedroom and a hall. You could have gates at the doors of other rooms that lead into the hall. Then the child would be able to play in his or her room and run out into the hall. He or she would be kept free from dangers by the various gates. Often this arrangement is more agreeable than a gated room to the child. It usually takes about four gates to compartmentize the average home. You might have a gate at the foot of the stairs or at the head of the stairs. Downstairs you should gate off the kitchen, the living room, or any area where there are many adult possessions.

In addition to the strategic gates, it is wise to have small hooks at the top of the doors. Then you can hook shut the closets and rooms you don't want him to enter without supervision. If you are renting you will have to cover up the holes with putty before you move but the effects on your child's development will be worth the extra work.

Let me emphasize again that all areas where the child plays alone, must be childproof. You must not leave medicines or cleaning solutions around. Small objects such as shelled nuts are very dangerous to children under five. It is easy for a small child to aspirate a small object into each bronchial tube and block off both lungs. So, be sure you put away the nuts right after the guests leave. Rooms in which your children play should be stripped. If you leave crayons, they will mark the walls. A blackboard and chalk are good for the playroom.

You must keep the toddler out of the bathroom. The toilet bowl is particularly fascinating to the two-year-old. He loves to put towels and other articles into it and then flush it. Some two-year-olds will take a small stool, climb up to the sink, and turn on the water. This can make a flood. If you cannot have a gate across the bathroom door, then you should hook the door shut. A small child should not go to the bathroom unless you are with him, even after he or she is toilet trained. He should use a little pottie in another room if you don't have time to supervise him in the bathroom.

If you cannot childproof your living room, you should keep your child out of there too. Two-year-olds love to tear up books, sales reports, and unread Sunday papers.

It is important to have a gate at the foot of the stairs to keep your toddler from climbing up the stairs and falling down. Also have a gate at the head of the stairs to keep him from falling. Your child can play upstairs while you are making the beds, taking a nap or doing paperwork. You must also have a gate at the head of the basement stairs and a hook on the back door so that your toddler can't go outside without your knowing it.

Many parents have made their basements childproof. If you have a recreation room in the basement, you must be sure that it is childproof if the children are to use it without supervision. The record player and valuable records must be put out of the way. The laundry and workshop areas and housekeeping chemicals must not be accessible to your child.

Childproof areas do not have to be fancy. One of my Infant Welfare mothers was extremely resourceful. She lived in an apartment and to support her family, she did laundry for her neighbors in the basement. She cleaned out a coal bin, wall papered it, and put a gate on it for her small children. While she washed and ironed in the basement, her children played in this coal bin. When these children went to school, they were extremely adaptable and overachieved -- made the dean's list in college (on scholarship) and are now established professionals.

THE GATED PORCH

Skip's parents bought an old house with an old-fashioned front porch. Most of their neighbors had taken off their front porches and had built modern porches in back. There was more privacy. Skip's parents could not afford such remodeling.

The old-fashioned front porch is a valuable method of compartmentation. Even in winter, your toddler, dressed in a snow suit, can play happily on the front porch. There is usually just enough traffic and people passing by to give him the amount of entertainment he needs. It is a shame when front porches are removed to modernize a house. If your toddler climbs over the railing, put chicken wire around the top to increase the height. Your child is more important than your neighbors opinions. Back porches, if they are made childproof, are useful, but, unless you back up to an alley, there is usually not as much entertainment in the back as in the front, and your toddler may get lonesome.

Every morning after his bowel movement Skip was dressed in a snow suit, stocking cap, and mittens, and put out to play on the front porch. He had a small truck with rubber tires that he parked around. He would lie down and look at it at floor level. The heavy tires made it look like a real truck especially from the floor. Making a noise like a diesel he pushed it back and forth.

Skip developed many friends in the neighborhood. The letter carrier always stopped to chat. Grandmothers walking by always spoke to him. Sam next door was five and a half and went to afternoon kindergarten. Almost every morning Sam climbed over the porch railing to play with Skip. He had big cardboard packing boxes that became elevators, ships, bedrooms and trucks. After about a half hour of play with Skip, Sam became bored and climbed over the railing and left Skip alone. Skip cried violently using every muscle in his body. His anger was so intense that his mother feared that he might have a stroke. Her heart turned over. She wondered if her pediatrician was right in this recommendation. Before she could do anything about it, Skip became interested in rearranging the boxes. Different from Sam's arrangement. Then a big truck stopped in front of the house. There was a delivery. The trucker stopped and talked to Skip.

This scene was repeated once or twice every morning. Skip learned to take his disappointments with less visible anguish. After a few months Skip could climb over the railing and join Sam in the neighborhood. Skip's father then increased the height of the railing with chicken wire. Sam couldn't get in and Skip couldn't get out. Skip's mother graciously let Sam in and out whenever he wished.

One Sunday morning, after examining the chicken wire nailed to the old fashioned wooden railing and beautiful white columns; the father of the neighborhood's non-compartmentized "bad boy" asked Skip's father:

"What kind of animals are you raising?"

"Children!" replied Skip's father with a straight face and calmness.

That fall Skip went to nursery school every morning. But the chicken wire continued to "deface" the neighborhood. There was a younger brother coming along. Both of these boys overachieved. Eventually the chicken wire was taken down and the porch was repainted.

The old-fashioned front porch is a valuable method of compartmentation. Even in winter, your toddler, dressed in a snow suit, can play happily on the front porch. There is usually just enough traffic and people passing by to give him the amount of entertainment he needs.

FENCED YARD

Fences need not be expensive to be effective. Snow fence is relatively inexpensive for a fifty-foot roll without posts. It makes an adequate fence, is not bad looking, and it can be painted. Chicken wire is adequate but it does not look as good. Be sure the mesh is small enough so that your child cannot get his foot in it and climb over. The ordinary farm fence has meshes that are too big. Cyclone fences and picket fences, although costly, work well. Sometimes young families, who plan to install these types of fences, tend to postpone it until the child is too old to need it. It is a mistake to wait. If you can't afford the expensive fence you want, buy a simple one when you need it. Then it is easier for you to get your child out of doors every day. He will flourish. He will sleep better and his appetite and disposition will improve. In reasonably good weather he should go out of doors as soon as he finishes breakfast. Your fenced yard should be arranged so that you can watch your child from a window.

It is important that you look the ground over carefully. Pick up the rubbish and broken glass. Be sure there are no dangers. Check with your local health department if you are not sure if certain berries are poisonous. Small toddlers put everything in their mouths and they can't be trained out of this habit before four years of age. Small stones are not as dangerous as pieces of glass and small sticks that do not show up on X-rays. You should not count on a hedge to serve as a fence. Children learn very quickly how to get through a hedge.

It is important to select the gates carefully for your yard. A smart two or three-year-old can learn to open a gate. A spring hook and eye is a good fastener. (See illustration.) Occasionally a two-and-a-half-year-old will learn to open that hook. Many parents use padlocks on their gates. The key for the padlock can be tagged and hung in the kitchen or the lock can have a combination to open it.

The door to your house should be fastened adequately so your child cannot enter at will and spoil the effect of the fenced yard. If the door is easily opened, he can bring his playmates into your house. This will make extra work for you. Then you will become overtired, irritable and frustrated and undo all the good training and relationship that you have developed with the pre-school child. Make your backyard interesting so your child won't want to come inside. Have safe toys, a sand box, packing boxes, boards, and a rope swing are a few of the things that fascinate children.

Older children may climb in and out of the yard. Usually by the time children have enough ability to climb over a fence, they have enough intelligence to be trusted to run loose in the immediate neighborhood. However, children should not be allowed to roam in most neighborhoods without some supervision.

At age four the child can run untethered in limited safe "Go north as far as the next street and south as far as the cross street. Don't play in the street!" When carefully shown these artificially delineated boundaries, most four year olds will obey for an hour or so if they have a wagon, or tricycle or an interesting toy. Sometimes an assertive four year old will deliberately run away if left alone for more than an hour. You have to check their play frequently.

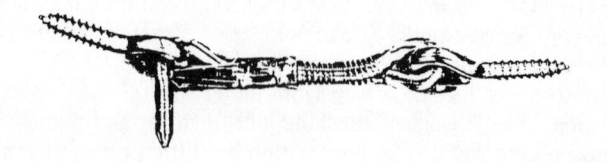

CHAPTER VII

TETHERING

If you live in an apartment and do not have access to a fenced yard, it is important that you learn how to tether your child out-of-doors so he or she can get some fresh air even when you can't be with him or her. You tie a small cord to his belt. A harness is not necessary. You can tie the rope around his waist with a bowline knot. Read the instructions in the Boy Scout Manual on knots. The other end of the rope should be tied to the bottom of a tree or pole. Be sure this end is tied low, so the child cannot choke himself if he gets tangled and falls. The pull must always be horizontal.

When you first tether your two-year-old who can run fast, he may fetch up too quickly when he gets to the end of the rope. Until he gets used to the rope, tie it to a fifteen-pound piece of firewood. Then, when he runs fast to the end of the rope, he will drag the log with him and not jerk himself. After a few days he will get used to the rope and you can tie one end to something stationary.

If you live in an apartment, you can tether your child in the back of the building. Remove dangerous objects from the area you plan to use. The child should have from ten to twenty feet of rope, but it should not be so long that he could get in the way of cars and trucks. It is helpful if you have a sandbox to which you can tie the rope. A child will play for hours on a rope in the back yard with a sandbox, pail, and shovel. You should start this sometime after the child's first birthday. Take her outside, tether her and play with her. Then quietly withdraw while her interest is absorbed in the sand. She can be momentarily out of your sight, but she should never be out of your hearing. There may be dogs or loud noises in the neighborhood that may frighten her. You should never let her cry for more than five minutes without finding out what she wants.

If you have a younger baby, tethering will give you time to pay attention to the younger baby while the older one is getting out-of-doors enjoyment. This freedom and independence for the eighteen-month and two year old will develop his personality. She will enjoy watching the trucks go by and seeing them unload. Life becomes full of new sights. The rope does not really restrict her for she is free from the grown-up "no." She is safe within the area. She is getting sunshine and fresh air and is making friends. She has become her own master within her little protected world and free from the frustration of trying to understand what her grown-ups expect from her. Soon she will be ready for the next compartment.

One mother, the wife of an underpaid intern, lived in a third-floor apartment. She had a new baby whom she was nursing and an eighteen-month-old boy. After much persuasion, I convinced her to tether her older boy. She put a sandbox out side and tied a rope to it. She tethered him there every morning. Some mornings, when she was a little slow in getting him out to the sandbox, her son would bring the rope to his mother as a signal that he wanted to be tethered outside.

The mother watched him from the back porch and saw many "cute scenes" talking to delivery people, etc. This child is doing exceedingly well. Tethering was the only way that this resourceful mother could get her older child outdoors in cool weather and still relax enough to nurse her little baby.

Another mother has written wisely, "I would be afraid to tether my child outside on a regular basis and then go indoors to an apartment even though I could watch him from the window. Tethering your child outside on a regular basis would give much temptation to child molesters such as in the case of Adam Walsh."

When we are constantly reading of missing children and are advised not to allow children to talk to strangers (feasible only after the age of four); she suggests sitting outside with the tethered children reading, sunbathing, gardening, shoveling snow, etc."

Law enforcement people tell me that in the eighties they get many calls about missing children every day. The kidnappers are usually one of the divorced parents. It is important to know your neighborhood. Ask your neighbors and your police department if they believe it is dangerous to tether your child outdoors.

One set of parents lived with three children under five in a new development where there was a "no fence" agreement for the neighborhood. Beautiful rolling lawns, that were kept like a golf course, connected the houses. For more than two years I tried to convince the parents to tether their children who were between the ages of one and four. They couldn't or wouldn't.

One summer one of the grandparents rented a house at the seashore for the season. It was a beautiful house with a gently sloping lawn that extended to a sea wall. Then there was a drop off into the bay. At high tide there was five feet of water. At low tide there was a seven foot drop to muddy sand. The parents did not know about this danger until they arrived.

One child was five, one was two and one half and the youngest was one year old and still breast-feeding. None could swim. The parents made a quick decision. They decided they must not have a worrisome summer. Father went to a hardware store and bought clothesline rope and two pieces of pipe which were driven into the ground as stakes. Tying a bowline knot around the waist of each of the younger children, they were tethered to the stakes on twenty feet of line. The pull was horizontal. They were tethered close enough to touch but not to become entangled. The older child was told not to play near the sea wall and he obeyed

It took a few days for the two-and-a-half and one-year old not to object to being tethered. They were tethered out after breakfast and after afternoon nap -- about four hours every day. The rest of the time the children played on the beach with one of the parents or grandparents. Of course some grown up was always watching when they were tethered on the lawn near the sea wall.

Two weeks after the tethering became routine, the two-and-one-half-year old stopped having nightmares and getting into bed with her parents. At home running freely from house to house in the "no fence agreement" few of the children slept the night through and they resisted going to bed at night. After my patient was tethered in the daytime routinely, she went to bed without a fuss and slept the night through.

The system (tethering) worked so well that the parents decided to continue the practice at home. The parents now had the courage to be different in their neighborhood where there was a "no fence agreement."

It is difficult to be different from your neighbors. You must make sure that you are right. But you must not be deterred from tethering because of gossipy neighbors. I had to write a letter defending one mother from "child abuse" because she had her two year old daughter tethered on the lawn between her house and that of her neighbor.

The neighbors will stop talking when they see how much happier your child is because he has four hours a day of freedom within his own world. You will also see how he flourishes by getting lots of fresh air and sunshine. In addition both you and your neighbors will be amazed how little your child frustrates you.

ON THE LEASH

In 1945, when I first began recommending that mothers walk their small children on a leash, elderly ladies would chastise the mothers for "treating their children like dogs." Now when the mothers walk their children on a leash, the elderly ladies congratulate them for having control of their children. If your two-year-old is on a leash, or if a strong cord is tied to his belt and to you, you can push a small baby in a carriage, walk, shop, talk with neighbors, and still keep your child from running into the street.

You will not dislocate his elbow by yanking him back and you won't have to drop your packages and chase him. You can keep him out of various dangers that the curious toddler investigates. When you go to the park, tie a long line to your child and attach the other end to yourself. Then you can lose yourself in a book while he plays, picks up sticks, and brings you things. When you go to the beach you can close your eyes and sunbathe while he plays at the water's edge. The rope will keep him from going out over his head, and he cannot disturb other people. You can relax while you are looking after your child. Do not let public opinion, which is shortsighted and thoughtless, deter you from putting your child on a leash.

Once I was the doctor for the annual yacht race from Chicago to Mackinac Island. At the beginning of the race, I sat with the race committee, a small group of distinguished gentlemen. Many of the sailors were young fathers; some were fathers of my patients. There were more than one hundred yachts in the race, and there were scores of fathers saying good-bye to their families. The grounds were covered with women and children. Many of the young mothers seemed harassed while they tried to watch their children. It seemed as though they could not wait for their husbands to be off. There was a great deal of confusion. One little girl fell into the lake. One young mother, however, stood out in the crowd. She had four children who were tied to each other by a clothesline so they were about six feet apart. One end of the rope was tied around her own waist. This attractive mother walked, smiling, with perfect poise through the crowd, greeting everyone. Her children were also smiling, happy, and under perfect control. This mother and her children were a sharp contrast to the scolding mothers and crying children around them.

I told no one that the four children who were tied together were my patients. With a belly laugh, one said, "Ha, ha. Mountain climbing." But one astute member watched them thoughtfully for a long time. He then turned to one of his friends and said in an understated tone "you know, that's not a bad idea!"

All four of those children are now professionals with post graduate degrees.

CHAPTER VIII
COMPARTMENTATION AND NURSERY SCHOOLS

Nursery school is another form of compartmentation. In most homes, the adult world and its demands on the pre-school child are so far beyond his capabilities that the child develops techniques of resistance and habits of disobedience that interfere with learning. In nursery school staffed with people who understand the normal stages of development, ask the child to perform only what he/she is capable of. The child gets praise.

At home, running free indoors and out all his waking hours, the child gets over tired and confused from the many "adult NO's" he encounters but can't comprehend to constructively modify his own behavior. He becomes fearful and resistant to all grown-ups, and eventually completely uncooperative.

Many nursery schools meet in churches. Check the yellow pages of your phone book or call church offices and ask if they have a nursery school. Some nursery schools advertise in the local newspaper, while others are very selective. Some enterprising mothers who need money take a few children into their homes to play with their own children. This very informal type of nursery school works well if the mother is smart, calm and likes children. The meeting areas must be stripped of valuable adult possessions and dangers. Outdoors there must be a safe, fenced yard with suitable toys. (Read sections on Strategic Gates, Fenced Yards, and Toys).

In Rome, in 1907, Dr. Maria Montessori took in fifty poor children and gave them the freedom to work or not to work, each according to his or her own ability, without interference from adults. No particular selection as to age is reported, but none of the fifty could read nor write. Each child did what he wanted to do. The children actually taught themselves. Child sized furniture, large sandpaper letters, and safe materials to make things with were ingeniously devised. Some children learned to read and write in short periods of time. Dr. Montessori's perception and vigorous defense of the rights of children attracted world-wide attention. Now there are Montessori schools all over the world. They are expensive because the equipment is expensive and the teachers have special training.

Montessori schools are good for children, especially those who are retarded or have learning problems. Many other nursery schools, however, do the job just as well without as much expense. In our culture today, I cannot pick out children who have gone to a Montessori school from those who have gone to another kind of nursery school. Those children who want to read at an early age will, whether they go to a Montessori school or not. Many learn to read from watching Public Television or from older brothers and sisters.

Dr. Arnold Gesell documented all his observations with motion pictures. One can go to the film library at Yale and find movies of all phases of child development: continuous uninterrupted growth, or age levels just four weeks apart. His nursery schools became laboratories to observe the natural activities of the infant and child. He wrote prolifically. One of his most useful books is the *Infant and Child in the Culture of Today.*

Most parents send their children to nursery school when they are about three years old. A child is ready for nursery school as soon as he is toilet trained. If he is more than two and one half and is normal in development, but is not yet toilet trained, you could send him to nursery school untrained. If he has no neurological defects in the control of his bladder, he will become toilet trained within a week after he enters nursery school. He will see the other children going to the bathroom all at the same time and will want to imitate them. Whenever he has an accident, he will become embarrassed because everyone will stare at him; thus, he will do anything to avoid having an accident in nursery school. This is quite different from his attitude with you at home, as wetting his pants in your presence is not embarrassing.

The reason he is not trained may be that he has developed techniques of resistance or habits of disobedience because he has not been compartmentized. Then he needs nursery school badly. It may be almost a necessity for you to keep your sanity.

You may wonder how you can tell if a particular nursery school is good for your child. You should visit one. You must see it in action. If you like the way the teachers handle the children, then that school is good for you. Generally, the nursery school program should not be highly structured. The purpose of nursery school is not to give your child instruction. He probably has had too much of that already from you, especially if he is the first child. The purpose of nursery school is to provide a place where children of the same age can play together at many different activities. In a good nursery school, the teachers are continually nodding their heads "yes" and giving approval. A poor nursery school is one where the teachers are continually saying "no, no." You should not have to pay a nursery school teacher to say "no" when you have probably over saturated him with "nos" at home.

Nursery school should get the children outside for part of the session each day, weather permitting. This is rather important; but to run a nursery school and to get the children outdoors every day is no easy task in the northern states. One of the ways that a nursery school solves this problem is by taking children on scholarship. In return, one or two mothers (of the scholarship children) spend the morning or afternoon helping the children put on and take off their outer clothing and boots. These simple necessities take too much of the teacher's time if she tries to handle them all herself.

When there are more than twenty children, usually the nursery school is divided into three year old and four year old groups. Such an age division is not essential. A good teacher can handle both ages together. Four year olds like a more sophisticated type of play. They fingerpaint, draw, and do minor carpentry work. Three year olds like to play with a big fire engine, large blocks, or boxes that resemble blocks of many colors. They run in and out of the playhouse.

Three year olds play parallel and do not depend on reactions from their contemporaries. The four year old is greatly dependent upon such reaction. The four year old goes into the playhouse and holds the door shut to keep the others out. She looks out the window to see who wants to get in. After a little wait, she lets another four year old in. Then both join forces to keep another out. One holds the door. The other looks out the window and enjoys watching the efforts of another child trying to get in. If nobody wants to get in, the playhouse is no fun for the four year old. The three year old is indifferent to all this. He follows the four year olds and goes in and out whenever he can, unaware of all the byplay.

All children like to listen to stories, but three year olds can't listen for as long as the four year olds. Both groups enjoy running around outside. They all use the sandbox, slide, and monkey bars. Swings are more dangerous and should be used with very strict supervision.

The nursery school program is not as important as the teacher. Talk to her: Is she warm? Does she have a heart? Does she love children? If she has these qualities, she will run a good nursery school. She does not have to have any degree or special training. Nursery school teachers are born, not made.

The teacher's characteristics are more important than the physical facilities, but certain things are necessary. The building should have a comfortable temperature and be well lighted; minimal toilet facilities should be available (potties are all right) and adaptable to your child's needs.

If your child has not been compartmentized, going to nursery school may be a traumatic experience. He may not want you to leave him there. He may cling to you with great fear. So, stay in the room and pretend you are one of the staff. You can show one of the other children how to draw a circle, a cross or a square. Be quite friendly with some of the other children while your child watches you in action. When your child becomes absorbed in something, you can leave for short periods of time and come back again. Linger and play with the other children each day and then quietly withdraw. Come back each time a little bit later. After about a week, your child will adapt to nursery school and enjoy it.

If your nursery school has a pickup service, your child may be too frightened to get into the bus. Rather than forcibly putting him on the bus, take him to the school yourself. If you are nursing a younger baby, take the baby along also. Linger and be one of the staff for a week or two. Don't push him. Gradually he will adapt and want to join the group. If your nursery school teacher does not go along with this procedure, or if she blames you for your child's reluctance, she may be correct, but she is probably not right for you. So look for another nursery school. It is not uncommon for a child who has not been compartmentized to be very much afraid to leave his mother. That is one of the reasons I recommend compartmentation so strongly. It gives the child self-confidence that he needs to be able to bear to be away from his mother and function well on his own.

When you send your child to nursery school, he will be exposed to a greater number of germs. He may get so many colds that it may be necessary to withdraw him from nursery school. It can be quite frustrating to have paid tuition for nursery school and then find that your child attends only a small portion of the time. This situation occurs more frequently in children who have not been breast-fed for several months. If the sickness is excessive, try to find a nursery school that meets every other day. Years ago, it was accidentally found in the Gesell nursery schools that upper respiratory infections were reduced when each group of children went on alternate days.

One group of children goes on Monday, Wednesday, and Friday. Another group goes on Tuesday, Thursday, and Saturday. It is important that neither group has contact with the other. Here is how it works: Billy who goes every other day, goes to school on Monday. He plays with Bobby who has a cold. On Tuesday, Billy does not have the symptoms of a cold, but he is contagious. By Wednesday, he has the symptoms, and his mother keeps him at home. He does not spread the cold to another child. If he had gone to nursery school on Tuesday, he would have spread the cold to another child before he showed enough symptoms so that his mother realized he should be kept at home. This alternate attendance reduced upper respiratory infections in the Gesell nursery school by as much as one third.

If you cannot afford to send your child to nursery school, you can make your own. Get together with three or four mothers who have children six months older or younger than your own child. Each mother takes all four children for one morning. Anywhere from two to five children make a nice workable group. Some mothers take care of the children in their apartments. Some take them to parks, beaches, or for walks in the woods. It is important not to over-organize the activities of these little children. Just the fact that they are together with their own age group is enough. Of course, it is important to meet regularly and have an arrangement for a substitute if one mother is sick.

Often it is too difficult to organize five women to run a cooperative nursery school. If you have a willing friend who has a child close in age to your own, you can take turns taking care of the children every other morning. That way you each have every other morning free.

Nursery school or a reasonable facsimile helps your child of three to four to adapt to life within your family. Also, it gives you, as a mother, a definite time to be away from your child. Every mother needs time off to think and to charge her batteries. You can become a better mother after you learn how to get scheduled freedom.

CHAPTER IX
HOW TO RECOMPARTMENTIZE

"My child won't stay in the playpen!" Lucy announced to her friend Vicky who also was a mother of an eighteen month old. Vicky who had succeeded in recompartmentizing just recently paused a moment and asked, "Tony can't get out can he? What do you mean Tony won't stay in the playpen. He can't get out unless you take him out!"

"That's right but he screams so loudly that the neighbors below, tap on the ceiling. I think that they are going to report me for child abuse."

"You should warn them that you are about to recompartmentize Tony so that they will know that you are not beating your child."

Tony had not been in the playpen for six months, since he had learned to walk on his first birthday. Lucy, his mother, was told to get him back in the playpen as a way of keeping him from having nightmares every night.

To recompartmentize a child who has been running free all his/her waking hours is more difficult than starting compartmentation just before your baby begins to move around.

To be successful at recompartmentation you will need to take a week off from your regular work at home to get your child back in the playpen or gated room.

This means that your typing, writing, painting, computer work, sewing or whatever will have to take a back seat for a week. You will find it extremely difficult to concentrate until you have taught your child to be compartmentized without crying.

THE THREE PHASES OF CRYING

You must also really understand the nature of crying so you can handle the pressure it creates. At first the toddler cries because he wants you to take him out of the playpen. After about five minutes of hard crying this "want" turns to anger because you haven't done what the child is asking.

Lucy took Tony out of the playpen after five minutes of loud crying because she could not stand it any more, and she was afraid of the neighbors. Tony sat on his mother's lap and chattered in a dialect that she could understand even though it was not yet English.

Tony pointed to the playpen and tried to describe the terrible ordeal he had just been through. As he sat on Lucy's lap he convinced himself that the playpen was an experience that must be avoided at all costs. He emphasized his mumbo jumbo by pointing to the horrible instrument of compartmentation to which he had just been made a victim.

After her discussion with Vicky, Lucy decided that she was going to win the battle of recompartmentation. The second time around she let Tony cry for fifteen minutes, the neighbors be dammed. Her toddler got red in the face and broke out into a sweat. Lucy was afraid that he might have a stroke. She picked Tony up and kissed him and wiped his flushed wet brow. In five minutes he calmed down and again spouted his dialect and pointed to that terrible device, the playpen. Tony's father who was not involved in process also got a vehement diatribe from his young son. At 18 months Tony was showing his capability of telling one parent about the bad actions of the other.

But Lucy had firmly resolved to win. She had reread the advantages of compartmentation and she did want to stop Tony's nightmares. She now let him cry in the playpen for 20 minutes. Tony's emotions shuffled from "WANT" to "ANGER" to "HYSTERIA". When she picked him up, he clung to her trembling. Tony shook convulsively. Lucy never realized that he had so much strength until he continued to cling to her. It took twenty minutes for him to stop shaking but it seemed like hours. Finally he fell asleep in Lucy's arms. It was the end of recompartmentation.

Dealing with the hysteria of the toddler was too much for Lucy. Fortunately there is an easier way to recompartmentize. It takes just as much persistance. But it is kinder because you can accomplish it by frequent demonstrations of love so you needn't wait until your child passes to the third crying stage -- hysteria.

The following is an example of how to recompartmentize successfully. First make sure the playpen is empty and then put your child into it and hand him one toy. When he objects to being put into the playpen, let him cry for about five minutes. Then go to him and kiss him. Do the minimum amount that will stop him from crying. Do not pick him up. Be brief in soothing him. When he stops crying withdraw quietly. He will cry again violently.

Let him cry another five minutes and then go to him. Give him a cookie, kiss him and soothe him. Leave the moment he stops crying. You may have to repeat this several times. After the tenth time, let him out. He wins this time, but more than an hour will have passed. That is all the compartmentation that either of you need for the first day. The next day, right after breakfast put your child into the playpen. Again let him cry for five minutes. Then go to him and give him a piece of toast or a piece of orange. Do the minimum that will stop his crying. When he stops crying, withdraw quietly. While he cries again, even more angry now, have your second cup of coffee. But again, go to him before he becomes hysterical. Soothe him.

Let me repeat the nature of crying. First the child cries because he wants you. Then he cries because he is angry that you don't come and because he is not getting his own way. From anger, he goes to hysteria. It usually takes about twenty minutes to become hysterical. He breaks into new thresholds of anxiety: from wanting, to anger, to hysteria. Each is more powerful and frightening than the next. Remember not long ago in the womb, there was no wanting, no anger, and therefore no hysteria. When he is hysterical, he no longer remembers what he wants. You should break the crying spell while he is still in the wanting stage. Your child has become hysterical if, when you pick him up he shakes in your arms for twenty or thirty minutes (Tony). This will upset you so much that you won't want to confront him with a playpen or gate again. This allows your child to feel that he is the boss, which, in turn, lessens his feeling of security. (Buzzie)

The hardest part for the parent to learn in recompartmentation is to stop hugging the toddler the moment he stops crying. The mother's instinct is to hug him for a long time. It is better to hug and pat him to stop his crying than to pick him up. The nursing mother can quickly stop his crying. The moment the child stops nursing, you must put him back in the playpen. Again this is against your instincts. Most breastfeeding mothers like to nurse the baby to sleep. When the child wakes up, however, he cries violently when you try to put him back in the playpen.

It is necessary to make the adjustment to the real world as comfortable as possible. There is so much newness all around and within himself; e.g., just the fact that he must "want" to be fed. This is new and potentially frustrating for him. He cannot adequately adjust to his emotions, and therefore, it is important not to force him to experience too much too soon.

In the process of recompartmentation, it is important to convince your child that you love him, but that forces beyond your control make it necessary for you to keep him in a playpen or a gated room. If you go to him every five minutes while he is in the wanting stage he will not reach the stage of anger or hysteria. Then you will succeed in recompartmentation. It takes persistence. It will help to re-read the sections describing the advantages of compartmentation. The second day you will have to go to him ten times before you let him out. The third day will be the worst of all. You will wish that you never heard of playpen or gates. If mothers quit trying to recompartmentize it is usually on the third day. You will have to go at least ten times. The child will cry more violently than he did on the first or second day.

During the past forty two years that I have been recommending compartmentation, mothers have always won when they persisted after the third day. On the fourth day a sham quality will appear in his crying. You will have to go to him only two or three times on the fourth day. The fifth day will be even better. After this five-day fight, you will have won. (Skip)

It is very important to carry out this mission at the same time each day. It is usually better to do this right after breakfast when the child has had something to eat and you are alone with him. You can interrupt his crying spells easily while you are doing some light chores around the house. You will find yourself becoming an actress. You will think of new things to say and how to be jovial. Make believe that you don't understand that he wants out. Sell him on the fact that you love him very much, but that you don't understand why he is crying. Don't ever try to compartmentize by locking him behind a solid door. You must always be able to see and hear him. Don't ever pick him up and cradle him for a long time when you are trying to recompartmentize. Don't give him prolonged hugs and kisses, but fondle briefly. Do the minimum that stops his crying. In this, you must go against your feelings. Make it up to him during the times you are not compartmentizing.

A good trick is to have two areas of compartmentation: a playpen and a gated room. Put your toddler in the gated room and let him cry for five minutes. Then pick him up and put him in the playpen. Place the playpen next to the window so that he can look out. Or, transfer him to a second gated room if he can climb out of the playpen. Let your child cry in the playpen for five minutes, pick him up, kiss him, and put him in the gated room. Let him cry there for five minutes, pick him up, and put him in the playpen. Go back and forth between the playpen and the gated room ten times before you give up and let him run around the apartment or house.

You can also have three areas of compartmentation: a front porch, a fenced yard, and a playpen outside. When the child gets bored in one place, you put him in another, after letting him cry about five minutes in each area. If you are not fortunate enough to have a fenced yard, you can recompartmentize by tethering. (Refer to the section on Tethering.) Move your child frequently; don't let him cry more than five minutes, and don't give up until you have tried to recompartmentize for three full days. You will win on the fourth or fifth day.

Recently a young mother told me that her eighteen month old baby, who had been out of the playpen for about three months, began awakening two or three times every night. She tried to recompartmentize him and did as I directed, so she said. But after two weeks of putting him behind a gate or in a playpen, he still cried even after going to him every five minutes for ten times. I told her that she was going to be my first failure in forty two years. She tried again but could not win; he still cried after going to him every five minutes for ten times. Finally, she consulted another pediatrician. He told her to let him cry behind the gate for twenty minutes. That did it. He stopped crying behind the gate and in the playpen. Also, he stopped awakening at three and four o'clock in the morning. In recompartmentizing some mothers have let their children cry for ten minutes straight. Ordinarily, though, I recommend only five minutes of steady crying before trying to break the crying spell. In handling persistent crying, it is wise to try to determine why your child is crying. Is he just being stubborn in wanting his own way? If this is your impression, you should let him cry longer (twenty minutes). The persistent ones will not become hysterical if you work up to longer periods of crying, but continue to break their crying spells by demonstrating love. All children need touching, handling, and talking mixed with learning how to play alone. Four hours total of each extreme is the ideal.

CHAPTER X

CASE HISTORIES OF SKIP AND BUZZIE
"GOOD FENCES MAKE GOOD NEIGHBOURS"

Mending Wall by Robert Frost
Something there is that doesn't love a wall
That sends the frozen-ground-swell under it,
And spills the upper boulders in the sun;
And makes gaps even two can pass abreast.
The work of hunters is another thing:
I have come after them and made repair
Where they have left not one stone on a stone,
But they would have the rabbit out of hiding,
To please the yelping dogs. The gaps I mean,
No one has seen them made or heard them made,
But at spring mending-time we find them there.
I let my neighbor know beyond the hill;
And on a day we meet to walk the line
And set the wall between us once again.
We keep the wall between us as we go.
To each the boulders that have fallen to each.
And some are loaves and some so nearly balls
We have to use a spell to make them balance:
"Stay where you are until our backs are turned!"
We wear our fingers rough with handling them.
Oh, just another kind of out-door game,
One on a side. It comes to little more:
There where it is we do not need the wall:
He is all pine and I am apple orchard.
My apple trees will never get across
And eat the cones under his pines, I tell him.
He only says, "Good fences make good neighbours."
Spring is the mischief in me, and I wonder
If I could put a notion in his head:
"*Why* do they make good neighbours? Isn't it
Where there are cows? But here there are no cows.
Before I built a wall I'd ask to know
What I was walling in or walling out,
And to whom I was like to give offense.
Something there is that doesn't love a wall,
That wants it down." I could say "Elves" to him,
But it's not elves exactly, and I'd rather
He said it for himself. I see him there
Bringing a stone grasped firmly by the top
In each hand, like an old-stone savage armed.
He moves in darkness as it seems to me,
Not of woods only and the shade of trees.
He will not go behind his father's saying,
And he likes having thought of it so well
He says again, "Good fences make good neighbours."

"Keep him in a playpen four hours a day," I advised Skip's mother at the eight month examination.

Shortly after Skip was six months old, his mother already had put him in the playpen, before he had learned to cruise about. He enjoyed lying on his stomach and watching his mother in the kitchen. Often she talked to him, and he laughed and squealed with glee. When he became restless, his mother changed his diapers. When he became bored, she put him in his six-year size crib until she had time to take him outdoors. It was convenient to substitute the crib for the playpen. Gradually, Skip spent more time in the playpen, so that before he could creep, he was spending a total of four hours daily in a playpen or in his crib. This was about one-half of his waking hours.

For another two or three hours, he was being fed and bathed. His parents, grandparents, and friends played with him at least two more hours during which he ran free.

Gradually, even at this early age, he was learning to play by himself. As he became older and more demanding, the method of compartmentation expanded for variety and relief from boredom. It was entertaining when the playpen was moved into the kitchen or near a window through which he could watch the traffic.

"What do you mean by compartmentation?" Skip's mother asked me at the fifteen-month examination.

I told her, "I began to use the word `compartmentation' in the fifties when teaching parents to separate the adult world from the child's world. As you recall compartmentation is based on the premise that the child has the ability to move about at the age of one, but he has no brakes until he is four. Therefore, for half his waking hours, he is relieved of the responsibility of trying to understand the adult `no' by spending four hours daily in the playpen, the gated room, behind strategic gates, or in a fenced yard. When these facilities are not available, he is tethered outside or attends nursery school."

"Do you advise that for the parent's or the child's benefit?"

"For both! The parents learn early how to keep control of the child who has no brakes. They also have a chance to recharge their batteries by doing other kinds of work or resting while the child is compartmentized. The child learns to play by himself. Instead of developing habits of disobedience, he develops a hunger to be with grown-ups and to please and obey. We have found that the compartmentized children have been overachievers in school compared with those who have run free."

"It sounds good to me," Skip's mother concluded as she left the office and went to visit Buzzie and his mother.

At Buzzie's house, the playpen was set up, but it was full of toys, and Buzzie was no longer in it.

"Why have you given up the playpen?" Skip's mother asked.

"He has outgrown it. He cries when I put him in it. The pediatrician said that it was good for him to explore."

Skip's mother put her child on the floor beside Buzzie. Independently, both boys toddled about the living room. Their natural curiosity took them to several fascinating and valuable adult possessions. When Skip reached for the cigarettes on the coffee table, his mother said, "No, no, Skip." He stopped and stared at his mother a moment, then toddled to her and hugged her knees. The pride that welled up almost brought tears to her eyes.

"You can see that he understands. It is foolish to keep him penned up. I don't understand why your pediatrician recommends it." Buzzie's mother exclaimed. "I read an article that said if you keep them in a playpen, they won't crawl; and if they don't crawl, they won't read."

Soon Buzzie reached for a cigarette. His mother had to be a little more emphatic than Skip's in order to stop him. With a glint in his eye, he stared at his mother with his hand poised like a statue, reaching for the cigarette. Over and over, she repeated the "No, nos". Finally, Buzzie lost his balance and sat down. His mother continued to recount what she had read about the correlation between crawling and reading.

The next time she looked, Buzzie was eating a cigarette. Quickly, she pulled the cigarette out of his mouth, slapped his hands, and wiped the tobacco off with a tissue.

"Sooner or later they have to learn," she explained.

Buzzie whimpered a little in his mother's lap, but soon both boys were smiling and reaching for one another while their mothers talked.

When Skip's mother got home, she put Skip in the playpen as usual. He cried a little while she began to prepare dinner. Having played with Buzzie out of the playpen seemed to make him more dissatisfied when put back into it.

"Is it wrong to keep a child in a playpen?" she asked herself. Who is right -- my pediatrician or Buzzie's pediatrician, who said, "The toddler must explore." The more she thought about it, the more she questioned my advice. She asked other friends, including Skip's grandparents, about the playpen. They were unanimous in their disapproval of the playpen. They thought of it as an unnecessary confinement. So, the next time Skip objected to being put in the playpen, his mother let him out. The more she let him out, the more he objected when he was in it. Finally, she gave in completely.

Skip's natural curiosity led him to explore all the pretty and dangerous things in the house. For two weeks, his response to his mother's "no" was consistently good. Like Buzzie's mother, Skip's mother now began to boast, "He knows." But then Skip's curiosity prevailed and he became insensitive to his mother's "no, no." The "no, no" became more emphatic. Often Skip would stop, shake his head "no, no" and then take what he wanted. His mother had to resort to slapping his hands. The need for slapping increased to several times a day. Afterwards, he looked at her with such a mournful expression she felt guilty for every slap. Some instinct told her she wasn't rearing Skip properly when she had to slap him so many times during the day. She asked her friends how they taught their children not to touch valuable and dangerous adult belongings.

Buzzie's mother said, "Slap him harder; let him know that you mean it. You must teach him not to touch things while he is young, otherwise, he will not have any respect for property when he gets older."

She read some of the books on child care. Almost all of them recommended that she put her valuables away, out of the child's reach. Her husband brought home safety caps to put in the light sockets. They seriously tried to make the five-room apartment childproof. What they could not lock in the closet, they stored in the basement. It was inconvenient living in a nursery, but Skip was worth it.

Skip now had the run of five rooms. The coffee table was made bare, and the valuables were put behind hooked or locked doors. The television knobs and garbage container were the only "no, nos". Now he seldom got his hands slapped.

Skip's mother noticed that Skip had lost some of his independence. Whenever his grandparents or a stranger came to visit, he became very shy and clung to his mother's legs or wanted to sit on his mother's lap. He did not laugh as much. Sometimes he seemed to be irritable. For no apparent reason, he cried more. Skip's grandparents and his mother's friends reassured her that all children go through a stage of clinging to their mothers.

"It means that he is developing the ability to decide what he wants and what he doesn't want."

"We like them to be afraid," another grandfather commented.

"It means that they are developing judgment," said another.

"You have given up the playpen," I told Skip's mother at the eighteen-month examination.

"How do you know?" his mother asked.

"He is too cautious to put the blocks into the cup. You have had to say `no, no' so many times now that he is afraid to do what I ask him. He does not understand the difference between these blocks that he is supposed to put into the cup and his father's books which you have told him not to touch. Instead, he just stares at me. He has become suspicious of all grown-ups because he is not old enough to understand what grown-ups expect of him. He now stares at me apprehensively. Even as he sits on your lap, he is too frightened to perform developmentally as he did at every previous examination. I imagine that when I examine him, he will object perhaps even cry. His recent past experiences have taught him not to trust grown-ups. His tears are telling me `go away, stranger. I don't trust grown-ups. I don't understand what grown-ups want of me.' I imagine that he clings to your skirt when his grandfather or any of your friends come to visit. He probably objects to having his hair cut."

"You are so right," she replied. "It started three months ago when he played with my friend's son who is the same age. She had given up the playpen sometime ago. She quoted her doctor as saying that it was good for the toddler to explore, to touch, and to manipulate a variety of objects."

"He can do that in the playpen or a gated room that has been made childproof."

"Most of my friends have made their whole apartments childproof."

The run of five rooms all the child's waking hours is too tiring for most two year olds. Even, when the whole apartment has been made child proof, five rooms is too much for the child before he has gone to nursery school. With free run all his waking hours the toddler gets too tired, then irritable and finally completely uncooperative." Some mothers, who are still breast-feeding two year olds, are getting adaptable children without compartmentation. After a child is weaned, he needs compartmentation until he goes to nursery school

When Skip's mother left my office, she was determined to recompartmentize him. Following my recommendations she planned to spend five days making compartmentation her top priority. During that time she organized her schedule to include nothing more than a light domestic routine. More involved activities were postponed. When she put Skip back into a playpen full of toys, he cried violently for thirty minutes and then sobbed convulsively in his mother's arms for twenty minutes.

She felt completely spent when she called me, but I told her, "You should not let him cry more than five minutes before breaking his crying spells. He cries because he wants you; then he becomes angry because you do not go to him. From anger, he shifts to terror and hysteria, and then exhaustion. Go to him every five or ten minutes, give him a toy or kiss him through the bars. Break his crying spell while he is angry and before he becomes hysterical. He will be happier when he is put in the empty playpen and then handed one toy. Only three toys are necessary. Rotate the toys every ten minutes." I advised.

After Skip examined the first toy, he cried to get out. His mother remained calm this time; and after about five minutes, she gave him a second toy. The moment he stopped crying, she quietly slipped away. Again he cried violently. In another five or ten minutes, she went back and gave him a third toy. Skip threw it away and continued to howl. She got down on her knees and kissed him through the bars. She stroked his hot forehead and rubbed his back; and he, in turn, patted his mother's face. While he was examining the toy, his mother quietly sneaked away. It was not long before he was crying again, and he had his arms up indicating that he wanted to be lifted out of the playpen. Mother called to him, "Just a minute," but she continued to wash the dishes. She let him cry for another five minutes; then she soothed him all over again and gave him another toy and took away the first. Still she did not pick him up. She quietly withdrew as soon as he stopped crying. She learned that the rotation of three toys was as good as 20 and better than a playpen full of them.

Obviously that first day of getting Skip back into the playpen was dreadful. Skip cried violently and his mother went to him ten times at five minute intervals before she let him out to follow her about the apartment.

The next day, as soon as Skip had finished breakfast and before she cleared the table of dishes, mother put Skip into the playpen again. He cried even more violently than he did the day before. After letting him cry for five minutes, she went to the playpen and kissed him through the bars and again washed his face with a cool wash cloth. She said, "Mommy is going to wash the dishes," and quietly withdrew. Again he cried violently. After about ten minutes, she returned and was affectionate with him; but the moment he stopped crying, she withdrew and began to put the dishes away. She let him cry another ten minutes before she distracted him. She swept the floor. He still cried violently fo another ten minutes. She became an actress who did not understand his signals to be let out. During these ten minutes of crying, she made the beds and then gave him a cookie. While he cried, she cleaned the bathroom. She broke the next crying spell by washing his face again and kissing him. In this way, she broke the crying spells always in a little different way. Over a period of about one and one-half hours. She got her work done, although for two days she had trouble concentrating.

After going back and forth to the playpen or the gated room several times to break Skip's crying, she took him for a walk. Experimenting with my suggestion, she put the newly purchased harness on him and walked him on a leash. Skip at first pulled at it, but he stopped while watching the trucks being unloaded in the alley. Later, in front on the sidewalk, an elderly lady stared at Skip's mother and Skip. "I don't care what that lady thinks," she said to herself, "I am going to win in this endeavor."

The third morning after breakfast, she put Skip in the room with a double gate. Again he stiffened, screamed and threw himself down. He seemed to be just as violent as on the second day of compartmentation. With calm persistence and resourceful good humor, she did her housework and went to her crying child behind the gate every five minutes for another ten times before she gave in. Again she explained to the neighbors what she was trying to accomplish. He cried even more loudly on day three.

Skip's mother found that she was more of a ham than she ever thought she could be. "Just a minute," she called, while washing the pots. "Pretty soon," she said as she put a cake into the oven. She made much sweet talk. She kissed him through the bars. She ignored his signals that he wanted out. She did not pick him up. She did not let him out until she had gone back and forth from her housework to her crying boy every five minutes for another ten times. Now she understood why most mothers gave up compartmentation of the third day.

The fourth day, after breakfast, began as the others. She kissed him every five minutes and did her housework between times. After a few trips, a sham quality had developed in his cry. He shut it off more quickly. He stopped crying when he heard her coming. Sometimes she took him to the toilet. Sometimes she gave him a new toy with which he now played.

The fifth day, she only had to break his crying spells twice. He played contentedly behind the double gate for two hours. She found that he enjoyed looking out the window. She remembered now that I had said that it was helpful when the areas of confined play were changed to another room, to a multiple gated area enclosing a room with a hall, to a fenced porch, to a fenced yard, or a gated porch like many of the families who came to me. She felt proud of herself that she had won without those facilities.

Skip was put behind the gate right after breakfast. She did not let him run around and then put him in the playpen. He would have objected violently after the freedom. He had the free run before lunch, and then his mother gave him her undivided attention. At first he required it because he seemed wild making new investigations. Within a few minutes, he settled down and lived in the adult world better than Buzzie who had not been compartmentized. Before dinner, he had at least another hour of free run. His father played with him when he got home. Eventually Skip became accustomed to being compartmentized just as his parents became accustomed to cleaning the house and caring for the garden. They may never have really liked doing these things but they became routine.

Never again did she attempt to let him "cry it out." She never forgot how Skip sobbed and shook in her arms when she had let him cry steadily for thirty minutes. She understood how such an experience made most mothers emotionally unable to achieve compartmentation. She was grateful for my explanation, "First he wants, then he is angry, then frightened. It takes him ten minutes to go through each phase. Pacify him before he gets hysterical."

With increasing confidence, Skip's mother had learned to recognize the cry for pain, want, sham anger, and hysteria. Calmly, she approached and resourcefully she distracted her crying two-year-old before he became really angry or hysterical. Now she could psychologically dissect his crying. Like an experienced actress, she had learned how to be charming, gay, funny, or sympathetic at will -- whatever was needed to distract her recompartmentized toddler.

When Skip's mother visited Buzzie's mother, she emptied Buzzie's playpen of toys and put Skip in it. Then Buzzie wanted to get into the playpen with Skip. When Skip was not in the playpen, Buzzie cried until he was let out. Because Buzzie's mother had given up compartmentation she complained that she needed roller skates to keep up with Buzzie. Skip's mother listened to her tell of her experience with compartmentation. She smiled when she was told that Buzzie's spirit was "too aggressive" to be fenced in. She suppressed a grin as an inner glow of satisfaction arose within her.

Skip's mother soon preferred to visit only with friends who also believed in compartmentation. The children could play together in a playpen or behind a gate, and the mothers could enjoy themselves without harassment.

Skip's mother enjoyed talking with the mothers she met in my office who compartmentized. All those mothers had much easier times with their preschool children. They didn't experience the harassment associated with the "terrible two's," about which much has been written. The mothers who had mastered compartmentation seemed to have learned to live with their children better than the mothers who had not mastered the art.

By doing developmental tests periodically, I can tell quickly when the mother has discontinued the practice of compartmentation. The child who is allowed to run all his waking hours during his pre-school years almost always develops techniques of resistance. This manifests itself by excessive caution in the test situations. It is usually more obvious in boys than in girls. Even at this early age, there is a marked difference in the sexes. The boys are reluctant to conform unless they completely understand. It seems that compartmentation is more urgently needed in the male than the female.

Some non-compartmentized pre-school children show a bold aggressiveness without purpose as an effective technique of resistance. Calloused against all direction, these children go their own ways and pay little or no attention to adults. These parents seem strict, and it surprises the casual observer to find that they have little control over their children. This disobedience begins because the parents expect more than the child can produce in his or her respective stage of growth. At first he can't do it. Instead of becoming timid and fearful like most, he learns to tune out. He becomes calloused and aimlessly aggressive as a technique of resistance. Disobedience become a habit.

"He is back in the playpen," I chortled when Skip came in for his two year old examination.

"He has just learned to climb out of the playpen. He spends more than two hours a day in a gated room. We also have gates in the kitchen and bathroom and small hooks high on the doors to keep him out of the closets."

"See how confidently he builds the tower of six blocks and makes a train with blocks. Noncompartmentized two year olds are scared and cry loudly when examined in the doctor's office. I am sure that if you continue to compartmentize, you will have an overachiever when he gets to school."

"How can you be so sure that achievement depends upon compartmentation?"

"I have been comparing the growth and performance of compartmentized and non compartmentized children for many, many years."

"Some of his calmness is inherited!"

"Of course but not all of it. No one knows how much is inherited and how much is acquired. It would be horrible to really know. You would take everything for granted and stop trying. Or you would try so hard and then blame yourself to the point of despair if your child were not successful. Nature was wise not to let parents know exactly how much is inherited and how much is acquired.

"I see here in Skip's chart that he did not perform at the 18 month examination. He cried when I examined him. I also see that you had let him out of the playpen and that he ran free all his waking hours. I must have given you my little speech on compartmentation and then you put him back in the playpen and the gated room."

"It was not easy. It was hard for me and hard on the neighbors. But I will say, compared with my friend's children, he is a lot easier to manage now. He is completely toilet trained. Just a week ago, he imitated his daddy. Now he tells me every time."

"I am glad that you did not spend a great deal of energy on toilet training. After two, the parent should leave the diapers off in the daytime; and then the child of his own volition will want to imitate his parents. It's healthy and natural that way. Those who fail to respond to that method usually have some mild neurological defect in the nerve supply of the bladder or of the bowel that makes it harder for them to learn control."

"We are looking for a house. My husband suggests moving into the new section of small houses that do not ask for a large down payment. We looked at one last weekend. They have an agreement in the neighborhood that no one should put up a fence."

"That's terrible. I would never move into such a neighborhood!"

"Why?"

"For years I have been making house calls on patients in expensive and inexpensive developments where there were `no fence agreements' in the neighborhood. I know well one area in particular where expensive homes have been built in a group with a `no fence agreement' among the dwellers so as not to spoil the view. One such development consists of about 20 homes with many small children. The kitchen doors face each other. One looks out at the beautiful rolling lawns but no fences. It seemed like having 20 sets of parents and about 50 children all living together. I followed many of these children over the years and they all developed various techniques of resistance."

"How can you say they become underachievers because they lived in a neighborhood without fences? The majority of new housing developments in America are without fences. Are you saying that all children reared in house developments without fences are underachievers? There must be thousands of such communities and hundreds of thousands of children who have grown up without fences."

"I am sure that there are more new housing developments in America without fences than with fences. Likewise, I am sure that there are more underachievers than overachievers. In my experience, the two go together," I insisted.

"I have a friend who has just moved into a new development. Beautiful lawns separate the houses. There are no fences. My friend's son, just Skip's age, runs all over these lawns from house to house. Everybody seems to have a wonderful time. They are all good friends. Why can't I move into that neighborhood with my friends? Skip will have been compartmentized for over two years. Running free after that won't make him an underachiever, will it?"

"I believe that he should be compartmentized until he is four years old. At three, he could go to nursery school. It would be just as good as a fence."

"I have never heard of anyone keeping a child behind a fence after three."

"The majority of mothers will not or cannot compartmentize from birth until the fourth birthday. Thirty years ago, among my practice, ten percent would do it. Now it's nearly fifty percent. Many quit at two because they don't come in to my office for regular check ups, and I do not have a chance to urge them to continue to compartmentize through the third year. Two years is better than not at all. It is a passing grade, but it is not the honor roll. I want my patients to do the best they are capable of."

"Won't Skip be better than average if I compartmentize him until he is two and then move into the new housing development among many of my friends? Shouldn't we try to live in a congenial neighborhood?"

"Do you know if any of the families who are now living in that housing development ever used a playpen, a gated room, a gated porch, a multiple gate upstairs, or did they ever tether their children outdoors?" I asked.

"Every mother I talk to does not believe in compartmentation. They want their children to have the free run of their newly acquired world."

"If you move there, you may eventually begin to think as they do. At first, Skip will seem to be very happy and very popular because he will be unusually friendly as he runs from one back door to another with children his same age. In the group, he will be in and out of many houses and have contact with several different mothers. He will be exposed to several different kinds of `no, nos' expressed in several different ways. He will become confused. In addition, running free alone or with the group will tire him greatly. With fatigue comes irritability. He will no longer be sweet and attractive.

I believe that if I examined the pre-school children living in that development, I would find techniques of resistance in every one of them. The majority will be over-cautious and will not perform. There will be a few who will be calloused against all direction and persist in having their own way against all directions from grown-ups. In all of them, various degrees of disobedience will become habitual.

At first, the grown-ups think they are cute and full of spirit. As they grow older, they may still be thought cute provided they are unusually smart. The average, however, will no longer be cute but a hazard to their neighborhood. A few parents will develop an understanding of growth and development of children and will have enough energy to direct the children's energies.

The majority of the parents will have lost the ability to communicate with their children as their children become identified with the group. This increases parents' frustrations when they can no longer think and plan for their families as individuals. This makes the children become more loyal to the gang than to their parents."

"How can you be so positive? Do you know that most mothers are urged to keep their children with them at all times. Togetherness is recommended. Do you realize that many mothers have been advised that it would dangerously frustrate their children and hurt their psyches if they were compartmentized as you recommend? If you think that you are in the minority because you persuade mothers to breast-feed, well, I can tell you now you are very much in the minority when you urge the use of the playpen, gated room, and building fences."

"I cannot help it if I am in the minority. The more I see, the more I'm convinced. Having watched my compartmentized toddlers develop over the years, I've compared them with those who ran free all their waking hours. The compartmentized, from an early age, have learned to play by themselves. From that, they've learned to work by themselves. Even those with average intelligence did above average work in school. Some are on the deans' lists in colleges.

Because of compartmentation, these young people never had to take time out to break a habit of disobedience which I have observed with much consistency in the noncompartmentized. You said yourself that you had much trouble getting Skip recompartmentized. I commend you for your accomplishment. Now you ask me for advice again. You want my opinion whether or not you should buy and move into a new housing development where they have a no-fence agreement. I would be derelict in my duty if I did not do everything I could to prevent you from moving into such a neighborhood."

"Couldn't I move there and still compartmentize?"

"You could, indoors. You could choose a room downstairs, make it childproof, and put a gate or screen door on it. Outside you could use fifty feet of snow fence and make an enclosure big enough to hold a sandbox and some cardboard boxes. Some of the neighbors might howl about the fence, but I doubt if they could legally make you take it down. You could tether Skip out back.

"If you move into a house in this development, you will be the only mother keeping her two-year-old behind a gate. You will have to learn not to be disturbed when you are considered different. You will have to be strong and thick-skinned. You could do it, but it would be easier for you and better if you stayed in your apartment until you can find the kind of house and neighborhood that would be suitable in which to compartmentize your children. You need a neighborhood that does not expect conformity."

"As you probably have noticed, Skip is going to have a baby sister or brother. How can I possibly get Skip outdoors from a third floor apartment and at the same time nurse a new baby?"

I proceeded to tell her how an intern's wife tethered her toddler to a sandbox and how the family tethered their pre-school children to keep them from falling into the ocean.

"One of my friends tried to tether her two-year-old outdoors and he objected so strenuously that she had to give it up. Do you think Skip will accept tethering at two when he is not used to it?"

"Now that Skip is accustomed to being behind a gate, he will adapt quickly to being tethered."

Skip's mother left my office determined to try to tether Skip to the back steps. She had already put a harness on Skip to which she attached a leash. She had practiced walking in the yard before taking him shopping. He was used to the leash. A grandmother stopped her on the street and congratulated her for her ability to manage the small child. "Using the leash the way you do is better than jerking his elbow out of joint trying to keep him out of the street," She said.

It had been useful having Skip accustomed to the leash. In the park, she tied one end of the rope to her ankle while she sat on a blanket with a book. Skip walked about collecting sticks. Likewise at the beach that summer, when Skip was twenty-one months old, she sunbathed while Skip ran in and out of the water. After she adjusted the length of the tethering rope so that he could not get out in the water over his head. She again lost herself in a book. This was especially useful after Skip had passed his second birthday. When his mother was again pregnant, she was finding it increasingly more difficult to keep up with Skip's greater speed on foot.

"We do not need to rush into buying a house," she told Skip's father one night.

Skip's mother went into labor spontaneously when Skip was a little over two years old. The younger brother was born easily after six hours of labor. He nursed well and slept. She had plenty of milk. Grandmother came in and cooked and took care of Skip. At first, grandmother did not want to walk with Skip on a leash, and she was reluctant to tether him at the back steps. But her daughter was so insistent, and Skip enjoyed going out so much, that she relented and tethered Skip in the same way that his mother did. Grandmother thought Skip was unusually smart and cooperative. He always looked forward to going outdoors. He did not seem to miss his mother. Grandmother fully enjoyed looking after her daughter's family. Just one thing prevented it from being perfect. It got to be quite a game at night. When everything was quiet, he could be heard pattering around and talking to himself. Almost every night she put him back to bed. Once his father put him back and spanked him. After that, he cried every time he was put to bed. He seemed to be afraid to be left in the dark. Grandmother suggested putting Skip in a junior bed with low sides to keep him from rolling out.

When I was asked about putting Skip into a youth bed, I said, "No," and suggested making an extension to the sides of the crib and putting a lid on top so that the toddler could walk around in the crib as described in Chapter V. Children are not ready for the bigger bed until they are four years old for the same reason that they must be gated or tethered. They do not understand artificially delineated boundaries until after the fourth birthday. A child of two and one half is not responsible if he climbs out of a bed any more than if he got into an automobile, started the motor, put the car in gear, and drove it over a cliff.

"Beds should be made so that the child under four cannot get out. In some pediatric wards in large hospitals an ankle cuff is used; and one ankle is tied to the bed to keep the child in bed. This prevents him from falling to the floor and fracturing his skull. Harnesses are not used any longer because the child can hang himself.

Skip was afraid of the dark. I explained, "Small children are really frightened of the dark. Arrange a night light, or keep the door of the lighted adjacent room open so that the two- year-old is not in complete darkness. Just because you have him incarcerated, do not abuse your power: Let it be a rule of the house that he should not cry more than five or ten minutes. At first, go to him every five minutes while he is crying. Do not give in until you have been back and forth ten times. In time he will learn to accept being alone and even the darkness."

Skip's parents developed a ritual about going to bed. Methodically, Skip's feet were tucked in. His favorite stuffed rabbit was placed by his head. The rabbit also was tucked in carefully. The lights were turned off. Then mother or father sat on the floor in the darkness. In a slow, monotonous voice, he recalled how the big bear at the zoo got into his cage. Then came the mother bear. Then came the small bear, and finally the little baby bear had to climb to get up through the doorway. Skip asked for a drink of water. His father got one for him without turning on the lights. In the darkness, Skip drank it and lay down again.

POWER WITHOUT BRAKES

Both Buzzie and Skip could sit by themselves at six months. They could cruise a little at seven months and crawl across the room at eight months. When put in the playpen, both wanted to be let out. When the playpen was moved into the kitchen or next to a window, where they could look out, it satisfied each for about a half hour.

While Skip's pediatrician instructed his mother to keep Skip in the playpen a total of four hours daily, the use of the playpen was not discussed at Buzzie's periodic examination. After crawling all over the apartment, both boys cried when put in the playpen.

Buzzie's mother did not insist that he spend a specific period of time in the playpen. She usually let him out if he made a real fuss. It did not take him long to find out that if he cried long, loud and hard enough, he would be let out. Buzzie's mother found that verbal restrictions were the easiest for the moment. She didn't put him in the playpen at all. He had the free run of the apartment for all his waking hours. His natural curiosity took him to many fascinating adult possessions for which he had no real appreciation; nor did he understand to whom they belonged. He really thought they were his own. When he first reached for a cigarette from the container on the coffee table, as he had seen his parents do many times, he responded beautifully when his mother said, "No, no. Don't touch." For about two weeks his response was consistently good. Proudly his mother boasted, "He knows." If this were the only "no, no" or even if there were only one more, Buzzie probably would have been all right.

Unfortunately, as he became quicker on his feet, his curiosity increased in geometrical proportions. He reached for books, vases, scissors, electric sockets, dishes, lamps, bureau drawers, toilets, stoves and medicines. Buzzie's mother became so concerned with the way Buzzie persistently got into adult dangers that she consulted her pediatrician. He advised putting all their nice things away and making their home as childproof as possible.

Buzzie's parents proceeded to make their apartment as childproof as possible. Buzzie's father bought plastic plugs for outlets so Buzzie wouldn't electrocute himself. They locked the wedding presents in the living room closet. They traded their old stove which had accessible handles for a new one that had knobs out of reach. Choice books were put on high shelves.

They heartily disapprove of the way Skip's mother had used the playpen and the gated room. They called it confinement." They wanted Buzzie to explore. His playpen was used for Buzzie's toys.

Buzzie's parents believed that they could live without their valuable possessions. They were convinced that they had made their apartment childproof. But soon they found that there were many valuables in the modern adult world that were not good for small children and which could not be put away. Living their competitive lives, without thinking of Buzzie, they brought in new possessions. There were cameras, briefcases, keys, medicines, new books and binoculars which to Buzzie were like new toys. He ran wild in an adult world. Again, he had to have more "no, nos" than he could understand, much less obey. His mother became a slave to his energy and his "disobedience" which was just normal curiosity. It annoyed her and made her nervous. Just to keep him alive, she had to watch his every move.

By the time he was two, he ran all over the house. He opened doors and pulled pans out from under the stove. Imitating his mother, he tried to light the burner, but he couldn't reach the right knob. The television picture was frequently spoiled by his manipulations. When his mother put down her pocketbook for a moment, he soon had its contents scattered all over the floor. He could climb now. His father's books again were fair game, and Buzzie edited them with his crayons. Sometimes he tore the pages out. He loved to put his duck and small boat in the toilet bowl as well as his diapers. Of course, he had to taste everything.

One day his mother forgot to lock the aspirin in the medicine chest, and Buzzie found the bottle. When his mother found him, he was sitting on the floor with the half-empty aspirin bottle. There were a few tablets on the floor, a crushed one in his hand, and two in his mouth. He was chewing and swallowing.

His mother screamed, "You didn't eat any, did you?"

Buzzie shook his head, "NO!"

More calm now, Mother asked Buzzie, "You ate some, didn't you?"

Buzzie smiled and said, "Buzzie ate; Buzzie's a good boy."

Mother and doctor decided that a trip to the emergency room and the emptying of his stomach was called for.

The unpleasant experience, although it tended to make Buzzie not like emergency rooms, failed to give him the brakes he needed to live with his grown-ups. He seemed to do something that he shouldn't when least expected and before his mother could react to stop him.[1]

There was no end to it. Buzzie didn't get into trouble; he stayed in trouble. In the evening, his mother was exhausted. Her patience had been so tried that she habitually resorted to shouting and slapping. She felt frustrated and abused. Both parents succumbed to the pressure and began to take it out on each other. Buzzie's father was in charge of feeding and putting his son to bed. But Buzzie would not let the day end when his parents wanted it to. Buzzie wanted Mommie, so she had to put Buzzie to bed. Buzzie wanted to "tinkle" again. Then he wanted a drink of water. He wanted the light on.

After all these desires were handled, he came into the living room again and was discovered sitting quietly by the door. Father got up again and put him back to bed. Buzzie was told he was going to be spanked him if he again got out of bed. Buzzie had no brakes and received his spanking. He was then afraid to get out of bed and cried himself to sleep.

Mother and Father then proceeded to pick up the broken pieces of their domestic tranquility. Because they were young and strong, they succeeded. That night Mother heard Buzzie call out to her in his sleep. He was having a nightmare.

The next evening Mother was so tired that she lay down on her own bed and dozed. Buzzie went to sleep beside her. Quietly, without waking him, she put him in his crib and went out to the kitchen to help her husband who was putting away the dishes. They both looked in on Buzzie. "How angelic he looks in his sleep," she murmured, touching her husband's hand.

Buzzie awoke in the dark. He was wet and hungry. He hiked one leg over the top of his crib, held onto the rail with two chubby hands, boosted his other leg over the side, and dropped to the floor. He felt his way along the wall through the open door of his room. Out in the hall, past his parents' room, he knocked over a small lamp and a chair, and toddled to the kitchen.

The big white box stood beckoning before him. He reached up, pulled open the door, and stared at the light. Finally, he chose his breakfast...two raw eggs and a stick of butter.

---

[1] This incident was typical of the 1950's before medicines had "safety caps" and mothers had IPECAC in their medicine chests to induce vomiting. After the age of four, I used to scare my own children about the dangers of sampling medicine, just as my mother used to tell horror stories about children playing with matches.

He sat on the floor, spread his legs, and broke the eggs. Laughing, he swished the eggs around on the floor like the finger paints his mommy let him play with when it was light outside.

Suddenly he felt hungry again and tried to scoop the eggs up to his mouth, but they slipped through his fingers. He started to cry until he remembered the butter. Then he unwrapped the package and took a big bite. He was surprised because he had to chew it. It was cold and hard, not at all like the butter his mommy put on toast when the sun was out.

Angry now, he spat out the butter. He pulled himself up and went over to the refrigerator, drew out the crisper, and took out a dozen oranges, one by one. These he threw against the stove. Again reaching into the refrigerator, with a crash, he pulled a half gallon of milk out. It ran all over the kitchen floor. When Buzzie's mother arrived, she found Buzzie sitting in a pool of milk surrounded by glass and oranges. By the time Mother had cleaned up the mess, it was nearly dawn. She took Buzzie to bed with her. She resented her husband for sleeping through the turmoil.

At two-and-a-half, Buzzie was even wilder. Many times he chased a ball into the street. He was scolded and spanked, but still he forgot the next time the ball rolled into the street. The four-year-olds stopped at the curb. Buzzie, without stopping to look, ran into the street to retrieve the ball. When his mother walked up to him, he remembered, threw the ball away, and began to cry.

Shopping with Buzzie was terrible. He knocked down the canned goods, or he rearranged the stacks of small packages. His mother's being pregnant didn't help. Sometimes she felt cramps and thought she would miscarry after she had chased Buzzie. In the evening when his mother told him that it was time to go into the house, he said, "NO!" "Doesn't Buzzie want to have supper?" "NO!" "Does Buzzie want to stay out?" "NO!" His mother emphatic now, took him by the hand and began to lead him. He kicked and threw himself down. His mother had to carry him kicking and screaming up the apartment stairs.

When he was hungry, he ate. At other times, he spilled or threw his food. There was no moderation. He was always into something. The pediatrician recommended nursery school, but there was no vacancy. He was put on the waiting list.

While Buzzie's mother was at the hospital having a new baby, Buzzie exhausted his grandmother and the two sitters who took turns taking care of him. Meanwhile, in the hospital, Buzzie's mother was very successful in breast-feeding. She had an abundance of milk and was very happy that she knew enough not to get cracked nipples as she had with Buzzie.

After Buzzie's mother got home from the hospital, grandmother left. She was more than exhausted. She could not stand Buzzie any longer. Then the sitters left. Buzzie's mother was alone with Buzzie and his baby brother. Buzzie seemed to be very fond of his baby brother and patted him frequently. Once in an exceedingly generous mood, he put a small nursery chair on top of him in the bassinet. Read Chapter XVII.

It was only when mother lay down to breast-feed that Buzzie became jealous and was compelled to get her attention. He opened the bottom drawer of her dresser and pulled out her underwear and flushed it down the toilet. It was not until the neighbors below telephoned that the water was coming through their ceiling that she saw the bathroom was flooded. Spanking did no good. He seemed to forget. It was not until the third visit from the plumber that she finally decided to give up breast-feeding.

It was not difficult to convince her husband that life would be better if, instead of paying rent on an apartment, they would make mortgage payments on a house. The next Saturday they looked at a house in a new development. All the houses were expensive, but new, and a large down payment was not necessary. Both sets of grandparents helped, and within a month they were moved in.

At times, Buzzie roamed the neighborhood with several other boys and girls of pre-school age. A few of the mothers invited all the children in and gave them cookies. But many of the parents in the neighborhood told the children to go home when they knocked on their kitchen doors.

At four, Buzzie seemed to understand a little better what was expected of him. He ran away, however, and was brought home by the police. The first time it really tested the policemen's ingenuity. His name was "Buzzie." That was all. His house had a red door. After sitting around at the police headquarters for two hours and trying to find out who he was, they set out to take him home in a squad car. They drove for miles, and it wasn't until the third passing that Buzzie pointed out his house. It was a "dark" red door.

After this episode, his father taught him his full name and address. Then it was easier for the police, and Buzzie enjoyed the rides in the squad car.

Buzzie's mother was worried. Her pediatrician always reassured her, but it was difficult for the doctor to give her the tangible help she needed. Growth came to the rescue, it seemed, because Buzzie developed brakes when he was four years old. That improvement, however, was not completely satisfactory. She did not feel as though she understood Buzzie and his unpredictable dependence.

Buzzie's mother lay awake at night thinking about her inability to communicate with Buzzie. All her friends told her that her problem was not one bit different from every other mother's problem with an aggressive pre-school boy. She did not tell her friends that she was worried about herself and her marriage. She thought her husband had lost respect for her because she frequently became frustrated in handling Buzzie.

The fights with her husband were more frequent and more bitter. After each battle, she tried to pick up all the broken pieces. After each, it seemed harder and harder to collect them all.

CHAPTER XI
WHAT COMPARTMENTATION CAN DO FOR YOUR CHILD

"I don't want it!" screamed four-year old Heidi.

"You can't swim, you must wear it!", answered her mother.

"No I won't you can't make me!", cried Heidi.

Neither Heidi's mother nor father could make her put on the life jacket. Her mother spanked her, but Heidi would not give in. Heidi was sobbing in her mother's lap when Skip came aboard. Skip put on the life jacket without complaint. Seeing Skip behave so well inspired Heidi's mother to make another try.

Still sobbing, Heidi shook her head no. Her mother took her below and she fell asleep on a bunk. Skip who was also four, sat quietly in the cockpit and watched the sails and the wind. When the boat tipped, Skip was not frightened as many pre-schoolers are when tipping in a sailboat for the first time. Skip had been compartmentized and he felt confident that the grown-ups knew what they were doing. He adapted and followed directions even though he did not understand why.

Heidi had well developed techniques of resistance to many new situations. She had developed a habit of disobeying.

Unlike Skip, Heidi had not been compartmentized. She showed the same resistance to wearing seat belts. Most children won't wear them without a fight.

In the seventies a national study indicated that only seven percent of the children in America used seat belts. It is better in the eighties since seat belts, or approved baby seats, are mandatory in many states. Among the boating population there has been no thorough study concerning life jackets.

The adult world is inconsistent and confusing to all children, but the compartmentized pre-school child will adapt to this world better than the child who runs free in it all the time. A small child must not be expected to understand the adult world. He cannot possibly understand why his parents sometimes forbid and at other times ignore the same action. Parents are often inconsistent in restrictions depending on the time of day, whether or not they are watching the child, and how tired they are. This seeming variability in grown-ups is extremely confusing to a child.

The compartmentized child has four waking hours a day when he doesn't have to try to understand adults. He, therefore, does not suffer as many frustrations as the noncompartmentized child. He smiles at strangers and is happy to meet people. People will compliment you and ask how you taught your child such good manners at the tender age of two. But you did not teach him. He grew into a happy child because he was allowed to develop at his own pace.

The noncompartmentized child is faced with the confusion and inconsistency of the adult world all day long. She cannot understand this world, so she learns to resist it. She develops habits of disobedience. She may be very shy and fearful because adults have always asked more of her than she is capable of giving. She will cling to your legs while you talk with your friends. She will cry when she gets a haircut, goes to the doctor, or is fitted for new shoes. She will be impolite to her grandmother. She will throw herself down on the floor and scream in a temper tantrum at the slightest provocation. It will be difficult to get her to stay in bed. Then she will have nightmares.

Sometimes, however, the noncompartmentized child is bold and over-aggressive instead of shy. He ignores adults unless they shout or slap, which they have to do to keep him out of danger. Because he is strong, he is capable of going his own way; but the adult world is too much for him. Often he is overwhelmed by the confrontation and collapses. He never completely regains his poise.

These techniques of resistance become well-developed in the noncompartmentized preschool child. He is saying, "Leave me alone. I want no more grown-ups." He is saturated with and exhausted by adult ideas. His survival depends upon his finding effective ways to protect himself from grown-ups. His protection is his disobedience. He pays little or no attention to you or any other adult. You reprimand him loudly at first; but when he gets out of reach, you are too tired or too frustrated to follow through. You avoid a confrontation because you do not want to precipitate a temper tantrum. In a way you are afraid of him, and he senses it. When he finds that his mother and father, whom he thought knew everything, are not infallible, he feels insecure.

Compartmentation is a state of mind in the parents, as well as a physical measure. It means not expecting more of your child than he is capable of giving, according to his developmental age. Many parents expect their small children to act about two years older than they are. A two year old can't possibly be made to understand the concept of "mine and thine" until he is four. So give the baby another toy and try to interest your two year old in a game of his own. If you expect too much of your child, you will create feelings of inadequacy in him and you will frustrate yourself by trying to get your child to do something he is not yet capable of doing. If he is in his own play area half the time, you won't have to spend fruitless hours trying to keep him away from the stairs and floor lamps. When he is running free, during the other half of his waking hours, you will have more energy to keep up with him because he is more adaptable.

THE COMPARTMENTIZED APPEAR TO LEARN FASTER

By comparing several hundred records of pre-school children; who were kept in a playpen, gated room, fenced yard or tethered for two to four hours daily (compartmentation) with children who were not compartmentized; it was found that the performances in the developmental tests (Gesell) showed accomplishments of the compartmentized to be, when compartmentation was the only variable, several months ahead of their chronological ages.

The compartmentized learned faster because they were not resistant to learning. They were able to embrace the learning experience and develop new skills instead of using their energy to disobey and resist. Among the noncompartmentized, there were many instances where rapport could not be established enough to test. Others performed at average or slightly below average levels using the same tests in the same way.

MORE SURE OF THEMSELVES

Several experienced nursery school, kindergarten, and first grade teachers have told me that they could spot the children who had been compartmentized. In several instances, the differences were a conversation point among kindergarten and first grade teachers. Sometimes, the feedback was that the children were conceited. I think this was because the compartmentized seemed to adapt to the classroom situations more quickly than those who were not compartmentized in their pre-school years. They had not developed techniques of resistance (too shy or too bold) or habits of disobedience that had to be unlearned. From the beginning, the compartmentized children were more sure of themselves. They did not show as many doubts when called on in class, they asked more questions and made decisions easily.

MORE ASSERTIVE

Children who have been compartmentized in their pre-school years are usually more assertive inside and outside their own homes. Even though they are assertive, however, they respond well to the adult "no" because they have not been super saturated with "no" or literally or psychologically beaten into submission, as are many pre-school children who do not get systematic, daily vacations from adults (compartmentation).

I have observed a carry-over of this assertiveness to the school. Because the child who has had a systematic, daily escape from having to understand adult wishes (compartmentation), he or she approaches all adults with eagerness through force of habit that he developed in his pre-school years. He volunteers in class and is not as shy. These children like to have the leads in school plays, become team captains and organize their own activities. Hence, compartmentized children give the impression of being more assertive in school and out.

Let's go to the birthday parties of Joan and Ruth who are both five years old. Joan clung to her mother's skirt's while greeting people at the door. She smiled and enjoyed opening her presents, but never left her mother's side. When it came time to blow out the candles she insisted on holding her mother's hand

She had to be urged to blow them out. Her mother seemed a little embarrassed when Joan passively followed her around while the cake was being served.

Ruth was quite different at her party. She greeted everyone, shook hands and showed guests where to put their coats. Ruth thanked everyone for her birthday presents and put them in a special place. She asked everyone to be quiet when she blew out the candles. Ruth even helped her mother serve her friends birthday cake and ice cream and asked each if he or she wanted a second helping. Ruth was everywhere, she functioned completely separately from her mother. Ruth was a charming little hostess.

Both Joan and Ruth were equal in intelligence. Both passed the reading readiness test. Joan answered but was shy. Ruth answered correctly and volunteered. She was the first to help a classmate find her lost homework. When classmates fought she laughed and hugged them both.

None of the parents were shy. In fact Joan's seemed more assertive than Ruth's. Both couples seemed equally loving. Why the difference? Joan's parents did not practice compartmentation. Ruth, on the other hand, was in the playpen, gated room and fenced yard. At three she attended nursery school. Compartmentation was 100%.

THE COMPARTMENTIZED HAVE FEWER ACCIDENTS

Many pre-school children are rushed to the emergency rooms of hospitals in America for treatment for the ingestion of poisons, for cuts, fractures, and burns. The compartmentized pre-school patients make fewer such visits. Only a few are hurt while being compartmentized. I have records of hundreds who were not compartmentized. Household accidents are the greatest cause of hospitalization in the pre-school child today.

It is easy to understand why the compartmentized have fewer accidents -- their compartmentized world offers fewer opportunities to be exposed to the hazards of modern life.

The results of my longitudinal studies indicated that there are significantly fewer accidents among the compartmentized in every age group: in the pre-school, school, high school and college students. Will we see the day when health insurance premiums will be reduced for compartmentation as the driving accident insurance premiums are now reduced for the high school students on the honor rolls?

THEY BECOME BETTER STUDENTS

I have records of significant numbers of children whom I have followed from birth into adulthood. More than one hundred were 100% compartmentized for four years. Several hundred were three-fourths compartmentized (three years). Still more were 50%, 37%, 25% or not compartmentized at all. That is, they stayed in the playpen and gated room for two to four hours daily until two years, 18 months, or one year of age or not at all.

The longitudinal data just completed, seems to suggest that children of equal intelligence earned grades in proportion to the amount of compartmentation they had received in their pre-school years. There are, however many conflicting factors that are mentioned in the EPILOGUE.

We know that the pre-school children who are compartmentized are more adaptable and more assertive. They appear to learn faster and seem more sure of themselves compared to the noncompartmentized. They have fewer techniques of resistance to new situations. This momentum of learning of the compartmentized carries into their school years. Other things being equal they become better students. Intelligence is probably mostly inherited. It plays an unknown part. Achievement from trying harder may play a larger part. The compartmentized may be better students because they try harder and have developed fewer techniques of resistance.

A CHART TO RECORD GROWTH AND PERFORMANCE

It is very easy and pleasant for the doctor to examine a child between one and three who has been compartmentized. This child usually cooperates during his physical examination and scarcely cries when he gets a shot. The noncompartmentized child in this age group hates to go to the doctor. He is terrified of the stethoscope and clings to his mother. It is often impossible to examine him and he has to be held down when he is to be given a shot. If the doctor gives him a developmental test, he will be hesitant about performing or not perform at all. The doctor can establish good rapport with the compartmentized child during the developmental test, and he will get a valid indication of the child's development.

Dr. Arnold Gesell began to use developmental tests in 1911 on institutionalized pre-school children. They responded well, probably because they spent much of their time in cribs and playpens. I am not advising you to keep your child in a playpen all the time -- just 2 to 4 hours a day. Later Dr. Gesell and his associates tested pre-school children who lived with their parents and were not compartmentized. They did not perform as well as the institutionalized children.

In 1940 I began to do brief modifications of the Gesell tests. Every well infant and child who comes to my office or Infant Welfare Station is given a developmental test before his physical examination.

The tests I use require the following materials: (1) the usual examining table, near which the mother sits and comforts her infant, who is lying supine or is supported in a sitting position, depending upon what tests are used; (2) a stethoscope; (3) about 12 one inch square blocks made of wood and painted bright red; (4) a dark colored pill about 1/4 inch in diameter, which can be rolled about on the table top (a small vitamin capsule is useful because it makes a noise; (5) a small wooden table measuring 14 X 10 inches, painted white, with 6 inch legs that are fixed or collapsible (the table top has a 1/4 inch rim to keep the pill from rolling off); (6) one aluminum measuring cup; (7) one red rubber ball the size of a tennis ball; (8) a one ounce glass bottle with a one inch wide mouth and (9) red and black lead pencil.

I approach the child quietly before I make the physical examination. I find it best to speak softly and not to stare at the child. I pretend to be interested in the test toys; frequently I ask the child to perform at half his age level to get him started. I try not to catch his eye or to direct my attention to him. For the doctor or any other adult to stare, to lock eyes, and exude personality will often make the pre-school child become shy or cry. If I catch the child's eye by accident, I quickly smile and look away.

If he still seems frightened, I usually ask his mother to hold him on her lap. Many years of watching one of my teachers, Dr. Douglas Buchanan of the University of Chicago, approach and examine children neurologically helped me to standardize these tests and to make them usable in my busy clinic and office practices.

During the last forty-two years I have noted considerable variation in response among children, and I have tried to discover why these variations exist. It is evident that the child's emotional reactions in the test situation are greatly affected by his mother's attitude. With some children I established rapport quickly, but most of the children between one and four stare questioningly and fearfully or cry and cling to their mothers. There are a few who always smile and do exactly what is asked of them. These children perform up to and beyond their developmental levels, even though they are not always smarter than their more cautious contemporaries. It is very interesting to watch the mother as I test her child. I have come to regard the child and the mother as a unit. It seems that the mother's degree of calmness or nervousness is one of the determining factors in the child's ability to perform in the test situation.

When a child has the ability to perform the tests but does not, usually there are adults in the home who are projecting their ideas upon him in such a way that he looks with questioning, frequently with apprehension, and too often with great fear at all adults, including the examiner. This excessive caution in the test situation usually begins at 10 months and lasts throughout the fourth birthday. Occasionally, instead of being cautious, the child is boldly aggressive. Calloused against direction, the child goes his own way and makes numerous swirling circles instead of one neat one. On the other hand, those who cooperate are truly unusual children. They smile a lot, cooperate during physical examinations, and barely cry when given injections.

I have developed a chart to record the performance of each child at each examination.

The chart on pages 58-60 is the actual chart I use in practice. This seemingly complicated chart combines longitudinally; the circumference of the head, the height and weight, the modified Gesell tests, and the amount of and type of compartmentation. Thus the doctor can see at a glance the physical, intellectual, and emotional growth of the child. This enables the physician to specify advice to fit the child's ability at the time that the problem arises.

For example a child of two and a half is throwing food all over the place and in general is obnoxious. It is helpful to know the number of "arrows" (lack of compartmentation) recorded on his chart. Are there no arrows or many? If there are many, he usually needs compartmentation to reduce his techniques of resistance (arrows). It is easier to modify his behavior after you have recompartmentized.

Before you try to solve all your problems with the terrible two year old by putting up gates (compartmentation); you must make sure that your child's in good physical health. Is he feverish? Is he coming down with an infection? Are his ears tender? Is he coughing? Are his bowels loose? Has he lost his appetite? Or is he just plain tired?

While making the movie to demonstrate non-adaptable behavior in a wild two year old; there was technical delay with the camera. The unadaptable two year old fell asleep in his mother's lap. One half hour later, when he awakened, he tested beautifully. As well as any of the truly adaptable who had been compartmentized. Gesell observed the same phenomenon years ago. The children tested better after a nap. They behave better too.

It's important that your doctor examine your child who is giving you trouble. Even if your child's behavior is good, it is important for the physician to make an appraisal of his growth as well as his health.

Your physician may use tests other than Gesell tests to determine adaptability. Many different tests are equally reliable. The whole field is an art -- not a science.

Not all the physicians caring for children in the 1980's are using the Gesell test as a means of testing for compliance in the art of compartmentation. The number is increasing as my students take up the cause. It will be better in the twenty first century.

Whether your child is Gesell tested or not, it will be easier to handle him after he has been taught and allowed to play by himself, free from danger and the adult no, for fours hours a day (compartmentation). Then he will imitate everything that you do. You will not have to teach him at all -- just love him.

On the first page of the chart the age in months for the first two years extends along the horizontal line or the abscissa. The developmental tests appear as symbols in capital letters along the vertical line or ordinate. Heavier horizontal lines extend from the developmental symbols to a diagonal line that intersects with the vertical line representing development. When you child performs, a small cross is made where the horizontal line representing age crossed the vertical line representing development. Also, the appropriate symbol along the ordinate for whatever tests performed are checked with pencil.

On the second page of the chart the abscissa shows the age in years from 2 to 18. The developmental tests up to the third grade are along the ordinate. In fine print along the ordinates of both the first and second pages are some of the usual developmental accomplishments, listed under the categories of smile, roll, sit, crawl, and toilet training. A cross is made where the line representing age crossed the appropriate horizontal. The information is recorded from what the mother tells us before the developmental or physical examination is made. I usually obtain this information while the child is getting acquainted with the test toys. You mothers are encouraged to read your lists of problems at this time, and questions are asked of you to enrich the brief developmental examination that immediately follows.

How the child performs is important, and such remarks as "good examination -- smiles, " "indifferent -- poor exam," "overcautious -- poor exam," "cries and clings to mother -- no exam," "good exam -- cried during physical exam," "wants to do it his own way -- poor exam," and "not up to his developmental level," are written in vertically, opposite the age. When there is no performance and the test has been tried for about a minute, an arrow is made along with the appropriate remark. In this way, it is evident at a glance just how often there is rapport with the child in the test situation. See pages 58-60. A smile is always recorded. When the child cries, the cry is recorded along with how abruptly he stops. When I get a good rapport with a child in the test situation, I find that this child has more than average adaptability for his age.

There are other factors that affect adaptability. The smartness and calmness of the mothers are important factors. Those mothers who are nervous and unintelligent seem to have children who are hard to manage. Lack of knowledge or a mistake in judgment as to what the child understands are the common difficulties.

The place in the family affects adaptability. The first child in a family usually does not perform the tests well because his parents are unfamiliar with growth. They expect their first child to perform at about twice his developmental level. These children are overly cautious or overly bold and do not perform the developmental tests.

These parents would be indignant if a school system tried to force their nine year old child to master calculus. Yet, many persist in teaching their two year old child the differences between mine and thine," not to spill food, not to suck his thumb, to give up his bottle, and many other habits that he is not ready to master until he is twice that age.

The eldest is usually less cooperative with grandparents, doctors, teachers, barbers, and shoe clerks. He will improve if he is compartmentized.

Boys are usually more cautious and less adaptable than girls. Girls are more willing to submit to something they don't understand. Boys are reluctant to perform unless they completely understand what is expected of them. Compartmentation is more urgently needed in boys than in girls, especially first born boys.

Prolonged breast-feeding increases adaptability. The child who can run to his mother and nurse for a moment or two when he is hurt is more adaptable.

There are other factors which affect the child's performance which are not environmental. Some children seem to be constitutionally more sensitive than others. This characteristic varies even among siblings. One may be so compulsive in his actions that he behaves differently from his siblings and parents. It seems as though his brain is made differently, or that it possesses a lesion that has yet to be detected neurologically. For the past forty-two years I have been collecting prenatal and natal irregularities which have just been computerized for statistical analysis.

The small child usually enjoys the developmental examination so much that, the few minutes spent doing and recording it, is more than saved during the physical examination, which is done more quickly and accurately with a cooperative child. Also, a quiet office, even when the child does not perform, puts the child's physician in a stronger position in counseling parents. The examiner's advice becomes more precise when a visit-to-visit record is kept on how you and your child affect each other. The weary mother is urged to use some form of compartmentation. The child's performance at the next visit tells me whether or not the mother has taken my advice.

Everyone who watches my testing methods agrees that they demonstrate great differences in individual children and parents. It is obvious that environmental factors effect the adaptability of pre-school and school age children. The permanency of these differences is still being studied. Experience teaches ever-increasing respect for the inherited constitutional differences of individuals. As a busy physician, I know that I change very little the basic constitution of you or your child. But, sometimes, I help you to live more simply. When there is success in teaching compartmentation, there appears to be more than a two-fold increase in adaptability in the school child and almost a four fold increase in the toddler. All techniques of resistance against adults correlate with the recording of a high percentage of refusals to perform the developmental tests. Also, both have a negative correlation with the amount of compartmentation, totally and longitudinally.[1]

From: *A Chart to Record Growth and Performance*

DIRECTIONS FOR USE

To use this chart to its fullest advantage it is recommended that the user read The Pediatrician Examines The Mother and Child by E. Robbins Kimball, M.D., J.A.M.A. March 24, 1956, Vol. 160, pp. 1033-1039.

The materials needed are an ordinary examining table near which the mother can sit and comfort her infant lying supine or support him in a sitting position depending upon what tests are used. In addition we need as listed below:

S = Stethoscope
B = Blocks one inch per side made of wood and painted bright red: about one dozen.
P = Pill, red in color about ¼ inch in diameter that can be rolled about on the table top. (A small hard shelled vitamin capsule is very useful because it makes a noise.)
Small wooden table measuring 14 x 10 inches with 6 inch legs which are fixed or collapsible and painted white. The table top is rimmed with a ¼ inch elevation to keep the pill from rolling off.
A cup — of measuring size
Red rubber ball, size of tennis ball
One ounce glass bottle with mouth one inch wide
Pencils, red and green

The tests are brief and geared to the child's growth so that we "interview" the child at his own level. The tests we use and their symbols are outlined below:

ONE MONTH:
 S_1 = He fixes upon the stethoscope dangling 10 inches above his eyes while lying supine but can not follow the stethoscope when it is moved out of his line of vision.

TWO MONTHS:
 S_2 = Follows the same dangling stethoscope 90 degrees sideways and 180 degrees up and down. (Supine)
 B_1 = Grasps block when placed in his hand. Supine or sitting.

THREE MONTHS:
 S_3 = Stares prolongedly at the dangling stethoscope. (Supine)
 B_2 = Takes a fleeting glance at the block on the table top. (Sitting)
 B_4 = Watches ball rolling on table top. (Sitting)

FOUR MONTHS:
 S_4 = Dangling stethoscope excites activity of hands and arms. Supine.
 B_3 = Stares at block on table top. (Sitting)
 B_4 = Looks at block in his own hand. (Sitting)
 P_1 = Watches a rolling pill on the table top. (Sitting)

FIVE MONTHS:
 S_5 = Closes in on dangling stethoscope with both hands. (Supine)
 B_3 = Puts block in his mouth when block comes in contact with his hand. (Sitting)

SIX MONTHS:
(All tests are performed with the small white table across his knees; or sitting at a table.
 S_5 = Grabs the stethoscope with one hand on the table top.
 B_4 = Picks up one block on sight, pays no attention to a second block.
 P_2 = Grasps pill with a fumbling motion of his fingers.

SEVEN MONTHS:
 B_7 = Bangs block on table top.
 P_3 = Rakes in pill with all fingers.

EIGHT MONTHS:
 B_8 = Passes block from one hand to the other.
 BB_8 = Picks up one block and looks at second block.
 P_4 = Rakes in pill with fingers but beginning to use thumb and index finger in pincer like movements.

NINE MONTHS:
 BB_9 = Picks up the first and then the second block on sight.
 P_5 = Plucks pill with fingers extended.

TEN MONTHS:
 BB = Compares blocks — one in each hand.
 P_6 = Plucks pill with fingers curled.

ELEVEN MONTHS:
 $\frac{Cu}{B}$ = Recovers block from under cup.

TWELVE MONTHS:
 $Cu\text{-}B$ = Imitates placing one or more blocks in cup.
 W_1 = Imitates scribbling.

FIFTEEN MONTHS:
 B_8 = Places one block upon another.
 P_7 = Drops pill into bottle.

EIGHTEEN MONTHS:
 $3B$ = Builds a tower of three.

TWENTY MONTHS:
 $4B$ = Builds a tower of four.

TWO YEARS:
 $6B$ = Builds a tower of 6 or 7.
 $6B$ = Imitates the making of a train with blocks.
 W_2 = Copies a straight line.

TWO AND ONE-HALF YEARS:
 $10\text{-}B$ = Builds a tower higher than 10 blocks.

THREE YEARS:
 O = Copies a circle.
 + = Copies a cross.
 BB = Imitates the making of a bridge with three blocks.

FOUR YEARS:
 □ = Copies a square.

FIVE YEARS:
 △ = Copies a triangle.

---

[1] "The Pediatrician Examines the Mother and Child, Inroducing a chart to record growth and performance", by E.Robbins Kimball M.D., *The Journal of the American Medical Association*, March 24, 1956, Vol. 160 pp. 1033-1039.

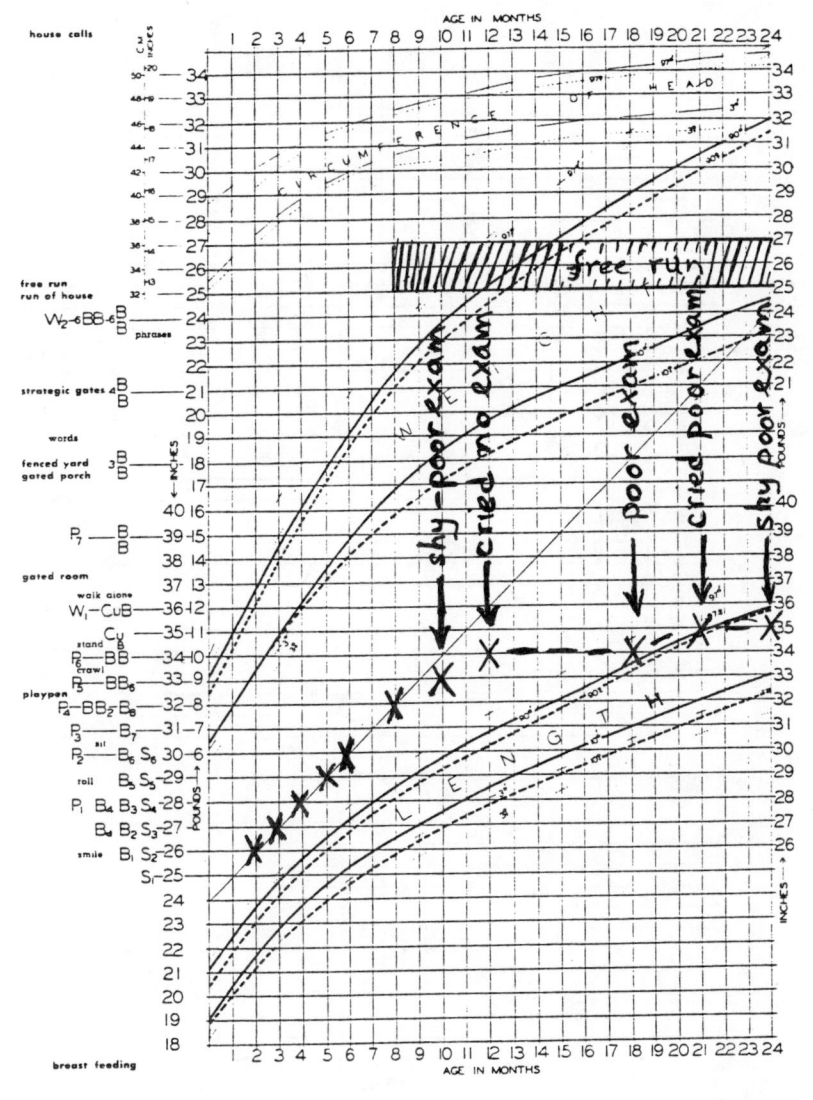

Chart of child behind in tests without compartmentation (free run) as shown by "X's" below normal developmental line — emphasized by arrows

CHAPTER XI / 59

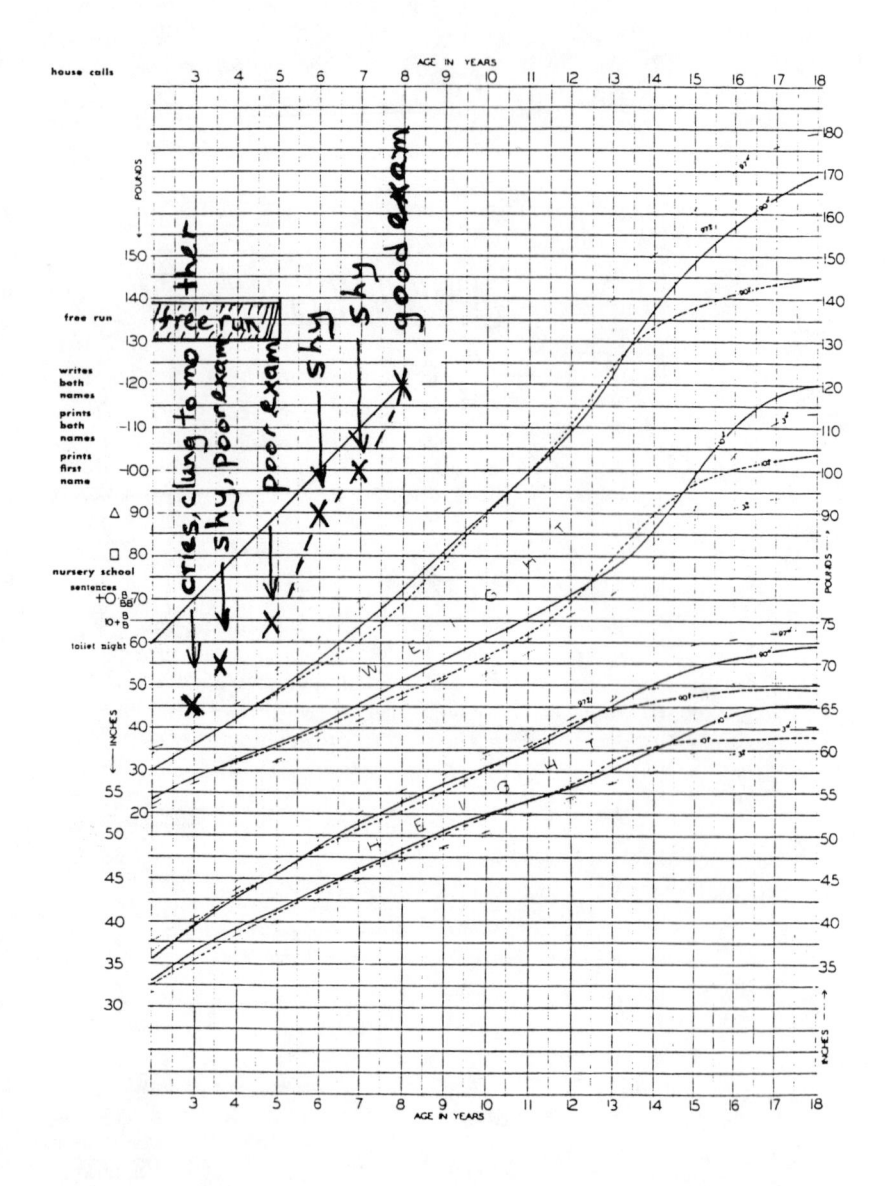

Same child catching up after going to school — a facsimile of compartmentation

CHAPTER XII
A CLOSER LOOK AT OVERACHIEVEMENT

"What do you mean by an overachiever?"

An overachiever is one who performs up to or better than he or she should based on his or her intelligence. As you know, intelligence is inherited. Achievement is acquired. The common complaint of parents in suburbia is that `My child's school work is not up to what it should be based on his intelligence.' He or she is an underachiever.

"How does the playpen or gated room in pre-school years relate to achievement in the school years?"

It is very simple. Elizabeth and Jessica have equal intelligence. Elizabeth was compartmentized until she was four. Jessica was subjected to many "no, no's" she never understood; so disobedience became a habit. Let me emphasize that both these little girls had equal intelligence. Both had easy births. Each child was well loved by her parents. Elizabeth and Jessica entered kindergarten together. Elizabeth immediately did what the teacher asked. She had never had to learn to question grown-ups as Jessica had.

Jessica had received so many "no no's", she did not know whom to believe or when. Sometimes she tore up paper and no one said a word and at other times she scribbled on order blanks and her parents screamed at her. Her parents were inconsistent. Why would her teacher be any different from the other grown ups in her life? Jessica had to overcome her habit of disobedience before she could equal the performance of Elizabeth. In first grade, Elizabeth performed before Jessica understood the question. Elizabeth continued to overachieve in grade school. Jessica still underachieved because she never overcame completely her habit of disobedience. She lacked the momentum to achieve that Elizabeth had developed.

"I don't understand why underachievement lasts years. I think it should disappear within months after compartmentation is used."

Underachievement usually doesn't last years, but in the growing child, it is easier to prevent bad habits than to correct them. The 15-month old will begin to overachieve (by Gesell testing) two weeks after recompartmentation. Also he or she will stop waking up at night. His temper tantrums become less violent. The four-year old who has never been compartmentized has habits of resistance that take longer to work out -- usually several months. If the techniques of resistance persist into the teens, it usually takes two years of rehabilitation.

Another consideration is that the noncompartmentized child so overwhelms his inexperienced parents that they lose the ability to communicate and control their child in his school years and in some instances, they never completely regain that ability. The parents of the compartmentized child live in harmony with him. They never lose their ability to communicate.

"What about the reports in some of the popular magazines that indicate children learn to read better when they have freedom to crawl?"

A few years ago there were many articles stating that it was good for your child's nervous system if he or she spent most of the waking hours crawling. The reason given is that cross-patterning associated with crawling -- left arm forward, right leg forward is important for the normal development of the nervous system. "If your child does not crawl, he will not read well," they said. I see no justifications for this position. Reading difficulties are familiar traits that have nothing to do with whether or not children crawled in infancy.

Furthermore the compartmentalized child has freedom to crawl in the playpen and in the other larger gated childproof areas. In addition, she has freedom from the adult "no" areas. When I have found reading difficulties among my young patients who have been compartmentized, I have found that they respond faster to individual tutoring than those children who were not compartmentized. Those who had run free had more techniques of resistance to overcome before they could get down to work to overcome their difficulties.

"I believe I have met overachievers who were not compartmentized in their pre-school years."

I am sure you have. A few of the parents of my patients have reared overachievers by childproofing without compartmentation. Most of these parents possess more than the usual measure of mother love. Without exception, they have more than the usual serenity. Often they came from farms and grew up with animals or had much experience in caring for small children. Besides childproofing their homes, they often use slings to carry their babies around on their backs.

When their toddlers become frightened or frustrated because of the over-expansion of their worlds, like primitive mothers, they suckle their infants. Most of these mothers are fanatical about breast-feeding. They nurse for one year regularly. They suckle irregularly whenever the child is hurt or frightened until three or more years of age. These mothers are completely dedicated to rearing their children. They are never concerned about their social positions. If the family income is below the average, it apparently never worries them. They are calm and intelligent and completely occupied with the task of giving everything to their children -- perhaps to the point of neglecting husbands, friends, and civic duties.

Their households may never be organized and seldom neat or clean. They are completely relaxed in their respective states of disorganization. These strong, fanatically dedicated mothers are able to rear their children without the help of compartmentation. These mothers are rare in my practice, but they produce overachievers without compartmentation.

Most of my practice has been involved with young couples. Many are business and professional people and well thought of in the community. When properly instructed these parents compartmentize their children. Those who are compartmentized become overachievers unless there is a neurological reason for not overachieving. Those who are not compartmentized develop techniques of resistance against grown-ups. In the noncompartmentized, these techniques of resistance develop into habits of disobedience until the parents lose control and rear their children without communicating with them or really understanding them. You know lots of them among friends' children. The school authorities call them underachievers. Their performances are never up to their abilities.

A Chart To Record Growth and Performance in packages of 100 can be obtained by writing to Sea Grape Press Box 4122 Boca Raton, FL 33429.

Recommended for professionals, a VHS format video tape demonstrating Dr. Kimball's modification of the Gesell tests used to measure compliance to the prescription of compartmentation, can be obtained by writing Sea Grape Press.

For talks on compartmentation or breast-feeding write Dr. E. Robbins Kimball, 14750 Beach Blvd., #23, Jacksonville, FL 32250.

CHAPTER XIII

WHAT CAN COMPARTMENTATION DO FOR PARENTS?

COMPARTMENTATION GIVES YOU MORE SELF ESTEEM

Buzzie wouldn't let the nice shoe salesman fit him with a new pair of shoes. He cried and he kicked. Even when his mother slapped him he would not hold his foot still. He was too quick and too strong to get a good fit.

"His father can bring him in," she said.

As she and Buzzie were about to leave, Skip, his mother and the new baby came in. Skip was tethered to his mother's wrist and the new baby was asleep in a sling.

Skip sat in the chair beside his mother and cooperated completely while the clerk fitted him with new shoes. Buzzie now wanted new shoes. Skip's mother held Buzzie patiently on her lap while the clerk fitted him with similar shoes. He was not as cooperative as Skip, but he didn't fight the clerk to a "no fit" as he had before.

That night as usual Buzzie had a nightmare. Mother brought him to bed with her and he immediately went back to sleep beside her sleeping husband.

Buzzie's mother could not get back to sleep. She kept thinking of shopping with her child and how little control she had. How can Skip's mother feel so confident to bring in two children and buy them shoes. She even took my uncooperative two and one half year old and held him so that the clerk could fit him too.

Skip's mother never had shown that kind of self confidence and patience when we were in college.

What's happened to me?

MAKES MOTHER MORE PRODUCTIVE

"I wouldn't be able to get any work done if I didn't keep Marty in a gated room for two hours every morning," said Mrs. Applegate who is a twenty-eight-year-old mother of an aggressive two-year-old. After graduating from college, Mrs. Applegate became a self-supporting art director for six years. Now she is a freelance artist to augment her family's income.

Compartmentation enables you to accomplish your work as efficiently as you did before your baby was born. You can complete your tasks while the baby is in the playpen and then be able to give him your undivided attention while he is running loose. You will know that you have a certain amount of time -- half the child's waking hours -- in which to do your work.

You will also have more time to yourself. While your child is in his gated room or fenced yard, you can work, read, take a shower, make phone calls, sew or take a nap. You'll have one ear open and probably won't sleep, but at least you'll rest. Having this time to pursue your own interests will make you more content and feel more like a mother and less like a slave. You will feel rested because you haven't spent the whole day chasing after your toddler.

The compartmentized child does not cling to his mother like the noncompartmentized child does. The clinger's mother tries to stop this habit and then feels guilty about it. You won't have this problem if you compartmentize. You will be proud of your child because he behaves better than the child who runs loose. Because he has had four hours in the playpen or gated room, he is not as tired or as irritable at the end of the day as the child who has been running loose all his waking hours.

MAKES YOU A STRONGER PARENT

Those who have compartmentized their pre-school children have told me how much more adaptable, happier, and easier to live with they are compared to those of their friends who were not compartmentized. I am convinced also that this initial advantage carries over into the school years so that those of average intelligence do better than average work. In addition to having a lasting effect on the child, compartmentation seems to make you a stronger parent.

You have had a chance to pursue other interests (2 to 4 hours a day) through the pre-school years. You have more patience and haven't had to learn to tune out because you got overtired or lost your temper and then felt guilty afterwards. Having succeeded in compartmentation, you have been able to handle your school child with more patience and objectivity.

You are able to shift gears each year to stay in tune with your child's changing abilities. For instance, you will give him or her a bicycle or pet animal when you see that your child is old enough to take care of it (eight years). You will teach him to row a boat before you teach him to sail (eleven years) or let him run a motor boat (sixteen years). You will not be afraid to give him an allowance that is smaller than that of his friends. You will know at what age to expect him to do chores (ten years). You will not pay him to work for you in his home after fourteen but help him to obtain work for pay outside his home.

By letting your child's activities be guided by his abilities, which is sort of a continuation of compartmentation; you develop a wisdom in your communications which exerts the necessary control through the tumultuous teens. Then there is less revolt, less use of drugs, and less loose sex among those teenagers whose parents practice some type of compartmentation which began in the pre-school years.

If compartmentation gives strength to parents then they develop more control. I have spent most of my professional life teaching mothers the art of compartmentation. I am convinced that the parents who have been exposed to the teaching of compartmentation have become stronger which in turn has made "parental love" more easily demonstrable and approving.

COMPARTMENTATION HELPS MAKE A BETTER MARRIAGE

In 1601 and before the Indian warriors of the Manhattan tribe were observed getting into their canoes and paddling up the Mountain River (Hudson). They hunted and visited various tribes along the banks and inland. They usually left in the spring and returned to their families before the cold weather. The warriors began to make these treks after seven years of domestic bliss. It was called "the seven year itch."

Many years ago (about 1925) Judge Ben Lindsay wrote in Liberty magazine about three periods in marriage when couples might divorce: after one year, after seven and after 25 years. If they divorced after one year, they never should have married.

After seven years of marriage husbands were no longer the dragon slayers on white chargers. Mothers were worn out chasing kids. Sex had become routine. Husbands and wives were no longer friends. They took each other for granted. The Manhattans solved it by paddling up river.

THE GOLF WIDOW

"I've had these kids all day. Now its your turn I'm going shopping." said Judy Abbott to her tired husband when he walked in the door. Her stress reaction was happening so often that Tom dreaded going home.

Abbott, Barnes and Cole had been on the university golf team. They had won the collegiate championship. Abbott and Barnes had gone into sales. Cole remained at the university coaching golf. No matter what, they seldom missed a week of playing together. They were good friends and competitors. They loved golf.

Lithely Judy took multiple camera shots of Tom Abbott: talking to customers or swinging a golf club. She directed with poise and her words were quiet and concise. Tom's company was one of her better commercial accounts.

Tom Abbott was his company's best salesperson. He was experienced, irrepressible, and extroversive. Judy caught his eye immediately.

Judy was valedictorian in her high school class and won a scholarship to college. After graduation she became the photographer for an advertising agency.

Judy had a temper. Even as a child everything was black or white. There was no gray. As she grew older her temper became incisive and quietly unrelenting. Tom now knew that he had never been in love before. Judy was fascinating and unfathomable. They had a whirlwind courtship. She walked the 18 holes with her camera and took many pictures but she did not want to learn to play golf. Her avocation was reading and her profession was photography.

They had a formal church wedding and a small stylish reception at his golf club. After a short honeymoon in Paris, they moved into the apartment where Tom lived as a bachelor.

Toward the end of her first pregnancy Judy gave up her job with the advertising agency. She read everything she could about breast-feeding and child rearing.

She breast-fed her first son for 21 months. She stopped when she learned that she was pregnant with her second. Two more followed. There were three under five. She breast-fed them all for over one year. They moved into a house.

Judy's reading and course in psychology were against compartmentation as I recommended it and she thought that either she or her husband should take care of their children.

The obstreperous behavior of the noncompartmentized pre-school children devastated both her and her husband. Both were awakened every night. Neither slept a night through. It dulled Tom's selling acumen. He played more golf.

Judy was proud of her husband's position and income level but she resented his golf. She was rude to his golfing buddies. She felt that her husband should have "his turn at taking care of the children." All the modern writings said that "fathers should share in the care of the children." Judy was given money to hire sitters but she seldom found them. She never got away with her husband without the children.

There was much shouting and threats of spanking, which they never got. The children had learned to pay no attention to her or any adult.

"Don't touch me," Judy often said when her husband tried to hug her out of her stress. As a family their "quality of time" together was rapidly deteriorating. Tom found that he could sell better when he played more golf and spent less time at home. He moved in with a golfing friend who was now divorced.

Tom and his friends frequently ate at a restaurant/bar where there was a dynamically attractive waitress. She had been a bar-maid since she was 15. She had two children by the time she was 20 and was a widow at 21. Helen reared her two children alone. They were now self supporting. She was a wise young attractive grandmother. Helen admired Tom's ability to make money and his prowess in golf. She became his confessor. She also organized a promotional party at the restaurant with his customers and friends. Judy was asked to photograph the party. Judy said that she would; but never appeared.

Judy consulted an attorney about a divorce. Tom countered by threatening to give up being a sales rep and becoming a golf pro like his friend, Cole. This frightened Judy into not seeking a divorce. Tom voluntarily increased his financial support to his wife and children which was already considerably higher than what his friends were required to give their ex-wives and children. Judy now had more money to spend than her friends.

Neither Tom nor Helen were very demanding of each other but she supplied all his needs. She increased his confidence in himself. His earnings doubled and his golf improved. He was generous with his money.

Alan Barnes also was a good salesman and provider. Their pediatrician differed from Judy's. When Sally Barnes no longer kept her toddler in a playpen, her pediatrician scolded her and told her how to use gates and how to tether as described in HOW TO RECOMPARTMENTIZE. Thus Sally kept her three children under control. Unlike Judy, Sally learned to play golf. She had learned the art of compartmentation. She kept a long list of baby sitters. She went on golf and business trips with her husband. When her husband's golf was too good "to let the customer win"; Sally graciously let the customer win. Alan got to depend upon his wife in his hobby and in his profession. Because Sally had learned golf Alan eventually learned to sail which had always been Sally's passion. With sitters she got relief from the chores of mothering for at least one whole day a week. In addition she made business trips with her husband several nights a month. These frequent respites rested her.

Because Sally was not frustrated, the "quality of the time" spent with her children was better than that of Judy's.

Bob Cole's income was steady but he was not the six figure money maker of his classmates: Abbott and Barnes. Linda continued to work after marriage. After the first baby she made arrangements to take her nursing baby to work shortly after his birth. She talked her boss into letting her baby sleep in a basket in a corner of the office while she resumed running the office. When he became mobile, i.e. could crawl around, she found a day care center nearby and continued to breast-feed in her lunch hour and during the day when called.

Linda continued in her full time career all through her children's grammar and high school. She taught her "latch key" children to call her at work every afternoon as soon as they got home from school. When her job prevented her from coming to the phone, one of the other women in the office took the call. The children's father and the stay at home mothers in the neighborhood were scheduled for back up availability for the children between the time the children got out of school and the mother got home from work. Despite her demanding job, she always knew where her children were. She was anticipatory. She planned thoroughly for the usual contingencies.

She repeated this "double career" with all three children. Linda never got the hang of golf -- but she did attend several functions just to be able to spend more time with her husband in an adult setting. Her husband reciprocated by taking her dancing frequently. She never resented her children, husband nor her double career. Like Sally, the "quality of time" that she spent with her husband and children together and separately was precious. Her children came first whenever they needed her, physically or psychologically, depending upon their levels of development. They remained well adjusted and overachieved in school and in their careers.

Day care centers seemed to be reasonable facsimiles to compartmentation. Linda was tired at night but she was not tired from chasing kids and she could relate more easily than the mother who stayed at home and was run ragged by her children.

Poor Judy was tired and resentful and didn't know how to correct the situation. Her children were not as well adjusted and did not achieve at the same level as those of the Barnes and the Coles.

In my study the "golf widow" was almost always associated with the lack of compartmentation or reasonable facsimiles such as: the day care center, nursery school; the nanny of the well-to-do; or just an ordinary mother's helper; breast-feeding from 3 to 4 years, (many La Leche mothers breast-feed today in America similarly to mothers before industrialization); living on a beach in the South, at the end of a dead end street, or on an isolated old fashioned farm. All these seemed to prevent the usual techniques of resistance. When some of the described methods of compartmentation were used in addition, the pre-school child never got out of control.

"The widow" syndrome was not always due to golf. Bowling, fishing, hunting, horseback riding, polo, sailing, auto racing, flying, and sky diving were often male attractions that made mothers become "widows."

COMPARTMENTATION WILL IMPROVE YOUR SEX LIFE

Barbara was a pretty co-ed with an outgoing personality. She always won the lead in the high school and college musicals. She could sing and dance. "Nothing will stop you," her proud father said. She was going professional.

After graduation she performed in the amateur shows about town but could not break into the professionals. She wanted to go to New York but her mother talked her out of it. She lived at home, dated a lot, did charity work, and amateur theatricals and she worked as a public relations person in her father's construction company.

After dating two years, she was reintroduced to a man whom she had known in her childhood. He seemed good natured, had looks, and they were soon very involved. He worked as a young executive in the family business. It was a story book wedding.

Barbara completely breast-fed their oldest daughter for six months. When she got so that she could take solids well, she stopped breast-feeding. A few months later she became pregnant again. This time it was a big strapping boy whom she breast-fed until he was nine months old. I told her about compartmentation but she would have none of it. Her courses in psychology in college taught that children should not be shut in.

When Barbara's daughter was four she went to nursery school and had gotten over "the terrible twos." Her two year old boy had not. He was all over the place and seven times worse than his older sister. His father had to spank him every night to make him stay in bed.

Every morning she awakened with her children and the dog in bed with her.

"The children are ruining my sex life." she said. "I am beginning to hate sex and kids."

I examined the robust two year old. He put the blocks in the cup (1 year exam) but he would not attempt to make a tower with the blocks which he had done before. He clung to his mother. There were lines about her mouth that were not there on previous examinations. Her eyes looked tired. She was disgusted with her children and with life in general.

I knew that Barbara was too frustrated to master the art of RE-COMPARTMENTATION. Yet I taught her to use STRATEGIC GATES (four) and told her husband how to construct a BEAR CAGE.

I advised her to complete the fenced in yard and she found a nursery school (Montessori) that would take her "tiger" before he was toilet trained.

A month later he performed the Gesell tests beautifully a little above his age level. Barbara's eyes now sparkled. Her son was no longer a problem. Her source of stress had vanished.

Barbara soon became pregnant again. She breast-fed and compartmentized her third child. She was able to attain outside fulfillment by acting in community plays and musicals.

Even at 14, Carol got "weak in the knees" when playing with boys. Her brother, two years older, kept an eye on Carol while they attended the large public high school. Their parents were very religious.

In the latter part of her senior year Carol became sexually involved with her boyfriend. She was discreet. Neither her parents nor her brother knew about it. Carol and her boyfriend graduated together. She won a scholarship to a prestigious university. He worked full time at the gas station.

In her freshman year at the university she made good grades and wrote letters to her boyfriend who was now several hundred miles away. In her sophomore year she joined an exclusive sorority. Carol became president of the sorority in her senior year. Also she became engaged to a quiet young scholarly executive, two years older, who also had been reared in a strictly religious family. They were married after she graduated from college.

Carol had a bad temper which surprised her quiet religious husband. Temper and swearing turned him off. He wasn't used to it; especially in one outwardly "so sweet."

They had two sons 18 months apart. She breast-fed both of them and everything seemed to be going well while she was breast-feeding. The prolactin in her blood excited her and the oxytocin made her sleepy. The combination of the two hormones gave her "the glow of breast-feeding." [1]

---

[1]Prolactin is a hormone produced by the anterior pituitary gland which is a pea-sized gland at the base of the brain. Its secretion into the blood stream causes "the making of milk" in the breast. It also makes the mother feel like fighting to the death for her baby.

Oxytocin is also a hormone made in the nerve cells in the base of the brain (hypothalamus). This hormone is stored in the pituitary. When the nipples are touched by the baby's suckling; (or husband's fondling) the pituitary squeezes out the oxytocin into the blood stream. This makes the smooth muscle around the milk ducts contract and drives the milk out of the breast. Dairymen call it the "let down reflex." It is turned on by hearing the

Carol never felt better nor looked more beautiful than when she was breast-feeding. It was when Carol stopped breast-feeding and the older boy ran wild in and out of doors all his waking hours that her frustration really began. She attempted to control him by shouting and slapping. It didn't help. It made him sneaky and afraid. Her mild mannered husband became shocked by this violence. He did not know what to do about it. Neither he nor his wife had ever been exposed to the art of compartmentation.

Almost always Carol got her toddlers to bed by spanking one or both of them. Then they cried themselves to sleep.

Her husband sometimes tried to help her put the boys to bed but he usually seemed more of a hindrance to Carol. The children took advantage of his mild manner. Her sternness and singleness of purpose worked better. Her husband was better at cleaning the dishes and putting them in the dishwasher.

After they got the boys to bed, Carol sought to relieve her stress by trying to get her husband to make love to her. The more stressful the day, the more sex she wanted. Carol was the opposite from Barbara. Chasing kids made Barbara not want sex at all. Carol's sexual aggressiveness turned her husband off -- often to the point of impotence.

In hurt pride Carol left the house for a late movie. Weeks later she visited a singles bar. After several affairs Carol's husband took her to court. The boys preferred to live with their father. Carol taught school. She was a dynamic teacher and became the head of her department.

She re-married; a man who was not at all intellectual but had a strong sex drive. After five years, he beat her up for infidelity. The divorce was life threatening. In fear of being the victim of murder or the cause of suicide, Carol moved to another city as soon as the decree was final. There she got another job as a teacher, and studied for a masters degree, and again became head of her department.

Finally Carol married for the third time -- another very physical, but non violent, man. Intellectually she could control him.

Carol's sons were now in college supported by their father. He never

---

baby cry, thinking of the baby or being a bridesmaid. The reflex is inhibited by anesthesia, anger, fear, worry or even answering mathematical questions.

Increased levels of oxytocin in the blood makes the uterus contract (cramps). Also the mother becomes sleepy. It is the same in the orgasm of sexual intercourse. The lactating woman will wet her husband with breast milk.

A generation ago, before breast-feeding became fashionable, a few male observers used to say that breast-feeding is like sex for the woman. Modern mothers tell me that is not correct. Their feelings are unique and different from any other experience. It is the "glow of breast-feeding." Artists have captured it. One does not have to ask a woman if she is breast-feeding. Just look at her!

remarried. He always spoke well of the mother of his sons.

The mothers who practiced compartmentation complained less about their marital dissatisfactions. There were more complaints from the parents who did not practice compartmentation. Communications had broken down. Too much sex was expected of them (Barbara) or not enough (Carol). After "the seven year itch" seldom was sex "just right." The most common complaints were of husbands' infidelities.

Those mothers who had compartmentized their pre-school children or had practiced a reasonable facsimile had a more open line of communications with their husbands. Their relationships as couples seemed to transcend their individual psycho-physio- sexual need (testosterone in the male and estrogen in the female).

I also observed fewer divorces in families who practiced compartmentation.

I believe, that if I had been given the opportunity to harness Carol's above average intelligence and organizing ability, in the art of compartmentation, her first marriage would have been less stressful. It might have been her only marriage.

PART II
SUBSTITUTIONS
FOR COMPARTMENTATION
CHAPTER XIV
BREASTFEEDING

NURSING

Usually well adjusted non-compartmentized children come from families where the mothers are calm and can anticipate what to expect from their children. In the eighties there is a growing group of women who breast-feed their children until they are three years old. Some also breast-feed a younger brother or sister at the same time. They usually carry their pre-school children around on their backs. Their children do everything with them.

I attend the conventions of La Leche League International[1] and speak to rooms full of nursing mothers with their babies and children. There are sometimes as many as 200 mothers with at least one child apiece. With so many children in one hall, one would expect bedlam, but there isn't. The two- and three-year olds run about at will. They are friendly and well-behaved.

From time to time there is a little crying as some little tot gets hurt or unhappy. Then the child runs to his mother and nurses a few moments and becomes quiet immediately. It is amazing how relaxed these mothers are and what good control they have over their infants and toddlers. One mother may finish nursing and then stand up and give an excellent talk. You have to see it to believe it.

The slogan of these remarkable women is, "Better mothering through breast-feeding." Their dedication to their children is complete. They are content to live in a "nursery". They care little about housekeeping, social position, or work outside the home. They are not ambitious in a worldly sense. Their children come first. Their husbands are proud of them and give them the love and moral support they need. Their whole lives center around their children. Whenever their children cry, they nurse them. If it's a three-year old, it's just for a few seconds for reassurance.

Some of these women have told me that they are against compartmentation as I recommend it. Yet, in a way, they are compartmentizing. By carrying their three year olds on their backs everywhere and nursing whenever they cry, they demonstrate a form of compartmentation. They are compartmentizing themselves and their children against the world.

While these mothers are strong and convincing, the majority of the mothers in the eighties run out of strength at the end of the day if they do

---

[1] For more information: *Womanly Art of Breast-Feeding* by the La Leche League International, 9616 Minneapolis Avenue, Franklin Park, Illinois 60131.
Nursing Your Baby by Karen Pryor. Pocket Books, 630 Fifth Avenue, New York, NY 10020.

not compartmentize. They become too tired to demonstrate mother love, so their children get confused signals about what they can and cannot do.

ONE PHYSICIAN'S APPROACH TO BREAST-FEEDING

"Doctor, can I have you for my pediatrician and not breast-feed? Everything I hear about you I like except for breast-feeding." One of many calls. I used to recite the statistical advantages of breast-feeding over the phone. I felt like a lawyer pleading his case before the jury. Usually the prospective mother was very polite and said that what I had to say was very interesting and if she decided to breast-feed, she would call me. Invariably, she didn't call. She engaged another pediatrician. He prescribed a formula. This happened repeatedly. It was discouraging. Finally when a mother called me to say that she wasn't going to breast-feed, I quickly replied, "you are the boss. Then I tried to terminate the conversation as quickly as possible.

When her baby was born, I made believe she had never told me she didn't want to breast-feed. I showed her how to hand express the colostrum, how to get the nipple and areola into the baby's mouth, how to lie, and how to hold the baby. I told her so much that she did not have a chance to remind me that she had called me before the birth of the baby and I had said she did not have to breast-feed.

This experience has been repeated many times. In only two instances did the mother remind me that she was not going to breast-feed. Usually, the mothers went right along with the program of breast-feeding without complaining and enjoyed it. *I learned that it is the job of the physician, nurse, father and all of the relatives to help the mother breast-feed rather than to only ask her what she wants.*

A very few mothers truly do not want to breast-feed. They have told me that they did not want their breasts touched by anyone, including their husbands. Their aversion seemed deep-seated. Breast-feeding made her want to vomit, one said. They usually made their wishes known. This rare and rather unnatural type of behavior was easy to recognize. As a physician, I had to respect their feelings and refrained from giving them the same push that most mothers need and to which most responded.

An obstetrician friend recommended me to a strikingly beautiful Hollywood actress and her newborn son as a patient. I saw them both in the hospital for the first time. I usually instruct mothers in hand expression of colostrum during a prenatal visit. Knowing my enthusiasm for breast-feeding, the obstetrician was emphatic in telling me not to ask her to breast-feed -- she was dead set against it.

After I examined her healthy son and told her as much, she explained her plans and described the baby's nurse, the nursery, bassinet, formula service, diaper service, baby crib, baby clothes. Bit by bit, I got it all with each daily visit. I told her how well her baby was doing - we did not have rooming-in then. I listened dutifully to her plans every day and every day I bowed left without mentioning breast-feeding. On the third day I noticed that her breasts were greatly enlarged, but we went through the same charade. On the fourth day she was much larger, very uncomfortable but still just as immaculately groomed and still very much in control. She was so obviously uncomfortable that I felt I could not contain myself any longer. I told her that I was instructed not to mention breast-feeding but, I said: "If you don't, you are missing something."

"All right, I'll nurse", she said and did very successfully, for several months. Later her second son was also breast-fed.

I was not so lucky with another attractive sheltered society girl who came to see me prenatally. When I attempted to show her hand expression of colostrum, using her forearm for demonstration, she stated that she did not intend to breast-feed. I gave her the statistics, but she still said no.

When her perfectly normal daughter was born, I proceeded with my usual breast-feeding instructions but she again said no. On the fourth day, like the actress, she was greatly engorged and weeping almost out of control. Nature was telling her to breast-feed, but she successfully fought off her popular obstetrician and me. Her pride would not let her change her mind. If we had held off selling breast-feeding until she was engorged; maybe, like the actress, she would have nursed.

Breast-feeding mothers used to have problems communicating with their non breast-feeding friends about infant feeding. Some had even changed friends. One breast-feeding Junior Leaguer told me that she just could not talk about infant feeding with her friends. Fortunately in the eighties the smart set wants to breast-feed and are not embarrassed talking about it.

When I taught medical students, I told each to organize a program according to his or her own individual personality. A program is necessary to lead the mother in an enthusiastic way if she is to be successful in breast-feeding. Why not just teach principle and not try to program? If there were no programs, the mother would not get the enthusiastic help that she needed in the hospital to overcome the difficulties that inadvertently developed. I felt fortunate that I was able to get 95% of my mothers breast-feeding.

Before World War II most mothers chose bottle feeding. About 20% breast fed in the hospital but more than three fourths of those quit nursing before the baby was two-months old. Those who continued usually had maternal grandmother or friend living in the house who had breast-fed successfully for several months and knew how to encourage a breast-feeding mother.

In medical school and in the hospital training programs in the forties, much time was spent teaching physicians how to feed formulas. Breast-feeding was considered best but few women could manage it. Pediatricians made international reputations discovering special formulas for babies like synthetic milk adapted (SMA). Acid and enzyme digested partly skimmed cow's milk mixtures were popular formulas when babies could not tolerate the most popular evaporated milk, water and dextro maltose mixtures. Colicky babies shifted from one pediatrician to another trying to find a good formula mix.

During World War II in North Africa, France and Germany it was quite different. Mothers nursed from necessity at anytime and everywhere. Both babies and mothers looked healthy and content although many of their houses had been destroyed. In the Dachau Concentration Camp, we went in right after the infantry - it was truly amazing to see the healthy contented babies nursing emaciated mothers. If starving Europeans can nurse, so can Americans, I vowed.

After the war I was invited into the office of the late Dr. Clifford Grulee: professor, chairman, editor, executive, author, and promoter of breast-feeding. My six years of association with him was like a post graduate course in pediatrics. There was a post war baby boom and with Dr. Grulee's help, I tried to develop a breast-feeding practice. Meanwhile Dr. Herman Meyer finished his scholarly book entitled *Infant Feeding* and found that the incidence of breast-feeding in America had decreased in a decade from 21% breast-feeding when leaving the hospital to 10% in the fifties. Because of Dr. Herbert Lussky's and my influence at the Evanston Hospital, 33% left the hospital breast-feeding. When the breast milk bank was established in 1953 the percentage went up to 66%. In 1983 it was 80% which is good considering that the babies are cared for by about 50 different pediatricians. It is the well-to-do college graduate mothers who are demanding their rights to breast-feed. Fifty years ago they led the movement away from breast-feeding, now they are leading the way back.

In my program I never asked a mother if she wanted to breast-feed. To ask such a question was like making a house call and finding a child with pneumonia and then asking the mother if she wanted me to give the child an antibiotic. If a mother engaged me as the physician, I knew that she expected me to make the correct diagnosis and to prescribe the proper treatment. If a mother engaged me to take care of her newborn, I felt as though it were a member of my family. In good conscience, therefore, I could never let the decision of whether or not to breast-feed be only the mother's decision. It had to be nature's decision. Why did I take such a positive attitude? I learned that most mothers didn't really know whether or not they wanted to breast-feed. They did not know enough about breast-feeding to have made up their minds. Some mothers who had decided against nursing took one look at the newborn baby and decided to breast-feed. A mother may have decided not to breast-feed because her best friend did not. After the birth of the baby, she was not sure about her decision. I found myself in a position to give the mother a push toward breast-feeding.

The advantages of breast-feeding are so overwhelmingly manifest that to give primary consideration to any alternative was a disservice to both mother and child. It is also a disservice to me as a physician. I felt that over the years, I had developed a breast-feeding practice which was more relaxed, less demanding and healthier than those of my colleagues who had not stressed breast-feeding.

A mother should be shown how to breast-feed rather than be asked whether or not she wanted to breast-feed. When a mother engaged me to look after her newborn, I proceeded to initiate a program that I had developed over the years to help her to breast-feed. If the baby was not yet born, I told her how to hand express the colostrum as a way of preparing her nipples and breasts for lactation. Mothers of the eighties are lucky that many physicians are now devoting much attention to helping mothers breast-feed their infants. If your particular physician is unenthusiastic; call the La Leche League and get a list of physicians who are able to help you over the particular difficulty you may encounter.

THE VALUE OF BREAST-FEEDING

"Nature is often hidden, sometimes overcome, seldom extinguished -" Sir Francis Bacon

Breast-feeding is better for your baby, for you, and for your doctor. Breast-fed babies are healthier than those who have been artificially fed. I believe breast-fed babies are healthier all their lives.

There are numerous reports in the literature comparing the health of the breast-fed and the artificially fed. One of the most widely quoted reports is that of Grulee and Sanford in the *Journal of the American Medical Association* in 1924. These two enthusiasts reported the incidence of illness in over 20,000 babies attending the Chicago Infant Welfare Clinics. The breast-fed babies had on-third the number of respiratory infections, one-seventh the amount of eczema (allergy), one-fifth the gastro-intestinal infections, and one-third the number of general infections that bottle-fed babies had.

More recent reports confirm Grulee's and Sanford's figures except that, since the antibiotics, there have been fewer deaths in both groups. Stevenson, Cunningham and others report that breast-feeding produces healthier children among the rich as well as among the poor. Dr Paul Gyorgy discovered the "bifius factor" that promotes the growth of a benign bacteria that coats the intestines of the breast-fed and thus prevents the penetration of virulent germs that cause death from diarrhea. Dr. Gaull has discovered an amino acid called taurine that is unique in human breast milk and promotes the covering or insulation of nerve fibers. Perhaps that explains the reports that the breast-fed walk and talk earlier than the bottle fed. Others have discovered enzymes and other chemicals - a new one every year that demonstrates the superiority of breast milk over other formulas for babies. The formula companies are trying desperately to improve their formulas to make them as good as breast milk. They are improving them so that they are much better than they were when I began practice in the forties, but when scientists study breast milk, they seem always to find some new ingredients unique to breast milk. When the late Dr. Paul Gyorgy, my teacher, was studying diarrhea in rats he found that he could cure the rats faster with human milk than with rat milk. We have always been taught that man is the dominant animal walking the earth because of his superior brain. We must give equal credit to woman's breast milk.

In 1959 I compared allergies among the breast-fed and bottle-fed babies in my private practice. I followed 1,377 children from early infancy into adulthood.

In 268 children breast-feeding was not attempted or was terminated in less than five days. Of these children, 31 (11.7%) were allergic. Two died, two had triple allergies (eczema, asthma and hayfever). In ten the allergies lasted more than five years and seven required prolonged treatment by an allergist. Eleven (35%) were allergic without a family history.

Of the 1,377 children studied, 528 were breast fed for six months or more - mostly nine months. Twenty-one (4%) were allergic. There were no deaths, three triple allergies, four double (eczema and hayfever), six prolonged allergy, and none with allergy without a family history.

Until recently breast-feeding has been decreasing in the cities of the world at the same time that allergy has been increasing. Some allergists have estimated that 25% of all children are allergic.

Since 1958 I have been urging mothers to give their babies nothing but breast milk for six months - not even vitamins. Several hundred of my mothers have been able to do this. Their children had fewer allergies and developed fewer infections than children who began to eat solid foods before six months.

When breast-fed babies develop infections, they are not as severe and do not last as long as they do in the artificially fed babies. Other physicians who have had much experience with breast-feeding have also found that children who have been breast-fed for nine months or more are tougher in fighting off illnesses. They respond to treatment better.

Breast-fed babies and children who get ear infections, boils and other infections respond faster to the appropriate antibiotics than those who have been fed artificially.

There is the same toughness among the breast-fed to the viral infections. I have not had a case of rheumatic fever, chronic nephritis, nor a severe collagen disease among those in my practice who have been breast-fed for nine months or more.

There are other advantages to breast-feeding that are less tangible. The infant and the toddler who have been breast-fed for many months have unusually clear skin and flesh that is soft and firm. You can almost recognize the child who has been breast-fed. He laughs more. She is friendly. He thinks grown-ups have treated him or her well. She seems to have no problems.

The complexion of the breast-fed child is very clear. An infant of four months who has been completely breast-fed has a different feel to his skin than the baby who had been fed artificially. The breast-fed baby's skin is smoother and feels like silk. As soon as solid foods or formula are introduced, there is a little more drag to the feel of the skin. Take the baby's shirt off five minutes before you try to feel the skin over his torso, always with your hand dry. The increased drag feels like velvet. The interns, residents, and I play interesting games trying to guess whether or not the young infant is being breast-fed completely. Ninety percent of the time we can tell by the feel of his skin if his mother has given him an occasional bottle or started solids. Anything given a baby that is not human milk makes him sweat a little, so your hand drags.

The clearness of the skin in the infant who is breast-fed lasts through childhood into adolescence. When such a person becomes a teenager, acne is usually not a problem.

Another value of breast-feeding to the teenager is the lack of necessity for prolonged and expensive orthodontia. Suckling at the breast for a prolonged time develops the jaw and jaw muscles in such a way that the permanent teeth are less crowded and tend to come in straighter. Very few of my breast-fed patients need orthodontia.

Breast-feeding is better for MOTHER. "It was the most beautiful experience in my life," one mother told me when her son was one year old. It broke her heart to wean him. Many mothers are ecstatically happy while nursing.

You, Mother, have a different look in your eyes from your friend who is feeding her baby artificially. You seem less tense. I watch you as you come in with your baby and sit with him. You have that look of serenity that artists have captured. I have seen that look in the faces of many of my mothers who are successfully and happily breast-feeding their babies. Physicians say it is your good health. Your husband thinks you never looked more beautiful. Is it the circulating prolactin which excites you or the oxytocin which makes you sleepy? Or is it the whole hormonal orchestra? A few psychiatrists, mostly men, say that you are being stimulated sexually whenever your infant suckles at your erotic nipples. But you act as though your feelings are deeply maternal.

It is healthier for you to breast-feed. Your uterus contracts to its normal size rapidly if you nurse. At your six-month check-up your obstetrician can tell whether or not you are nursing by the firmness of your uterus.

The very act of nursing necessitates intimate handling of your new baby. You get acquainted more quickly. Right away you have to handle your baby with confidence. You feel good inside when you find that you can satisfy your baby's hunger, stop his crying, and make him smile.

There is statistical evidence that mothers who breast-feed are less likely to develop cancer of the breast. In Japan, where it used to be the custom to nurse children until they were four or five years old, cancer of the breast was almost unheard of. Since World War II, the American methods of artificial feeding have taken hold in the cities of Japan. Now breast cancer is occurring there almost as frequently as it does in this country. I have seen only one woman with cancer of the breast (an intralobular non-malignant type) who had breast-fed for one year or who had breast-fed for several months and then hand expressed a drop or two of her milk each day until her baby is one year old. I recommend this hand expression if a mother is unable to breast-feed for one year.

It had been said that the baby's nursing makes the mother's breasts less shapely and saggy. I do not believe this. The sagging of the breasts is a result of bearing children and old age. The woman who becomes heavy in lactation should wear a brassiere that supports her breasts, but does not bind them inwards. There should be a "sling type" of support. This will prevent overstreaching of the fibrous tissues of her breasts. When breast-feeding is terminated, the breasts will involute evenly so that they are even more shapely than before.

Breast-feeding strengthens your marriage. To breast-feed successfully, you must learn quickly what you can do, and what you cannot do. And still get the let-down reflex. You can not let yourself get upset emotionally. Otherwise you have a crying baby. Your husband learns fast how to handle himself, you, and the baby. You do not indulge in the kind of fights where you both cry and then make up. Your marriage shifts into a quieter gear based on a new mutual respect. You have changed. Your husband's feelings toward you have changed. He now admires you because he sees you as representing the best in womanhood. As you practice being quiet with each other, your love deepens. This is the atmosphere I have observed in the breast-feeding families. Both parents give of themselves more completely and enjoy the giving.

It seems that all the members of a breast-feeding family are healthier. I know the children are healthier. Some of my colleagues believe that the reason that I have healthier children in my practice is not due to breast-feeding. They say it is because I have made such a fuss about breast-feeding that the mothers who come to me are those who want to and can nurse their babies. And the mothers who are able to breast-feed are healthier than other mothers and have therefore given their children a greater inheritance of good health.

The only way I could answer that strong argument would be to have my mothers nurse every other child. But you know that is impossible. Once you have breast-fed, you want no part of formula feeding. But I do have some families in which the natural children are breast-fed and the adopted children are bottle-fed. Although the heredity is different, the comparison of the adopted babies and the breast-fed natural babies makes breast-feeding look better than artificial feeding.

Breast-feeding is better for the DOCTOR. At first, it is usually easier for the physician to write a formula than to try to push the mother into breast-feeding. In 1950 most mothers had to be pushed. In the 1980's most mothers want to breast-feed. The longer I practice, the more I am convinced that the doctor must refrain from asking the mother if she wants to breast-feed. He must tell her to breast-feed and let nature make the decision as to whether or not she can succeed. Unfortunately many competent physicians honestly believe that it is not worth the fight. Perhaps the majority of the physicians would like their mothers to breast-feed, but they are too busy, too tired, and do not know how to help them easily.

Years ago, most physicians were raised on farms. They milked cows when they were boys. They understood the let down reflex. They learned fast that they had to be nice to the cow to make her give milk. Usually some relative was breast-feeding a baby. They knew much about lactation before they studied medicine.

Now most physicians come from suburban areas and have never seen a cow being milked. The small animals used at home and in the classroom to teach mating, birth, and lactation are inadequate compared to the cow to teach the physiology of lactation. In the 1950's only one or two in a class of medical school seniors had ever heard of the let-down reflex; none understood it. They had been so busy learning the details of the phenomenon of disease that there was no time left for a subject of such nebulous value as breast-feeding.

You must be patient with your physician's lack of knowledge of the womanly are of breast-feeding. You must respect him or her for the knowledge of disease and how to treat it. Then he/she will respect you for your ability to breast-feed. If you feel that his advice in breast-feeding is not right, ask other women who have succeeded. Refer to the chapter La Leche League.

If somehow you and your doctor get through the danger weeks (the first eight) you both will be grateful to each other. You, because you have confidence in the functions of your body as a woman. Your physician will secretly admire you, as your husband can openly admire you, because you represent to him the best in womanhood. This mutual respect will last your lifetime. Ninety-nine percent of women are physically and hormonally equipped to breast-feed, if they want to and can be handled properly.

In my study I had a less hysterical practice because I encouraged breast-feeding. Breast-feeding seemed to be a part of the total family attitude. Such parents were less brittle. It seemed that it was the parents of the non-breast-feeding family who insisted when they called about illness; "Doctor, you must see him right away. It's serious." I was lucky to live in a community where the mothers had free choice of doctors. If they wanted to breast-feed, they could come to me. If they felt guilty about saying NO to breast-feeding, they stayed away although I preferred that they didn't. It was gratifying to watch my breast-fed babies grow up and demonstrate over and over they had better than ordinary health.

In the eighties American mothers are returning to breast-feeding - now over 50% - higher than in any industrialized country. Probably because of the newly discovered advantages, the same smart group who led Americans away from breast-feeding a half century ago are now leading the movement back. Young doctors, nurses, students and hospital personnel are busy now learning the art of breast-feeding so they can encourage mothers meaningfully. The La Leche League is growing geometrically and it is heartening.

PRENATAL PREPARATIONS (THE BEGINNING OF BREAST-FEEDING)

For your first baby you should consult a specialist in obstetrics to check everything; even if you plan to have another physician deliver your baby.

You need a good diet: proteins, fruits and vegetables, not starches. Also ask your doctor about minerals and vitamins.

For nausea in the early months frequent snacks of what you like with sips of thin liquid helps. Do not take any medication for nausea or vomiting. Obstetricians tell me that they are afraid to give even aspirins to pregnant women. It took a long time to learn the Thalidamide story.[2]

No alcoholic beverages, please, during pregnancy. The fetal alcohol syndrome was recognized as a disease in the seventies and more than a hundred cases of mental retardation with typical facies were described in which the mothers were chronic alcoholics or went on one or more binges early in their pregnancies. Two of my patients are retarded due to their mother's alcoholism. Alcohol also has been associated with prematurity. Probably an occasional social cocktail or two separated over several hours are harmless, but it is safer with no drinking at all during pregnancy. The observation of my great grandfather: "drinking people don't have good children" may have merit.

Eat well and get plenty of exercise. Some work until their labor pains begin. You are allowed to gain 30 pounds, assuming you are in the normal weight range for your build and height. In the 1950's you were allowed to gain only 20 pounds. If you are overweight, you should have a glucose tolerance test for diabetes - a disease that should be rigidly controlled throughout your pregnancy. You should be routinely checked for syphilis, tuberculosis and whether or not you are immune to German measles.

You should have loose-fitting clothes that are comfortable and good looking. Go to a maternity shop. You need a well-fitting brassiere of the uplift type to support your growing breasts. The brassiere should be loose enough so that it doesn't flatten your nipples.

HAND EXPRESSION

As your pregnancy progresses you may notice some colostrum, a yellowish fluid, leaking from your nipples. This mucus fluid precedes the flow of milk in your breasts. During the last three months of your pregnancy your should hand express the colostrum every day. It is important that you learn how to hand express.

Place your right hand on the left breast. Keep your thumb and forefinger stiff. Place your thumb on the skin at the edge of the areola (the darker area around the nipple). Keep your forefinger on the skin near the edge of your areola. Keeping each joint stiff, bring your thumb and forefinger together. The motion should parallel your rib cage. In fact, you should push in a little to kink the ducts. Do not pull out when you bring your thumb and forefinger together. Keep your hand still and move only your thumb and forefinger. When you get a drop of colostrum, keep your hand in the position that produces colostrum. Then rhythmically work the thumb and forefinger together. Move your hand only to find the best location to make the colostrum flow best; it should not hurt. If you hurt

---

[2] In the fifties Thalidamide was given to pregnant women to help nausea and vomiting. It caused deformed extremities in the babies -- their arms and legs became like "flippers".

yourself, you are not doing it correctly. **See illustration.**

Do this every day and you will gradually find you become quite adept in expressing the colostrum. If you are successful in this, you will have less engorgement after the baby is born. It relieves the tension within your breast when you get the colostrum out. You will also have manipulated your nipples enough so that the baby's sucking will not hurt so much. It is helpful if the nipples are handled as much as possible before the baby is born.

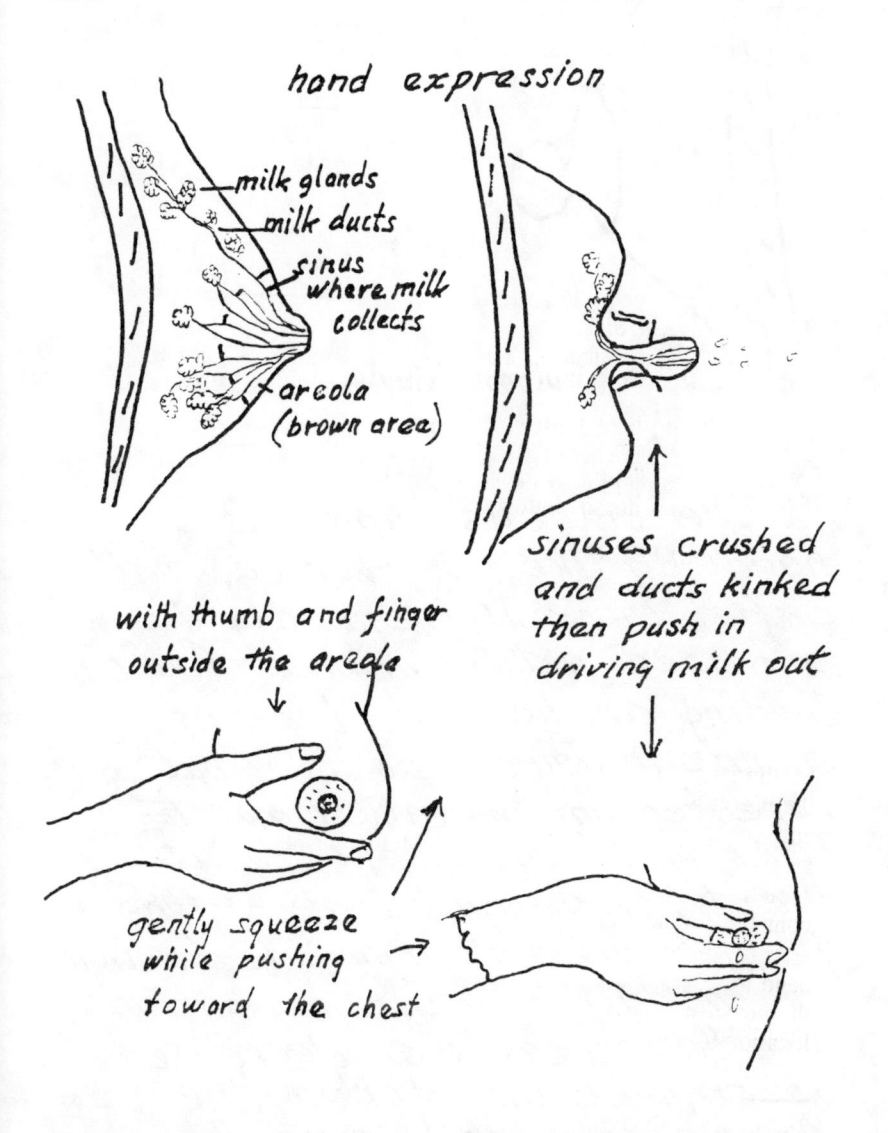

hand expression

- milk glands
- milk ducts
- sinus where milk collects
- areola (brown area)

sinuses crushed and ducts kinked then push in driving milk out

with thumb and finger outside the areola

gently squeeze while pushing toward the chest

Bulbous Nipple

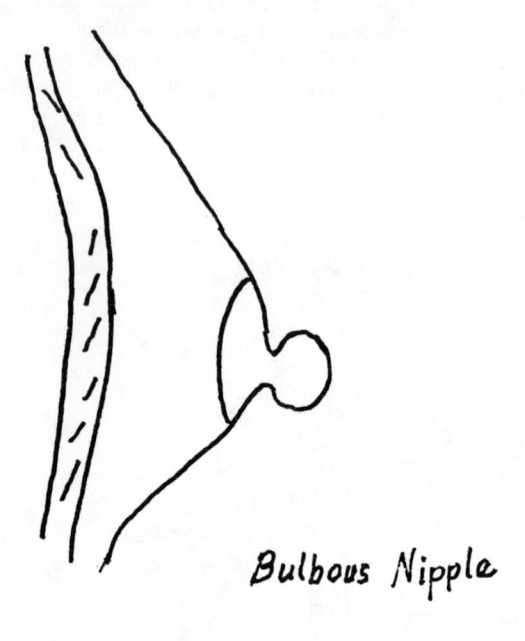

The bulbous nipple is a handicap like the inverted, small or flat nipple. It frequently discouraged mothers in breast feeding. Suckling can be limited to one minute in any one position but repeated innumerable times by twisting the breasts, using both breasts, or changing position of the baby to prevent injury. The duration of suckling in any one position can be increased or decreased according to pain. Working the areola into baby's mouth helps.

NORMAL LACTATING BREAST AND NIPPLE DURING THE LET DOWN REFLEX

- MILK GLANDS
- AREOLA
- ONE OF 18 LAKES AND RIVERS OF MILK

Should you get uterine cramps, desist. A few years ago one obstetrician reported cramps and premature labor, but for the many years that I have been advocating the expression of colostrum prenatally, not one cramp has been reported to me. A few women seem to have an antipathy toward having even their babies touch their breasts. You will find that by giving birth to a child and breast-feeding, you will be doing much which you previously never thought you could.

A few years ago it was recommended that the nipples be washed with a washcloth and warm water and then dried after the expression of colostrum. I do not believe this is necessary. The nipples and areola secrete a protective wax that should not be washed off. Just wash your nipples like any other part of your body. The use of hardening agents, astringents, or scrubbing with a brush is probably harmful. If these are used too much, the skin may become hard. Hard skin on the nipple is more likely to crack than soft skin. Soft nipples withstand suckling best. It is important that the nipples be exposed to air. You should sleep without your brassiere.

Retracted nipples that are poorly formed are a common anomaly. These should be treated in the prenatal period. Read the section on SORE NIPPLES.

As your time approaches, you should get your bag packed and ready to go to the hospital. You will need your nightgown, house jacket, slippers, extra nursing brassiere, tooth brush, tooth paste, soap, perfume, and an interesting book. Your first baby usually goes several days beyond the due date, but you have to be ready.

BREAST ANATOMY AND PHYSIOLOGY

The amount of protuberance of the human breast varies considerably among women but usually averages one or two inches. Each breast weighs one-third of a pound or less when not pregnant nor lactating and usually increases at least three times its weight to nearly one and one-half pounds when lactating. For some unknown reason the left breast is usually a little larger than the right. The central portion consists of glandular tissue which is rather constant in amount and adequate in ninety-nine percent of women to nurse at least one baby per pregnancy.

The glandular tissue is located in the center of the breast and consists of 15 to 20 lobes that are arranged radially around the nipple. Fibrous tissue surround the clusters of milk glands that look like clusters of hundreds of tiny grapes. The fibrous tissue holds the glands in place and when dissected look like little pockets for the milk glands to fit into. Some of this fibrous tissue is connected to ligaments that course vertically through the breast from the ribs to the skin. These contain elastic tissue and are called Cooper's ligaments. These elastic bands which abundantly course through the breast are responsible for the shape of the lactating and non-lactating breast and keeping it attractive.

Each lobe is separate and has its own separate glandular and duct system that empties into its own separate reservoir (ampulla) which in turn has its own duct which passes through the nipple. When the let down reflex occurs the muscles around the ducts and ampulla contract and drive the milk out the nipple. Usually one sees several streams squirting out but not all eighteen at once. Read LET DOWN REFLEX. (**See illustration,** page 85.)

The size of the breast has little to do with a woman's lactating ability. The adipose tissue surrounds the glandular tissue in many women make up the bulk of the non-lactating breast. The variations in the amount of fat around the glandular tissue is one reason why the non-lactating women have breasts in a variety of sizes. When lactating the glandular tissue increases at least three fold and the adipose tissue diminishes. The reverse occurs when the breast stops lactating, but in some women all the adipose tissue does not return to the degree that it was before pregnancy. That is why some women have noticed that, after prolonged nursing, their breasts are smaller.

That is why the lactating breast which has become three times heavier must be supported by a brassiere that gives lift so that Cooper's ligaments do not become so badly stretched that they do not function. Then the breasts become pendulous. You have seen pictures of primitive African mothers.

The cells that produce the milk are cube shaped cells with oval nuclei that are arranged in such a way as to make a sac called the alveolus. In the non-pregnant state the alveolus is small partially collapsed and filled with cellular debris and a little fluid that is similar chemically to blood serum. Early in pregnancy the cells making up the wall of the alveolus become elongated and develop a second nucleus. The part of the elongated cell that projects into the sac (alveolus) develops fat globules and a number of granules have been observed. The breast is made ready, but its secreting activity is held in check until the expulsion of the baby.

How the milk is made by the tiny cell is a miracle. Each animal has adapted its milk to the special needs of its own young. For example, caseinogen (a protein) is lower in human milk than in any other animal (1.2%) because it is not needed. The human infant doubles his birth weight in 180 days. The caseinogen is 9.5 percent in the cat's milk because the kitten doubles its weight in seven days. In cow's milk the caseinogen is 3.02 percent because the calf doubles his birth weight in 47 days.

In contrast lecithin (a protein) and taurine (an amino acid) is more abundant in human milk because the human infant has so many more neurons (nerve cells) and nerve fibers (electrical wires) that need to be covered (insulated) so that the electrical nervous impulses can travel within, and to and from, the brain.

During the past 20 years, new unique ingredients in human breast milk have been discovered every year.

THE MIND OF THE MOTHER

As soon as you give birth, all your concern is for your helpless new baby. This quality in the mother is the substance by which the species have perpetuated themselves for millions of years. It is beautiful to watch the sudden development of concern and excessive courage in the mother animal protecting her young. The ewe becomes hysterical when separated from her lamb. The human mother is no exception, but the changes come more gradually in the woman.

Domestication seems to dull this instinct. The bitch who has become a family pet has to he helped in mothering. Eva, the over-bred racing mare, completely rejected Wonder, her first born, but with help she accepted Glory, her second. Six thousand years of civilization has diluted the fierceness of mother love in the human, as well.

Women seem to have an inborn adeptness at handling babies. An inexperienced girl will be more confident about holding a baby than an inexperienced boy. Women can spend long periods of time just watching babies. But education, emancipation, careers, and ambitions tend to smother modern woman's maternal instincts. Modern women therefore need help in developing their instincts. Together with this psychological need, humans also require more help physiologically than do the animals. A mare gives birth after one or two contractions and after a few minutes she stands up and can run if necessary. A woman usually labors for hours as she slowly molds a round head through the oval boney encircled passage within her pelvis. She needs help; some women need much more than others. Some women can give birth without any medication at all; some need to be completely sedated. If a mother watches and helps her baby to be born and is permitted to nurse him while she is still on the delivery table, she will have a good start toward developing her maternal instincts to the fullest.

Although the changes are gradual, they are profound, particularly in the way you think. Your mind in childbirth seems to be subject to your emotions and physiology. The gradual adjustment to gestation has been thrown into a sudden confusion with the expulsion of your baby. Your judgement is at its lowest ebb. The more education you've had, the more dependent you feel. You ask over and over in the delivery room, the student nurse, the nurse in charge of newborns, and finally your pediatrician. You worry about the shape of your baby's head. Will it become round? Why doesn't he open his eyes? Will his nose always be crooked? Will that extra fold on his ear always be there? Why does one eye open wider than the other? Is that a bruise or a birthmark on his eyelid? Will it go away? You are full of questions spoken or unspoken. Unspoken because you may be sleepy.

If one of your doctors or nurses should be slightly unenthusiastic about how wonderful your baby is , you become suspicious all over again. Your physician may have felt too tired to be enthusiastic or the nurse too preoccupied. There is a wildness in mother love that does not become quiet until you get your hands on your baby and can hold him. It does not satisfy this new biological urge for the nurse to hold your baby at your bedside and only let you look. You must touch, feel, hold and cuddle. You must see him completely undressed and examine every square inch of his body surface. It then helps your chemistry become quiet if you are told by those around you that you have produced one of the finest specimens they have ever seen.

Finally, although still irrational you regain your strength and the doctors, nurses, hospital, and all its staff have become the best in all the world. All is wonderful. Your baby is going to get the best of everything. You are in a glow.

THE TECHNIQUE OF BREAST-FEEDING

Strong, dedicated mothers will succeed at breast-feeding with or without supervision. But most mothers need vigorous encouragement and detailed instruction. Some weaker women, who have not been taught how to nurse or those whose friends or relatives discourage them, may lose their milk before they learn how to make themselves good lactating mothers.

Before your labor pains become too distracting, you remind the resident and nurse that you intend to breast-feed your baby. Then they will not give you drying up pills or a dry-up injection. If by chance you do get the pill or injection by mistake, don't worry about it. Lactation will be depressed for only a day or so. Most women have such a strong lactating ability that they produce milk even though they've had a few doses of lactating suppressing medication.

More and more women are breast-feeding as soon as the baby is born. Some women are allowed to nurse their babies on the delivery table, after the cord is cut and the baby is cleaned up. While you are still on the delivery table, ask the nurse to place the baby on your abdomen so you can let the baby try to nurse. If your baby's trip into the world has not been too strenuous, he will suckle a little.

If you had your baby without anesthesia, the baby will take one or two sucks and then fall asleep. You should discuss this with your doctor before your baby is born. In most hospitals, this policy is becoming more popular but, some nurses and delivery staff do not appreciate this request. However, this is your baby and you have certain rights. You should not hesitate to make your wishes known.

If your baby won't nurse on the delivery table, don't feel unhappy. Just having your hands on your baby will make you feel good. Don't hesitate to feel him. Go over every square inch of his body. He'll probably be sleeping, and you'll be reassured that you have touched him.

THE FIRST DAY OF NURSING

Your baby will probably be brought to you to nurse, regularly in most hospitals, when he is about twenty-four hours old. Before that, he is kept in the central nursery. This may seem like an unnecessary precaution to you, but the experienced nurses and doctors like to observe the babies for the first twenty-four hours. The baby is given sterile water to see how he swallows and if he can swallow without spitting up. His urination, the passing of the meconium plug, and subsequent bowel movements will be observed. If you have not held your baby on the delivery table, you will be very impatient to see and hold him often. Make your wishes known to the doctor and nurse. In modern obstetrical floors they will bring your baby to you before he is twenty-four hours old for you to hold and practice breast-feeding. If the nurses are too busy to do this, you will have to insist.

Your baby will be wrapped in a small, sterile receiving blanket. Small babies like to be wrapped so they are snug and warm. This simulates the enclosed feeling the baby had while in the uterus. Babies cry less when they are wrapped.

On the delivery table you were probably too exhausted to completely examine your baby. When you get him for the first time, you will undoubtedly want to unwrap him and examine every inch of him. After you handle him for the first time, you will know he is perfectly all right. Feeling him makes you sure. If the nurse who brought the baby to you stands over you, you may not have the nerve to undress and look at him. If you have any doubts, you may ask the nurse to help you to put him to your breast.

I recommend that you learn to nurse lying down while you are in the hospital. This is a relaxing way to nurse, and later on you will be glad you learned how. Ask the nurse to pull the curtain to screen you from your roommate. Privacy will put you at ease. In some military hospitals the breast-feeding mothers are in one ward and the formula mothers are in another. The breast-feeders help each other.

Lie flat on the bed on your side. Your baby lies flat on the bed on his left side, facing you. Your right arm goes around the baby's feet to keep him awake. Your left hand directs your right nipple into you baby's mouth. Roll your body slightly to regulate the height of your nipple. You may hand express a little colostrum at this point, to moisten the nipple so that the baby gets a taste. That may entice him to grab on and suckle. (To learn how to hand-express read PRENATAL CARE). Use your left hand to stroke the baby's cheek with your nipple. Eventually you can work it into your baby's mouth. If you stroke his left cheek he will open his mouth and turn toward the left. Then you can guide the nipple into his mouth. He may suckle vigorously to the point of hurting you or he may just sleep.

It makes no difference. Don't feel as though he has to nurse at this time. When your baby does take the nipple, gently work the entire nipple and areola (darker area around nipple) into his mouth with your left hand.

While you are lying on your right side, you should feel perfectly relaxed and comfortable. You do not always have to look at your baby. You can put your head down on the bed. **(See illustration)**. Put a pillow under your head if you want to. You will almost be able to doze while the baby nurses. When you get home you will be able to tuck the baby in bed with you for his wee-hour feedings.

If your baby is unusually vigorous, he may grab hold very hard. It may hurt. Now be sure to work the areola into his mouth every time he opens his mouth a little. **See illustration on next page.** The areola is tougher than the nipple. He may take just one or two sucks and fall asleep. Let him sleep. Snuggle him to you.

If your baby is a barracuda, who sucks vigorously and steadily right from the beginning, you will have to stop him after a minute or so, so he won't injure your nipple. On the first day, let him nurse a minute at each breast at each feeding. The most efficient way to stop a baby is to pinch gently his nose until he opens his mouth to get air. This usually takes about 30 seconds. Or you can put your index finger in the corner of his mouth to break the suction. Some mild, sleepy babies can be stopped by pushing on the chin with the index finger. Never pull the baby off the nipple -- it will hurt and may injure your nipple.

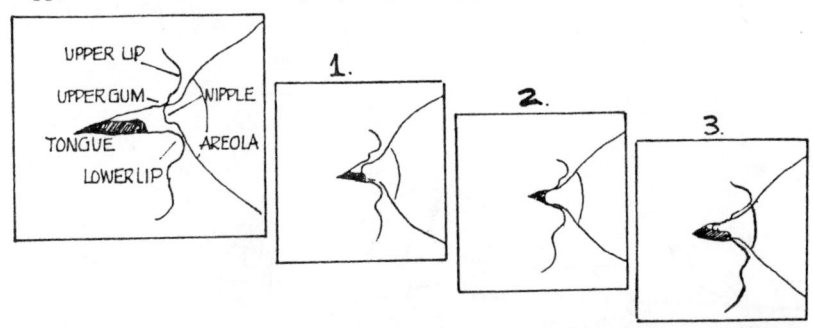

As soon as your baby lets go, you will notice that your nipple is pulled out more than it has ever been. This is good. Then gather your baby in your arms so his body faces yours and his face rests between your breasts. In this position, you roll over to your left side and get your baby started on your left breast, just as you did on the right. **(See illustrations on next page)**

Don't be disappointed if the baby does not nurse at the left breast as vigorously as he did at the right breast. He may not nurse at all. Don't worry, he just wants to sleep and this is a practice session.

If your baby does nurse as vigorously on the left side as he did on the right and hurts your nipples, be delighted. This very vigorous and aggressive nature means he came into this world with a minimum of injury.

It is important to make sure that you work the whole areola into his mouth and that he does not just suck the nipple. There is an abundance of nerves in the nipple compared to the areola. Besides hurting more, sucking just the nipple does not put enough pressure on the reservoirs of milk (ampullae) to force the milk out the 18 milk ducts within the nipple. Every time he opens his mouth while suckling, push with your forefinger a little bit more of the areola into his mouth until the upper edge of the areola is hidden by the upper lip. See diagrams and read: BREAST ANATOMY..., PRENATAL PREP..., AND SORE NIPPLES.

Again, let him nurse for one minute, and then hold his nose to make him let go. If he still wants to nurse again, roll over and let him try the right breast for a second time during that feeding. This time, you give your breast a little twist so that he gets a little different bite on your nipple and areola. This will be discussed in detail later.

Usually your baby will just want to sleep while you cuddle him. Just relax and doze until the nurse comes in to return him to the nursery.

CHAPTER XIV / 91

Don't worry if the nurse scolds you if you have undressed your baby and bundled him up again the "wrong" way. She, like you, wants what is best for the baby, even if your ideas differ from hers. But undress your baby again later if you want to. He's yours.

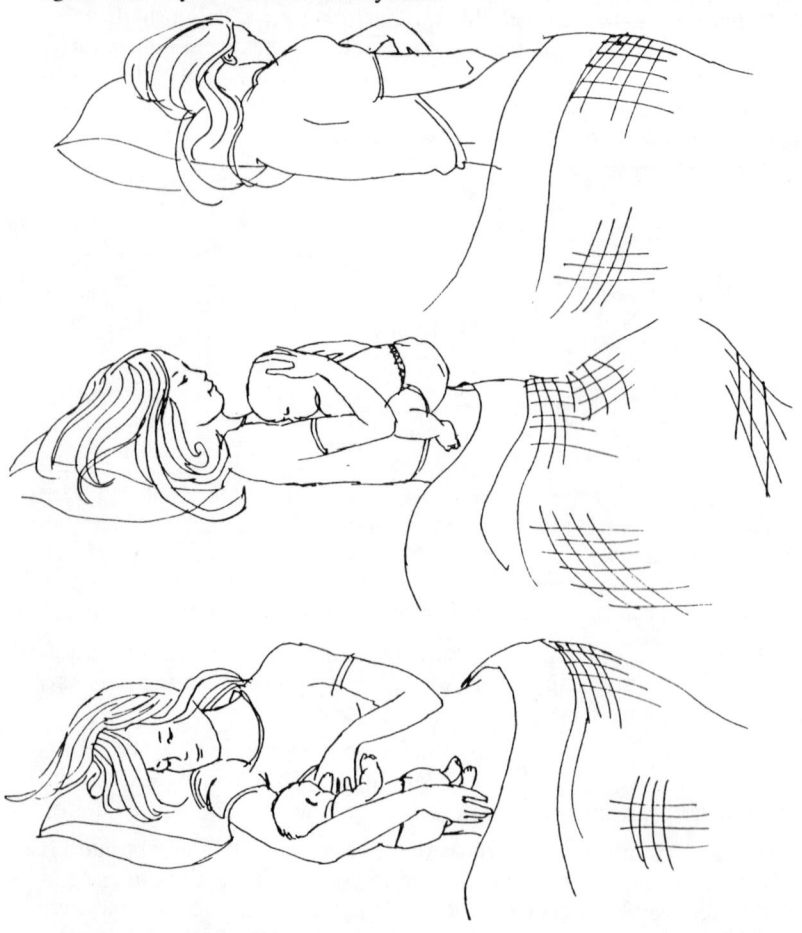

The nurse will take your baby back to the central nursery and offer him some sterile water. The water may seem unnecessary to you; but some babies need it because they do not suckle strongly enough to get the colostrum. Many babies need water to flush out the sedative and anaesthesia that their mothers were given during labor. It would be too difficult for the nurses to keep track of which babies were to get water and which weren't. So they offer it to all the babies. In some hospitals the mothers give the water after each nursing. It does not hurt the baby to be given water even if he does not need it.

If this is your first baby, I would advise you to have "rooming in" if it is available at your hospital. Read the section ROOMING IN. With rooming in you can nurse your baby whenever he cries, which builds up the milk supply sooner. However, it does not interfere with breast-feeding if the baby is kept in the central nursery and brought to you every four hours. Ask that the baby be brought to you every four hours around the clock. Also let it be known that you don't want your baby to receive any formula. That might take away his appetite for his nursing. The nursery personnel can give water between feedings or bring him to you if he cries. It is surprising how well the breast-fed babies adapt to the four hour feeding schedule in the central nursery when they are breast-fed. Don't be disappointed if your hospital is not set up for rooming in. You will be able to nurse your baby on demand when you get home.

THE NEED FOR WATER

Your baby probably could get along with no water at all. All babies are born with an excessive amount of water in their tissues. They lose about ten to fifteen percent of their body weights drying out. When they become thirsty, they get breast milk. Most mothers produce enough milk so that the baby does not need water. Formula-fed babies get enough water in the formula. However, there are a few babies who become excessively dehydrated and get lethargic. 15 to 20 percent of all babies become jaundiced. These babies need water to flush out the by-products of excessive blood destruction, which causes the jaundice. In most maternity divisions these babies are in the minority. However, it is impractical to set a schedule so that bottles of sterile water are provided only for those babies. You will be given sterile water in small bottles of three or four ounces to give to your baby. Don't be alarmed if he doesn't take it. If your milk is flowing well, he wont want it. However, if he refuses the water and seems excessively dehydrated or jaundiced, ask the nurse to help you. Don't ask the nurse not to give your baby water. It is easier to prepare water for all babies than to try to keep the books straight as to which ones need it and which ones don't. Such individualization is too difficult in a maternity hospital.

When your baby gets home, he will need water only if it is very hot outside, above 90 degrees. Otherwise, breast milk is adequate. Occasionally he will need water between feedings, if he cries a lot or has hiccoughs. On rare occasions giving him a little water between feedings will quiet him when nothing else will except breast-feeding.

ROOMING IN

Rooming in is the term used when the baby's bassinet is brought into the room with the mother so that the mother can learn how to take care of her baby under supervision before she has the full care and responsibility at home.

Rooming in has many advantages. You become acquainted with your baby more quickly and many of your questions will be answered before you leave the hospital. The nurses will encourage you to hold, feed, diaper and bathe your baby. They will teach you how to care for his navel and circumcision; or clean her vagina. You will recognize the shift from meconium to breast-fed stools and how frequent they are; how often he urinates; the way he sleeps, the irregularity of his breathing, and many other different little idiosyncrasies. Also it is pure joy just to lie quietly and watch your baby sleep. Your husband will be able to hold the baby and you will both feel more confident of your ability as parents by the time you go home.

When rooming in was established at the Evanston Hospital in 1960, my colleagues and I noticed that we got fewer calls from the new mothers after they got home if they had chosen rooming in at the hospital.

Being able to nurse your baby whenever he seems hungry is helpful for the new mother in learning how to breast-feed. Dr. John Montgomery from Detroit in the 1950's reported on the frequency that some babies suckled in his new rooming in section: there was a gradual increase in the frequency until on the third day most nursed about ten times a day. One champion nursed fifteen times but only for one or two minutes each time. They all slowed down the fourth or fifth day to every three or four hours and nursed longer each feeding. Sore nipples, he said were no problem.

Hospitals in America began experimenting with rooming in during the 1950's in an effort to make the mother feel that she was not on an assembly line when she had her baby in the hospital. Dr. Preston McElendon of Washington, and Dr. Edith Jackson of Yale were early advocates of this plan. Some maternity hospitals are specifically constructed with single, double, or quadruple bassinet nurseries separated by glass from the mother's room. The baby's crib can be moved to the mother's bedside or can be kept in the sound proof nursery and the mother can watch her baby through the glass.

At Yale, the facilities were very simple: three adjacent rooms big enough for four beds each were designated as the rooming in unit. The mothers slept in the end rooms and the babies' cribs, all eight of them, were wheeled in and out of the room between which was considered the rooming in nursery. In some hospitals the crib is left with the mother as long as she wants it, and at night put into another central nursery. It is not advisable to allow rooming in babies to be out with mother, father and visitors all day and then be returned to the central nursery where they are taking care of sick newborns and prematures. It is also not advisable for a new mother to have "twenty-four hour duty" in the care of her newborn right after delivery. She must be able to get her rest especially at night.

Also most staff people like to observe the new babies for 24 hours in the central nursery where highly trained neonatologists work. There, the more experienced personnel, can observe the breathing, mucus in the nose and throat, the type of spit up, and how soon jaundice appears. A few mothers resent not getting rooming in right after delivery. Fewer, who have had rooming in right away, have gotten overtired and rooming in had to be discontinued.

Rooming in takes a certain philosophy of the staff and more than average intelligent flexibility to make it work. More than half the hospitals have rooming in or some modifications of it. Even the "bring-the-baby-to-the-mother-when-he-cries" system takes more staff than the average central nursery system. There are excellent maternity hospitals that do not have rooming in and have just as high a percentage of breast-feeding. I insist, however, that only water be given to the babies in the central nursery and that the baby be brought to the mother every four hours around the clock.

Rooming in is extremely valuable to the first-time mother who has never held a baby in her arms before, but the experienced mother, whose only vacation is her stay in the hospital after the birth of a baby, usually prefers the luxury of letting someone else look after her baby and, when not breast-feeding, having her meals in bed.

THE SECOND DAY OF NURSING

Now you can let your baby nurse two minutes at each breast twice at each feeding. You give your breast a little twist so he gets a different grip on each nipple the second time on each breast. If you feel you are able to nurse for longer periods of time, consult your doctor. He will be able to tell, by the shape of your nipples and the amount of pigment in the areola, if you should increase the time. Blonde and redheaded women have less pigment in the areola and it is a little more susceptible to injury. Brunettes have darker pigmentation and their nipples and areolas are a little tougher. All women have different thresholds of pain, and you must decide how tolerant you are to the pain of sore nipples. Some mothers have very sensitive breasts and can barely stand to have them touched. If you have expressed the colostrum and manipulated your breasts during the last three months of your pregnancy, they are probably tough and can stand longer periods of nursing. Read the section on PRENATAL PREPARATIONS.

Today you might want to nurse your baby sitting up in bed. When nursing with the right breast, your left leg should be partially extended. Draw your right leg up so the knee helps to support your right arm, which is holding the baby. Your right arm should surround the baby and his buttocks should rest in the palm of your hand. Your left hand will be free to direct the nipple into the baby's mouth. If you lean forward slightly, you can bring your breasts closer to the baby. For the sake of comfort, try this position first without the use of a back brace or cushions. **See illustration on next page.** A pillow under your right arm may help. Reverse the process to nurse with the left breast. Nurse the baby two minutes on each side lying down, then two minutes on each side sitting up. By then he'll probably be asleep. Don't try to burp your baby; this will come later. Don't wake him by burping him. Many breast-fed babies don't have to be burped at all.

If the nurses don't bring your baby to you for the 2 a.m. feeding, feel free to ask. If the hospital personnel are giving you a bad time about nursing, ask your doctor if you can go home early with your baby. Many of the La Leche League and modern mothers go home after one or two days to save money. Then you can nurse your baby on a self-demand schedule at home. If you do go home early, it would be wise to have some household help. Read the section HOUSEHOLD HELP.

If you have painful stitches, hemorrhoids, severe cramps, or if you cannot urinate, be sure to tell your doctor. He can help you. Now you will feel dependent and a little bit insecure while your so-called hormonal orchestra rearranges itself for lactation. You may feel as though you don't have the energetic, intellectual drive that you had prior to the birth of your baby. Don't be dismayed, these feelings are normal and temporary. You will be overanxious but happy.

Support baby with both thighs

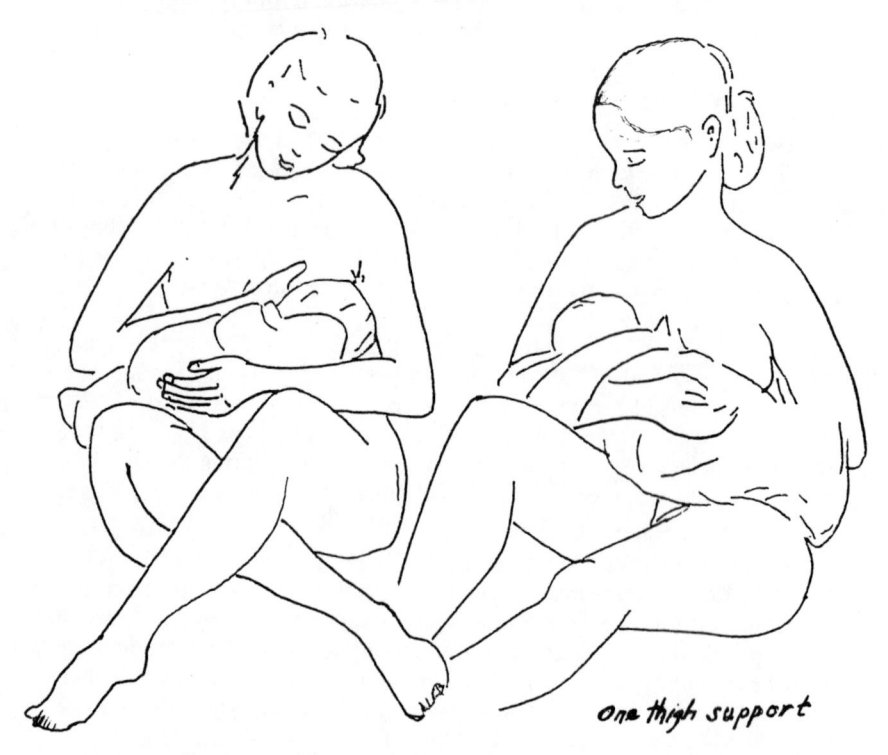

One thigh support

THE THIRD DAY OF NURSING

When your baby is about three days old, your breasts will begin to feel swollen, hot and may be painful. You bra will be too tight so don't wear it. You don't need support or protection for your breasts while you are lying around in the hospital. When you get home and are walking around, you should wear a bra. You can buy a regular nursing bra with flaps that opens to expose your nipples. Don't use the kind with plastic linings. Your nipples need air. Leave the flaps down as much as possible. In the 1940's you would have been told to wear your bra or even an old-fashioned binder in the hospital, but you really don't need to in the eighties.

If your breasts become engorged, your nipples will be flat and the baby won't be able to grasp them. Apply heavy bath towels, which have been wet with hot water and wrung out, to your breasts for about half an hour. Your breasts will become softer. Then express a little milk to bring your nipple out so you can work it into the baby's mouth. If you have rooming in, you can do this whenever the baby awakens. If your baby is in the nursery, apply the hot towel about half and hour before you expect him to be brought in . If the baby still can't grab the nipple, ask the nurse for a nipple shield. You apply the shield to your breast so that it covers your nipple and areola; then put the nipple end into your baby's mouth. The baby will suck and draw your nipple out a little. If the shield is uncomfortable, you can use a regular nipple from a nursing bottle. After a minute or two of suckling, you can shift him directly to your breast.

If the shield fails, hand express ten minutes on each breast every three hours for a few days until your breasts become softer. You can also request an electric breast pump. Most mothers are able to get through this stage of engorgement without having to feed the baby human milk from a bottle.

The past several years hospital costs have increased so much that most mothers go home the third day before the milk has come in. In such an instance, read DIRECTIONS FOR GOING HOME then THE FOURTH DAY OF NURSING.

Also more mothers are going home the second day and the day of delivery. When their households can be arranged so that they can spend three days in bed, they have been very successful in breast-feeding.

EXCESSIVE ENGORGEMENT

The engorgement of the breasts may occur any time after the third day. The breasts become hard, tense, and hot. The veins are dilated and visible under the skin. Your breasts are extremely painful and you may have a fever. Engorgement comes on suddenly and usually occurs between one feeding and the next. The areola is stretched out and the nipple is so flat that the baby cannot grab hold. Hand expression or the breast pump do not yield much milk and are painful. This engorgement is due to the fact that your breasts are overfilled with blood, not milk. There is probably plenty of milk or colostrum, but it can't get out because the blood vessels have swollen, causing pressure which congest the tissue around them.

It is important for the mother to hand express her colostrum during pregnancy so she will be adept enough to do it when her breast are engorged. Remember that when you get pregnant again. Read the section HAND EXPRESSION.

If excessive engorgement is ignored, the future milk producing ability is in danger. Many women who have stopped breast-feeding have told me they had too much milk to start with and then had no milk at all. When questioned more carefully, it was found these women had severe engorgement after the third day. The engorgement blocked the ducts so that the little milk that was produced was never released and the breasts dried up before they even got started.

If you have engorgement, apply hot towels to your breasts and hand express often. Nurse your baby frequently for shorter periods of time. Nurse 12 to 15 times a day if necessary. Rooming in is helpful to a mother with engorged breasts. In some instances the electric breast pump has helped, but generally its pull is too violent to help much. Ask your doctor for some pain pills or have your husband bring you some wine or beer. Within 24 hours you will begin to see a little milk flowing from your nipples. Then you are over the hump; your letdown reflex is beginning to work, and you are well on your way to successful nursing. Continue to hand express. If the baby still has trouble with your nipple, you can hand express the milk right into his mouth.

THE LET DOWN REFLEX

Farmers gave the letdown reflex its name. When a farmer milks a cow she either does or doesn't let down her milk. It's very dramatic. If a boy or a dog chases a cow from the field into the barn right before she is milked, frightening her, she will only let down enough milk to cover the bottom of the pail. If the farmer feeds her, talks softly to her, and gives her a chance to relax, he will get a whole pail full of milk. A woman's lactating mechanism works similarly. It is a nervous, hormonal, and circulatory cycle. The tactile stimulation of the nerves about the nipple is transmitted to the spinal cord and are sent to the brain. From there they go to the pituitary gland, which squeezes out a hormone known as oxytocin. The oxytocin goes into the bloodstream and circulates through the body. When it reaches the woman's breasts and nipples, it causes a contraction of the smooth muscle in the nipples, which makes them erect. It also causes the smooth muscles around the ductules in the breast to contract, which squeezes out the milk. In some women this flow is so dramatic that several streams of milk will squirt from the nipple in a spray. I've seen it spray as far as twelve inches. Usually the milk just flows or drips. It usually takes 30 to 90 seconds after the baby starts sucking for most women to get the letdown reflex. You might feel a tingling sensation in your breasts or you may feel nothing even though you are letting down the milk.

You may also experience abdominal pain. This is because the oxytocin is causing a contraction of the muscular wall of your womb, which will lead to an excessive flow of blood. Occasionally the cramps will last for several weeks, but it is good for you because it makes your uterus return to normal more quickly. The ocytocin also makes you feel relaxed and at peace with the world. The letting down of the milk usually lasts three to five minutes. During this time most babies get about 75 percent of the milk at that feeding.

The letdown reflex sometimes fails to work when the mother is upset, nervous, worried, or is entertaining company. This usually happens at the end of the day when the mother is getting dinner for her husband and the other children. She may only give the baby half ounce of milk, when she usually gives him six. Then the baby will be colicky at night and will have to be nursed every half-hour or hour several times.

If your letdown reflex fails to work, drink one cocktail or a glass of wine and go to bed. Or sip tea and rock in the rocking chair. Or give your mother-in-law some mending to do in another part of the house. Do whatever will relax you within reason. After you've rested for twenty minutes, nurse the baby again. This time you'll fill him up.

It is very important for you to learn how to relax and to avoid situations which will prevent your letdown reflex from working, and of course be careful not to become dependent on any external stimulus to achieve this.

A consistent letdown reflex is the most important physiological activity for a nursing mother to be successful in breast-feeding her infant. The lack of it is the reason why 80 percent or more women stop breast-feeding, instead of learning how to live so that the letdown reflex will work. Dr Michael Newton and his wife, Dr. Niles Newton, have published some interesting research on the letdown reflex. They measured how much milk a woman produces by weighing the baby before and after feeding. They put this woman's foot in ice water and then she nursed and gave her baby only one ounce. Next they asked her to solve mathematical problems. She listened and gave the answers under the threat of having another electric shock. She only produced one ounce of milk. But when she was allowed to nurse peacefully, she produced her usual six ounces of milk. Dr. Charlotte Naish, mother of five, and an enthusiast for breast-feeding in England says, " A woman who is nursing her baby should not be consulted in any decision unless it concerns her baby directly." Read the section THE DANGER WEEKS IN BREAST-FEEDING.

The letdown reflex presents a great challenge to every nursing mother to learn how to make it work. Mrs. F. gave up nursing because her baby cried all night. Her physician told her she was too nervous to nurse her baby and to put the baby on bottles. When the next baby came she wanted very much to nurse. She had moved and I was the pediatrician. I made her spend her first three days at home in bed. She was a nervous woman so I told her to drink a highball in the evening before she nursed. She liked the idea and it worked. Her older child was compartmentized, so she didn't have to worry about what he was doing while she nursed the baby. The baby gained well and Mrs. F. looked wonderful and was very happy. She nursed her baby for nine months. When the third baby came along she nursed her, but was not dependent on the highballs. She had learned what she could and couldn't do to achieve the let down reflex.

Mrs. G. was a teetotaler, so the cocktail method wasn't an option. Her alternative was when the baby cried in the evening, her husband walked him. Mrs. G. sat in the rocking chair and rocked and drank warm water. It would usually take her about 15 minutes to relax. Then her husband would give her the baby and she could nurse him. A few moments of quiet contemplation was what she needed to let down her milk. So be sure you have a comfortable rocking chair in the house as an alternative of choice.

Each of you must learn what makes your letdown reflex work; also what prevents it. If suddenly at one feeding you don't feel it, and you usually feel it regularly, your baby will be fussy after nursing. Then you must do what ever makes you relax and nurse him or her again.

THE FOURTH DAY OF NURSING

The fourth day of nursing is usually either a day of great encouragement or discouragement. Mothers who quit nursing usually quit on the fourth day. By this time you will probably feel the letdown reflex. But some very successful nursing mothers don't feel it for a few months; a few mothers never feel it at all. Your nipples may hurt on the fourth day, but when you see your baby nursing vigorously and know he's getting your milk, you won't mind. (Read the section SORE NIPPLES).

Time today's nursings from the time the baby begins to swallow and allow him to nurse for four minutes on each side -- twice on each breast. If you have an abundance of milk, he will get most of it during the first four minutes. He may get so much that he will spit up a large quantity of it. He may be hungry, so nurse him again. By the fourth day, you will know what kind of nurser your baby is . He may be a vigorous barracuda or a quiet, sedate susan. Both are normal.

Don't be discouraged if your breasts are still engorged. Use hot towels, hand expression, and nurse your baby every one, two, or three hours if you have rooming in; or go home. If you are feeling well and chose to go home, stay in bed three days. Then you will be able to nurse as often as you and the baby want to.

If you haven't had much engorgement and you are not getting much of a letdown reflex, or if your nipples are small and tender, or large and bulbous, or partially inverted, read the section SORE NIPPLES. If your baby is a barracuda, nursing may be so painful that you want to quit. In this instance ask for a pain killing sedative or drink a little wine or cocktail before nursing and be sure the baby gets the whole areola into his mouth. Nurse lying down and then sitting up. Do not let him nurse more than four minutes without changing his position. If you do not get the letdown reflex and he is still going strong, go back to the first breast. Nurse on both sides each for four minutes. If he still will not go to sleep, repeat the nursing on both sides in a different position or give your breast a twist so that he gets a different bite.

If your nipples are swollen, red, and tender, expose them to the air. Don't even cover them with a nightgown or the sheet. The exposure will heal them. If they are kept moist and warm, they will become macerated like your fingertips do after they have been in water for a long time.

If your baby will not nurse because he is dysmature or premature or has had more than the usual amount of asphyxia and concussion in birth, learn how to hand express. Or ask for an electric breast pump to keep your lactation going.

If you have a lot of milk, your baby will have gained an ounce or two on the fourth day. But it doesn't mean you won't succeed if your baby is still losing weight. Even if you only produce half an ounce a day , you can nurse him well and completely. Just nurse him often to build up your milk supply.

FAILURE TO SUCKLE

If your baby is not suckling by the fourth day, something must be done or you will lose your milk. By the fourth day, the sedative or anaesthesia you had to help deliver your baby should be worn off. (Most women today have some help by sedatives or anaesthesia but an increasing number are giving birth without any medication.) If the baby still refuses to nurse, and if the nipples seem to be all right, and if no engorgement has set in, find out if the baby is being given formula in the nursery. If he is, he may not want to nurse. Ask the nurses. If the baby is quiet when he is brought to you, it is likely he's getting formula. Ask the nurses not to give him formula.

If you can't have rooming-in ask your doctor to leave instructions for the baby to be brought to you every three hours to nurse. This may not be possible because it would upset the hospital routine, but more hospitals are becoming flexible about this. If you can't have the baby that often, see if you keep him for an hour each feeding. Whenever you feed the baby, hand express a little milk into his mouth to entice him to want more.

Jaundiced babies are particularly sleepy and often do not nurse well. They must be fed often to get enough fluid to make their kidneys work better. Frequent nursings, ten or twelve per day, is the best procedure for jaundiced babies. If this cannot be arranged in the hospital, go home as soon as you can. (Read the section JAUNDICE).

Sometimes mother and baby cannot get together. The letdown reflex is slow to come and this makes the baby angry. The mother should express her milk a few minutes before she plans to feed the baby so the milk is flowing when the baby goes to the breast.

FAILURE TO NURSE BECAUSE OF ASPHYXIA AND CONCUSSION

Man has "out evolved" himself. The brain of the infant has developed to such an extent that it is a large round object that has to come out of a smaller oval-shaped opening in the bony pelvis of the mother. It has to mold, be pushed and squeezed, and the mother often has to be sedated and anesthetized. For half a century the procedure has been routine; those strong women who were capable of giving birth without anaesthesia or sedation were in the minority in the 1940's and 50's, but their numbers are increasing, led by the advocates of natural childbirth. By the end of this century most strong women will give birth without sedation or anaesthesia. Now obstetricians trained in the university centers are doing much work to try to reduce the incidence of cerebral asphyxiation and concussion in newborn babies. Fetologists and neonatologists who are spending their lives studying newborns, are contributing immensely to the understanding of how to get a baby with a large head out of a smaller pelvis without anesthetizing the mother excessively.

A bigger problem is concussion, which occurs when the baby is expelled through the birth canal too fast, and the changes take place too quickly. But if the second stage of labor (the pushing stage) is too long, there can be trouble with the circulation to the brain. Especially if a mother loses control because of the pain and in the process of being born, the baby doesn't get all the oxygen that he should.

However over the years, newborn babies have adapted to and recovered from this temporary condition. In the majority of instances, this state of asphyxia and concussion is over by the time the baby is 72 hours old. But in some instances it may last longer. When your baby is brought to you and does not go to breast right away, the nurse might stand there impatiently and pinch the baby to make him cry. You then try to force the baby to nurse by squeezing his mouth open and putting him to your breast. This is likely to frustrate him and by pushing him into the nipple, you will make him pull back. Your letdown reflex has begun to work, your milk is in, but still your baby does not suckle well. You can put your finger into his mouth, and he will not grab hold of it. This baby is probably suffering from a mild brain concussion from which he will recover completely in about a week.

It does no good to shake him, poke him, pinch him, or force him to nurse. Let him lie beside you in bed and don't try to put him to breast at all. Hand express your milk or use and electric breast pump or the Kanesson-Marshall pump to help you to keep your milk coming. Your baby can be fed human milk, either yours or from the milk bank.

The baby should then be fed with an eyedropper or a fast flowing nipple, slowly so that he doesn't choke. He should be fed at frequent intervals and allowed to sleep in between as much as possible. Discuss this situation with your doctor so that frequent and prolonged attempts to nurse are not exaggerated. The best way to tell if your baby has a mild temporary brain injury is to put your finger in his mouth to see if he suckles strongly. If he doesn't have a strong sucking reflex, it is best to let him rest until his brain recovers from the difficult trip into the world. This usually occurs sometime after he is a week old. Occasionally I have seen it go on longer, but invariably the baby recovers. These babies can be completely breast-fed. They should be breast-fed rather than fed formula. So it is very important for you to keep your milk coming and your lactation at its best by hand expression or the electric pump or the Kanesson-Marshall pump every three or four hours so that when your baby is strong enough, he is able to go to breast and suckle well. Read the section PREMATURES.

The late Dr. Douglas Buchanan of the University of Chicago, one of the greatest child neurologists of this century, used to say that "every baby born is asphyxiated and concussed, it was only a matter of degree." He also noted that "the brain had tremendous power to recover if it was made right". He taught that learning disabilities and mental retardation, conditions that show up in later childhood, were never due to birth injury but to genetics and difficulties when the brain was being made during the first four weeks of pregnancy. The "brain injured" babies grew to become normal in intelligence and often honor students.

SORE NIPPLES

I am sure that mothers in primitive cultures do not have trouble with their nipples that the civilized white women do. One reason is that many mothers wear a bra all day and a nightgown or pajamas at night. Seldom are her nipples left uncovered. It is like a person who wore shoes all his life and then had to take a long walk barefooted. Also I have the impression that many of the first time mothers whom I have pushed into breast-feeding (read ONE PHYSICIANS APPROACH TO BREAST-FEEDING) have never had their nipples manipulated enough. Husbands please note. That is why, whenever I see a mother pre-natally, I instruct her in the technique of daily hand expression of the colostrum during the last three months of her pregnancy. (Refer to PRE-NATAL PREPARATIONS). Not only does she learn the valuable technique of hand expression, but her nipples get manipulated and thus the cracked nipple is prevented.

In my experience when a mother is left on her own to nurse and is not guided by someone who will look after her nipples, her doctor, husband, nurse or lactating friend; she may end up with such sore nipples that she has to stop breast-feeding. Or the pain my be so severe that she can not get the letdown reflex which is equivalent to the stopping of breast-feeding because the baby's hunger will not be satisfied if the mother does not get the letdown reflex. (Read the section LETDOWN REFLEX).

My own wife, nursing our third child let him go for twenty minutes the first time and got sore nipples; fortunately she had enough grit to continue nursing until her nipples toughened up. Whenever I take the lactating ability of a new mother too much for granted and fail to examine her nipples daily and guide her in taking care of them, she may telephone me after she has been home a few days, stating that her nipples are in shreds. Unfortunately for her, it hurts too much to laugh. In this situation, I usually find a crack about one-quarter to one-half inch long at the base of the nipple at twelve o'clock, if she has been nursing lying down. The crack is at two o'clock on the left nipple and ten o'clock on the right if she has been nursing sitting up. **See illustration.**

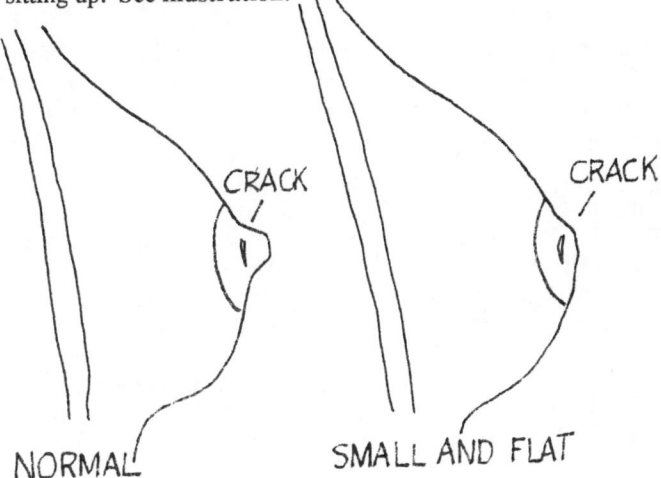

CRACK OCCURS IN RIGHT NIPPLE WHEN MOTHER NURSES – SITTING UP – AT 12 O'CLOCK WHEN LYING DOWN

It is the pressure from the upper jaw on the nipple directly that makes the injury. The tongue covers the lower jaw. If someone shows the mother how to work the whole areola into the baby's mouth, and not allow the baby to suckle just at the nipple, then the pressure and shearing action of the jaws do not hurt the more sensitive and highly innervated nipple. Instead the pressure is borne by the less sensitive and more resilient areola. Since I have insisted that every nursing mother know how to work her whole areola into her baby's mouth with her index finger every time her baby opens his mouth, I have seen less cracked nipples

In illustration #2 in FIRST DAY OF NURSING see how the jaws and tongue of the nursing baby work. Also note that when he opens his mouth more of the areola can be pushed into it so the pressure of the upper jaw can hit the areola. I have seen the pressure of a suckling baby's jaw in some "barracudas" to be strong enough to cause a black and blue mark should the baby inadvertently suckle on his mother's arm instead of her areola.

Some nipples are not really cracked but have become red and swollen to about twice normal size reminiscent of a finger struck by a hammer when the nail is missed. These nipples are so tender that even the weight of a sheet over them is unendurable. In these situations nursing must be discontinued temporarily while a mother hand expresses her breast milk -- placing her finger and thumb at the edge of the areola away from the injured nipple. See HAND EXPRESSION. Or she can pump her breast and give the milk to the infant by medicine dropper, spoon, or bottle and nipple. After a few days, depending on the severity, she can put the baby back on the breast by letting the baby suckle after the letdown reflex has been started by hand expression. Always start the baby on the less tender nipple and again remember to work the whole darker area into the baby's mouth with your index finger every time he opens his mouth. Some mothers have used nipple shields in these situations. but I have not had much luck with them. The nipples still hurt and only rarely can the baby get enough milk through the nipple shield.

In the beginning when resuming nursing on the tender side, limit the time to one or two minutes then hold his nose for 30 seconds to make him let go. Then put him on the good side. When you go back to the sore side again that feeding, change your position by lying down or sitting up or putting your baby's feet over your head or giving your breast a twist clockwise or counter-clockwise. **See illustrations, next page** and reread FIRST DAY OF NURSING. All these maneuvers cause the baby's upper jaw to hit the nipple in a different place. Frequent nursing for short periods of time is better for nipples. Don't forget; with each change, work the whole areola into your baby's mouth.

When going back to nursing, if you cannot stand suckling long enough to lower the intralobular pressure in your breast to maintain your milk production, then you must hand express or pump your breast with the sore nipple to maintain lactation until your nipple heals. A forty-watt bulb at 12 inches for fifteen minutes after nursing and exposure of the nipples to the air for 2 hours after nursing helps. Antibiotic ointments help if the fissures become infected. It does no harm if the baby suckles after the application of the ointment. Large quantities of ointment do no more good than about one-sixteenth inch out of the tube rubbed thoroughly but gently. Alcohol or astringents or rubbing vigorously with a towel injures the nipple and does not prevent cracking.

I repeat: the best treatment for sore nipples is prevention, and it should start before the baby is born. Every mother should learn the art of hand expression and express the colostrum during the last three months of her pregnancy. The gentle manipulation of the nipples toughens them so they're not as likely to crack after the baby is born and suckling begins.

The shape of the nipple plays a part in the tendency to crack. If the nipple is inverted when the woman is not pregnant, the surface of the nipple is concave. With the birth of the baby and the stimulation for breast-feeding, the concave surface becomes convex. The increased pressure the baby puts upon this outer surface makes it crack. **See illustration.** It becomes very painful to nurse. The best treatment for this condition is to use the Plastishield, (Plastishield, Inc., Minneapolis, Minnesota), (**See diagram**). The shields can be worn during pregnancy. They are carried by most large drug stores. The evaporation of the warm air beneath the shield tends to create a gentle suction which brings out the inverted nipple.

Plastishields should be worn beneath the bra when pregnancy is contemplated.

strain

Inverted   Inverted Nipple pulled out

Suckling must be carefully monitored. See page 84. Before 1940 nipple variations were a common reason for not breastfeeding.

Hand expression during the prenatal period also helps bring out the nipple. If after the baby is born, the nipples are inverted, an electric breast pump can also be used to pull the nipples out. The baby must have a large part of the areola in his mouth and not suckle too long at any one time or in any one position.

The complexion of the mother is another factor in cracked nipples. The pigment increases in the areola and nipple during pregnancy. It seems to be nature's way of toughening the nipple for the task of nursing to follow. The bulbous nipple is also apt to crack unless a special effort is made to work the areola into the baby's mouth.   With the first baby especially, the time of nursing must be carefully limited and increased carefully so that gradually the nipple will toughen.

An important variable is the vigor of the baby. the so called

"Barracuda" will be more apt to injure his mother's nipples than the sleepy or the lazy baby who does not suckle vigorously, but the "Barracuda" suckles beautifully when the areola is pushed completely into his mouth.

As a nursing mother, if you are aware of what can happen to your nipples, then you will learn to adapt gradually to this new physiological function the same as the student with soft hands learns to work at pick and shovel, with gloves first until his hands toughen. Try not to get hurt, but if you do, tomorrow it will be better.

SMALL WHITE SPOTS ON THE NIPPLES

The small white spots on the nipple are small cysts. The suckling baby usually breaks them and they disappear. Some mothers have broken them with a sterile needle. They have nothing to do with the phenomenon of "plugged duct" and breast abscess which is associated with a "lactating indiscretion." Read section: PLUGGED DUCT AND BREAST ABSCESS.

Sometimes the nipple itself becomes infected, swollen, reddened and very tender. Usually the breast is pumped and the mother is treated with an antibiotic. Then breast-feeding can be resumed.

JAUNDICE

With the fetal circulation by-passing the lungs, the number of red blood cells the baby has while in the uterus, is more than he needs after birth when the blood is oxygenated by going through the lungs. Hence the extra red blood cells that he has to break up, releasing hemoglobin into the blood stream, become bilirubin which causes jaundice. In about a third of the babies the jaundice can be seen (over 12 mg. per 100 cc.) because the liver and kidneys have not yet begun to function well enough to clear the bilirubin out of the blood or because some gets bound to the blood proteins and lingers. Jaundice above 20 mg. per 100 cc. scares people. Some are scared at 10 mg. per 100 cc. In the 1950's, when the Rh. babies died, it was found that their brains were stained with bilirubin which made the neurons malfunction. Those who lived with high bilirubin levels (above 20 mg percent) were at risk for having trouble with long division at eleven years of age. Thanks to exchange transfusion and the discovery of RHOGAM, Rh. babies are a disease of the past. But from the Rh experience there has been lingering fears that jaundiced babies will grow up mildly retarded and we still have blood type incompatibilities. Florescent lights (bili-lites) and sunlight metabolize the bilirubin in the skin and dramatically reduce the jaundice.

Breast-feeding in a few instances, not completely understood, augments jaundice and stopping breast-feeding for 24 to 48 hours clears it up. It might be necessary for you and your physician to decide which is best; to substitute formula for a day or two to help the jaundice, but risk allergy, or continue breast-feeding uninterruptedly and help prevent allergy; but risk inability to do mathematics. In my longitudinal studies of completely breast-fed babies, before everyone knew so much, all my breast-fed babies with bilirubins in the high teens and low twenties did well in mathematics and many became honor students.

My study showed no correlation of high blood bilirubin with mental defect even with the prematures who were at greater risk. I agree with the late Dr. Douglas Buchanan who observed that the causes of cerebral defects have many more associations than high blood bilirubin levels -- among them are multiple minute cerebral hemorrhages due to congenital weakness of the walls of the cerebral capillaries.

Fear should not sabotage your breast-feeding. You and your doctor will make the right decisions unemotionally. New information in this field is continuously becoming available.

GOING HOME FROM THE HOSPITAL

No matter how nice they were at the hospital or how good a time you had, you will be eager to get home with your new baby. You may not be able to get into the skirt you had planned to wear home, but don't worry. With time and proper exercise, you will get back into shape and all your pre-maternity clothes will fit you again. Nursing will help your figure to return to normal much quicker; it stimulates the uterus to contract.

If possible, have your older children out of the house when you return home with your new baby. After your rigorous morning of getting ready to come home, you will be exhausted. Your baby will feel this excitement. So get undressed, go to bed and nurse your baby. It is much better for you to receive the welcoming tumult in bed, and nurse the baby. It is natural for the older children to be eager to see their mother and the newest member of the family, but for your own sake, hold them off for a little while.

Keep the baby's bassinette right next to your bed, so you can just lean over and pick him up to nurse or change his diaper. Have all the baby's equipment near you so you don't have to get out of bed. If father is under pressure in his job and awakens easily, encourage him to sleep in another room for a few weeks or until lactation is established.

You must stay in bed for three days after you get home. Get up only to go to the bathroom. Your household has been functioning without your personal attention while you were in the hospital, and it can continue to do so for three more days. If you do not have household help, your husband can cook the meals and bring them to you in bed. If you have visitors, dive into bed the moment they arrive. Most people will offer to help so don't be shy about asking them to make sandwiches or take your toddler for a walk.

I am adamant about these first three days in bed. Almost invariably, if a mother has not stayed in bed, she doesn't get the letdown reflex on the second day. Then the baby suffers. He cries, has colic, and doesn't nurse well.

After three days, you may get up for a while. For the first month, you should take three one-hour naps a day. If you rest between feedings, you will have plenty of milk for your next nursing. Nurse lying down as much as you can, as this is very restful. Elevate your feet as often as possible. Try to nap in the morning after your husband and older children have left the house. Nap again after lunch and just before the dinner hour. After supper let someone else have the kitchen duty; you lie on the sofa and discuss the day's happening with your husband. Rest and relaxation is important to be a successful nursing mother. You must learn to put things aside for these first two months. Mothers of first children have to learn not to worry; those, with more than one, not to get tired. Being successful in lactation will make you a stronger, happier and a more fulfilled woman.

HOUSEHOLD HELP

It is almost impossible for a young family to obtain household help these days. When I first started practice, many mothers had baby nurses. Frequently grandmother treated the new mother to a practical nurse for two weeks. These nurses were trained in an era when sterility was more important than breast-feeding. Often they went into a room, sat in a rocking chair, rocked the baby, fed the baby, and kept father out. Sometimes they let the father look at the baby, but not touch. Their attitude toward the mother was, "You produced this baby, but now I will show you how to make the baby grow." If the mother decided that she wanted to breast-feed, that was horrible.

Breast-feeding was old-fashioned and unnecessary. They kept the babies clean, showed the mothers how to bathe the babies and how to prepare the formula. They were skillful in the techniques of artificial feeding, but they were not interested in housework nor in looking after the other children. They drove them out of the baby's room. They truly loved the babies and there were tears when they left. I do not recommend such household help for new mothers; and fortunately, such devoted baby nurses are harder to find.

What you need as a mother is another pair of hands and a spirit of encouragement and helpfulness. She must fit in well with your temperament, your needs, and your goals. If you have been so unfortunate that you have not been able to compartmentize your older children, you must have household help who will take your two-and-one-half year old for a walk, or will take the four-year old to the store. Refer to COMPARTMENTATION. She should do some of the shopping, carry some of the groceries, put a roast in the oven or microwave. Helping to prepare and cleaning up after meals would be very helpful. These are the kinds of services that will help you. It is better to go without help, however, if your only choice is a baby nurse.

If you cannot find or afford a full-time cleaning lady or maid, a neighborhood girl, a junior or senior high school student, is usually excellent. Part-time as long as it is quality time is often enough to provide a little relief periodically.

Your mother is fine, if you get along with her. Your mother-in-law should be avoided. In forty-two years of practice, I have seen only eleven mothers successfully breast-feed with a mother-in-law in the house. It is not what you say to your mother-in-law that stops your letdown reflex. It is what you don't dare say. Sometimes your friends may have the same affect on you.

In my study, in the northern suburbs of Chicago, the average family income was over $50,000 per year in the 1960's. Mostly the young mothers graduated from highly competitive colleges as did their husbands. Usually one or both were raised with one or more servants and were used to them. A few had English nannies. Most of the young mothers were active in charity work; especially the Junior League which was demanding. Being well educated, they appreciated the advantages of breast feeding and made it fashionable again.

The husbands of these strong women were often very competitive in their jobs. They were rapidly on their way up and many spent most of their waking hours thinking about their careers. They worked hard and played hard. Many fathers did not have the stamina for house work, but went off hunting, fishing or playing golf resenting the "squaw work". Mothers often got angry when they had too much work to do, and resented watching their husbands relax at home or away. The letdown reflex didn't work and they lost their milk. These mothers needed household help to keep this from happening. The new mother needed the kind of household help that would keep her calm and relaxed. The experienced mother, the kind that would keep her from getting tired.

Gradually practical nurses became available who were better trained in the art of breast-feeding and physicians became more enthusiastic about breast-feeding. Modern high schools gave courses of instruction in this art. La Leche League members and physicians gave talks in many high schools and colleges all over the country.

A few couples had no money for help. Father took his vacation when mother went to the hospital to have the baby. Father was mother's helper. She was usually successful when father favored breast-feeding. Read IMPORTANCE OF FATHERS IN BREASTFEEDING.

Many of the young mothers in America in the 1980's do not want household help. They feel more comfortable with their husbands helping them. Most have all the conveniences including microwave and disposable diapers. Housework is simple. Meals can be prepared in five minutes and fathers are just as adept as mothers in preparing meals, cleaning up, and changing diapers.

More and more fathers are attending childbirth education classes and have become interested and supportive of mothers through their natural childbirths. They understand their wives and how to protect and support them in breast-feeding. These are the fathers who have forty hours per week jobs that are not ulcer producing. They leave their worries at their places of work and they become intrigued in helping take care of the new baby.

Fifty percent of the young mothers work until just before going into labor and return to work when the baby is a month old; either because they want to or financially have to -- they think. Fortunately, most are learning to breast-feed and hold down a job at the same time; thanks for the increasing opportunities to bring babies to work and the development of good day care centers. Refer to WORKING AND BREASTFEEDING.

It is important for each mother in the 1980's to know her priorities and those of her husband. If your husband can earn $100,000 a year in the 1980's, you must forgive him if he is not handy around the house and short of patience with the children. You must be smart enough to hire compatible help to keep your chemistry of mother love going.

Often I have felt that the full time homemaker needs two husbands. One to bring in the money; another to help her with the children. Of course, if she compartmentizes, she can get along better with or without help.

FLUCTUATIONS IN THE AMOUNT OF BREAST MILK

The amount of breast milk can vary a great deal from hour to hour in any mother. In the morning when you are rested, you have more than enough to satisfy the baby. The infant usually sleeps soundly following this feeding and may even sleep through the next feeding. The second time in a day that you breast-feed, you have enough. It isn't until about six o'clock in the evening, if you have been very busy fixing supper, preparing the other children for bed, and greeting your husband that you find that you cannot let down the milk You give practically nothing to the baby. You will probably produce six to eight ounces of milk at the early morning feeding, about five or six ounces at ten o'clock in the morning, about three ounces at two o'clock, one ounce at six o'clock, one-half to one ounce at eight o'clock, and another one-half ounce at nine o'clock. All through the evening the baby screams and gets less than half an ounce of human milk at each try. This fluctuation in the amount of breast milk can be remedied if you relax and rest. You must get off your feet before the early afternoon feeding. You should lie down while you nurse. Beer, wine or a weak cocktail will help you relax. If you do not drink, you can ask your doctor for a mild tranquilizer. Some mothers are able to relax by just sitting in a rocking chair and drinking warm water. Do anything that will help you think sweet thoughts and ease the strain.

The adults around a nursing mother can also affect her milk supply. One of my mothers entertained her husband's spinster aunt and mother when her daughter was six weeks old. While the relatives were passing the baby around, Mrs. P. prepared dinner. When the baby began to cry for her dinner, Mrs. P. started to nurse her in the living room. A horrified silence fell.

"You mean you do that in front of people?" the aunt exclaimed. Mrs. P. was as stunned as if she had been slapped. She took the baby to the bedroom to feed her, but she could not let the milk down.

Grandmother tried to quiet the baby while Mrs. P. worked in the kitchen. The broccoli boiled over and the baby continued to scream. Grandmother told Mr. P. to mix some formula and when he went to the bedroom to phone me, he found his wife in tears. I told Mr. P. to give his wife a cocktail and put her to bed. Thirty minutes later her milk began to flow and she nursed the baby to sleep.

A nursing mother should not entertain anyone until the baby is six-months old. Also, if you have children between one and four years of age who are not compartmentized, you are in serious trouble because your mind will be on the children while you are trying to nurse the baby. Read COMPARTMENTATION.

Another way for you to improve your evening milk supply is to borrow or rent an electric breast pump. The more the breasts are stimulated, the more milk they will produce. In the morning after the other children are cared for and your husband is gone, sit down and pump your breasts, about ten minutes on each side with an electric pump, or a Marshall pump. In my practice, I have found that very few mothers can succeed in the art of hand expression. The small bulbed breast pump which can be purchased at every drug store has a suction that is too weak to be effective. The electric model must be set at ten pounds of vacuum. That strong pull will usually get two or three ounces from the mother. It can be put into a bottle and placed in the freezer. Additions of freshly pumped breast milk can be added to the frozen milk until there is about four ounces. Melt it in the evening and give it to your baby if your attempt to satisfy him by frequent nursing fails. After you have tried the breast once an hour three times, you can offer the entire four ounces. One or two ounces of human milk diluted with water to make four ounces will suffice.

Often when you are on a trip, you will have an excess amount of breast milk. When you return from a cocktail party, you will have so much milk, and the letdown reflex will work so violently, that you will have to wake your baby to relieve yourself. To relieve yourself of this fullness when you are at the theater for a four-hour play, you can go to the washroom and hand express the milk.

NO SCHEDULE, PLEASE

Successful breast-feeding depends upon a letdown reflex that works well. Since mothers cannot always get the letdown reflex when they want to, it is foolish for a mother to try to impose a schedule for nursing her baby. The baby of average size needs about 14 ounces of human milk per day to gain properly after he is two weeks old. But sometimes you may produce less than an ounce per feeding. If you tried to stay on a four-hour schedule, obviously the baby wouldn't get enough to eat. Sometimes you must nurse your baby twelve to fifteen times a day without any schedule so you can stimulate milk production. The longer the infant suckles, the more the intralobular pressure is decreased and the greater is the stimulation to secrete more milk.

This kind of milk has a higher fat content and more calories. This is the way it works. When you let down only a small quantity of milk, say half an ounce, that is all that is stored in the ductules between feedings. But the hungry baby will continue to suckle and decrease further the intralobular pressure. This automatically triggers the glands in the breasts to make more milk. The prolonged suckling makes the baby tired, and the milk he receives is rich in fat, which assuages his hunger and helps him sleep. If he does not get enough fluid or caloric intake, he will awaken in an hour or two. But while he sleeps, a greater amount of breast milk has been secreted into the ductules because the intralobular pressure was greatly reduced.

More milk gathers to fill the void in the ductules. Then when he nurses, your letdown reflex will expel a greater amount of milk than before. Thus by frequent feedings you make more milk.

On the other hand, if your baby gets a large amount of milk, four to eight ounces in the first few minutes of suckling, he will be satisfied before the intralobular pressure decreases as low as before. The breasts are not asked to make as much milk, so the next time will be less. Thus the baby controls the milk production, which is what Nature intended. A baby should be fed when he wants to nurse, not when the clock says he should.

It is inaccurate to refer to the breast as being emptied. That is anatomically impossible, because the breast is made of tissue which contracts. Breasts are like a lot of little balloons. It is impossible to really empty them. The baby only decreases the pressure within them, which stimulates the manufacture of more milk. The secretions of milk is dependent upon the innate efficiency of the glandular tissue of the breasts and the completeness of the woman's hormonal physiology. 99 percent of all women have sufficient glandular tissue and hormones to breast-feed a baby. The expulsion of milk, however, is dependent on the letdown reflex, which is dependent upon how the mother thinks. (Read LET DOWN REFLEX).

In my experience, the mothers who try hard to get their baby on a schedule always fail. If you can get yourself in the frame of mind so you don't care whether or not your baby is on a schedule, before you know it, he will sleep from six to six and nurse only four times a day. This will continue as long as you are not upset. If something bothers you, your baby will awaken several times in the evening because you did not let down enough milk at the last feeding. Do not be afraid to dedicate yourself completely to the task of breast-feeding. Let the baby control your schedule.

Let him nurse whenever he seems hungry, whether it is four or fifteen times a day. But don't let him sleep all day without nursing. Then he'd awaken every hour or two at night. If your baby sleeps more than four or five hours straight in the daytime, you should awaken and nurse him. You do not need to wake him at night to nurse. Don't be afraid of spoiling the baby. Nurse whenever he cries and enjoy it.

THE DANGER WEEKS

The first time mother has many adjustments to make about her new feelings. Read section: THE MIND OF THE MOTHER. She may also have concerns regarding sore nipples and her ultimate ability to satisfy her baby who cries a lot. Read SORE NIPPLES and HOW MUCH IS ENOUGH.

When I received the telephone calls during the second week at home it was usually that the baby was awake most the evening but sleeping and nursing all right during the day.

"Did you spend the first three days in bed when you got home from the hospital?" The answer was always "No!"

"Do you have company?"

"Yes!"

"Do you feel the letdown reflex?"

"Not in the evening!"

"Have you been taking three one-hour naps during the day?"

"I haven't got time for naps!"

Then a didactic schedule of rest was re-emphasized. For the first month, mother was told to take three one-hour naps even if the house was on fire!

After the first month she was told to take two one-hour naps or one two-hour nap for as long as she nursed.

In my study during the 1950's, I found that 76% of the mothers who were successful in nursing followed these instructions for naps 75% of the time. In the 1980's it was the same, but the smart mothers did not have to be pushed into breast-feeding. They were nursing because they wanted to and the danger weeks were not as conspicuous. There has been a change in the wind as predicted by Karen Pryor in her brilliant book, *Nursing Your Baby* (Harper & Row, 1963). Except where there were cultural aversions, beer, wine, highballs or cocktails were discretely encouraged before the rest periods. Read LETDOWN REFLEX.

The babies determined the schedule; six to twelve nursings per day were frequent during the first months.

The mothers were instructed to nurse from both breasts each feeding - about ten minutes from each breast. Between the second and eighth week of breast-feeding, when the babies slept all day and cried all night, the mothers were told to hand express or pump their breasts about an hour after the two morning feedings. Breast milk was then given to the babies at night when they were not getting enough. Within two weeks the mothers rose in milk production so that they satisfied their babies in the evening without having to give breast milk from a dish with a spoon or from a bottle.

It seemed to take a mother about eight weeks to feel secure in breast-feeding. To learn what she could and couldn't do and still get the letdown reflex. A baby cried; the mother nursed, and then baby smiled at her. That gave her confidence and a feeling of pleasure in what her body could do. The first time mother is subject to worry; the mother of more than one is subject to fatigue. She must understand that it takes a woman two weeks to learn how to breast-feed and two months to become adept.

In my study I felt sorry for the mothers who quit breast-feeding before two months. They remembered all the difficulties without experiencing the rewards. When I was successful in brow beating the mothers into breast-feeding beyond two months (the danger weeks), they became joyously addicted to breast-feeding and didn't want to quit. I felt it was my duty as a physician to do everything that I could to help a mother complete her sexuality by breast-feeding for at least nine months or for as long as the baby wanted to breast-feed. Most thanked me for not letting them miss that part of womanhood, with all the emotional and chemical benefits that they gave their babies. But it was for something more that they thanked me; it was perhaps the realization of themselves as mothers, in the most complete sense of the word.

IMPORTANCE OF FATHERS: IN BREAST-FEEDING

One of the most important roles for a father whose wife is breast-feeding was taught to me by the late Dr. Clifford G. Grulee, an eminent professor of pediatrics, a practicing pediatrician, a consultant, and an author of textbooks. Shortly after the end of World War II, I had the good fortune to move into Dr. Grulee's office. At the time he was the executive secretary of the Academy of Pediatrics and ran the academy from the adjoining room. During my early days of practice, I often had chances to ask him questions about how to practice, about diseases and the handling of patients. When our oldest son was born I was in fear of how successful my wife would be in breast-feeding. I had heard stories about how hectic it is for the lactating woman in a pediatrician's home. Dr. Grulee told me: "Tell your wife to spend the first three days in bed after she gets home from the hospital." I did just that. I told the woman who was going to help us that I didn't want anyone to ask my wife any questions. (My wife always got up and got things for people whenever anyone asked where anything was.) She blinked in astonishment, but was very helpful. When she left two weeks later, she said that in thirty years experience this was the first time that she had seen a baby completely breast-fed.

When I've said, "Stay in bed three days." to mothers going home from the hospital, they invariably laugh and take it as a joke. I know they don't do what I tell them. But if I have the opportunity to tell the father to make his wife stay in bed, the wife is more likely to do it.

To insure success, I emphasize that this also gives father something definite to do. He is no longer left out. If he is interested in breast-feeding, he will see to it that his wife does spend the first three days in bed and doesn't have the harassment of thinking that she has to catch up for lost time getting the house back in order. Over the years, I have felt that next to the members of the La Leche League, the husbands were the most important helpmates in breast-feeding, regardless of my inherent bias.

For one thing, they insisted that their wives get enough rest. They gave them moral courage. They offset the propaganda against breast-feeding among their friends who poked fun at them or made discouraging remarks. Grandmother might say, "I was never able to nurse my children." The neighbor who says, "I tried, but nursing only upset my baby." I have found that many mothers feel as though they want to quit, but keep on because their husbands want them to. If the husband is for breast-feeding, then the wife will be also.

I recall one very successful executive whose wife was nursing their first child. Friends came to celebrate and see the first-born son. After the mother was finished nursing, she put the baby down and he cried. She nursed again and he cried. Her husband said, "She is just not a cow!" This was all she needed to get discouraged. She gave the baby a bottle every evening. At first it was one feeding, then more and within a week she was not nursing anymore. Read the section SABOTAGE.

That baby is full grown. All through his late childhood and manhood he had severe allergies, and there is no family history of allergies. When he married and had his first child, he was bound and determined that his wife should breast-feed. He insisted that she stay in bed for the first three days when she was home from the hospital. He insisted that she take three one-hour naps the first month and two one-hour naps after that. He asked her to keep no schedule, and he made no demands for meals, housework, or cleaning. He allowed no company to spend no more than a few minutes in the house until the child was six months old. This child showed some allergies to some of the immunizations so he was determined all the more, that she would continue to breast-feed. She kept it up until the child was 18 months old. That child is now an adult and has no trace of allergy. the same young couple had two more sons. They were all breast-fed for over a year and none of them have any allergies.

When the going is rough during the danger weeks of nursing, many mothers have been ready to quit. I don't like the husband to ask his wife how she feels. He knows how she feels by how quickly the baby goes to sleep after the night feeding. If the baby doesn't settle down and is restless during the dinner hour, the wise father takes the baby in his arms and walks with the baby. He gives his wife a cocktail and tells her to go lie down. Or he wraps the baby up in a sling and goes into the kitchen, takes over, and prepares the meal. If there are older children to be fed, he takes care of them. He knows automatically that his wife is upset or over-tired and she cannot get the letdown reflex at the dinner time.

It is nice when father can do this without awkwardness, but each mother seems to make her family adjustments when her husband is in favor of breast-feeding. Father never must indulge in snide remarks about doing "woman's work". He does it because of deep love and because he wants his wife to be successful in breast-feeding because he knows it is better for both the baby and the mother. One word of disapproval as to the way the house is run and his wife would stop nursing immediately. Then I would usually get a phone call asking for a bottle for the evening feeding. One conscientious mother cried hysterically, "I owe my husband more than I am giving him." That husband should never have let her get into such a state. Always it would be the failure of the letdown reflex from not getting an afternoon rest, harassment of relatives and friends who were not in favor of breast-feeding, or lack of compartmentation of the other children. The husband is in the position to protect his wife from worry and fatigue if he wants to.

One All-American college football star who was breast-fed for nine months became a husband and father of four boys and also very successful in business. With each baby, his wife started out nursing well with plenty of milk, but trouble began with the dinner feeding. She felt she'd lost her milk and changed to the bottle within a few weeks. She told me that it was because she didn't have any support from her husband in breast-feeding.

After her last child, her husband's attitude toward breast-feeding, I believe, caused her to have a mental depression. Now their children are nearly grown. The father has become a good father and is very interested in athletic activities for his children, but none of them enjoy the health that he himself still enjoys because none of his children got the nine months of breast-feeding that he had.

Some fathers expect their wives to keep a neat house, and will never be a help to their wives in breast-feeding. Many women change doctors because they do not find a doctor sympathetic to breast-feeding. The father who understands the nature of a woman and helps his wife breast-feed learns another dimension of marriage and love.

In one of the talks by one of the fathers of the LaLeche League to other fathers, the father spoke of how nice it was to be able to sleep all night because his wife would get up and feed the baby. He said that if the baby had been bottle fed, he would have to get up. I found out later what he didn't say --- that was that he saw to it that his wife got rest in the afternoon. He protected her from people, not in favor of breast-feeding, who bugged her. At work he bragged about his wife and convinced other fathers that maybe their wives should breast-feed. His office was divided into two camps: one consisted of the men who believed in breast-feeding and those who did not.

In short, the nursing mother, especially in the danger weeks, needs all the support that she can get, and I think that the husband and father of her child is the most important support that she has. I recommend that fathers learn as much as possible about the physiology of lactation, the mind of the mother, and then take over and see to it she is successful in breast-feeding.

HOW MUCH SHOULD I SOCIALIZE WHILE I AM BREAST-FEEDING?

You should socialize as much as you want to. Do what you like to do, but don't get too tired. Don't do things that make you nervous. You can swim, play tennis, ride horseback, and go to parties. Accept every invitation you get to go out, but do not reciprocate until your baby is six months old. I have yet to see a nursing mother successfully breast-feed after entertaining. The baby will have twenty-four to forty-eight hours of severe colic because you will not be able to let down your milk.

One of my mothers wanted to go to an out-of-town football game while she was nursing her baby. I encouraged her to take the baby with her because she didn't want to wean him. So she took her little boy on the train with her husband and friends.. She checked into a hotel, hired a baby-sitter, went to the game, came back, nursed her baby, and went to a tea dance. She always got the letdown reflex.

Usually your letdown reflex will work better when you are having fun. Go skiing, to the seashore, to weddings, cocktail parties, and on business trips with your husband. Every time one of my nursing mothers was a bridesmaid, her letdown reflex worked so well and her milk flowed so much that she ruined a nice gown. It was the music. If you are going to be a bridesmaid, wear plastic linings inside your bra. Ordinarily plastic linings are not good because the heat and perspiration generated around the nipple, combined with the lack of evaporation, make the nipples tender. Your husband's handkerchief folded inside your bra ordinarily gives you the protection you need. But you are not a bridesmaid every day.

It takes planning to find sitters away from home. It is worth the bother to be able to attend business meetings, seminars, luncheons and cocktail parties with your husband. Also you will find that it is easy to nurse your baby discreetly in public. The La Leche League have some good tricks for nursing in public which they are happy to share. The League has a phone number in the telephone book of every large city. If not, call Chicago before 3 pm 312/455-7730, or write La Leche League Inc., 9616 Minneapolis Avenue, Franklin Park, Illinois 60131.

LA LECHE LEAGUE (pronounced Lah Laychay)

It started at a picnic. In September, 1956, a small group of mothers and children from Franklin Park, a suburb of Chicago, took their children and babies to the park for a picnic. This picnic was unusual because two of these mothers were breast-feeding their children while at the picnic. When the other mothers saw these two babies nursing, they began to discuss their own attempts and failures to breast-feed. Both of these mothers had not been able to nurse previous children as long as they would have liked, but now they were breast-feeding very successfully. Therefore, these mothers were very sympathetic with the stories of the failures. They could identify with the feelings of defeat in those mothers who were not successful in breast-feeding. Several of these mothers thought there should also be a way to communicate encouragement in breast-feeding, as well as a way to communicate the difficulties that each mother encountered and how these difficulties were overcome. From the conversation at this picnic, there developed the idea to hold meetings for the transmission of information to those mothers who wanted to share their experiences with other mothers and potential mothers. Seven nursing mothers made up the original group and called themselves the La Leche League. They took their name from the Spanish title for the Madonna: Nuestra Senora de la Leche'y Buen Parto (Our Lady of Bountiful Milk and Easy Delivery). One mother was a doctor's wife. They all agreed that the doctors were too busy to talk about breast-feeding, and most doctors were men, and unless their wives breast-fed, knew little or nothing about breast-feeding. Those who breast-fed in 1956 were definitely in the minority, and people knowledgeable on the subject of breast-feeding were hard to find.

These remarkable mothers read all they could about the physiology of lactation and invited interested doctors to talk to various groups. Armed with the statistics on the advantages of breast-feeding and facts about their own children that they were successfully nursing, these seven mothers held a series of meetings for their friends who were expecting babies. Besides the advantages of breast-feeding, experiences in overcoming difficulties were discussed. One of the doctors who early became interested as a medical advisor was Dr. Herbert Ratner, who was the Health Commissioner of the nearby suburb of Oak Park. In addition to giving very good advice to the women, Dr. Ratner conducted classes for fathers and held meetings where fathers discussed the advantages of breast-feeding from father's point of view. Intelligent advice was given by husbands of women successful at breast-feeding to prospective fathers. Advice was given such as:

- Do not demand that your wife be a neat housekeeper; make her relax.
- Don't allow her to give personal service to anyone but the baby.
- Don't invite company until lactating ability is established, but accept every invitation that you get and take the baby with you.
- Take pride in your wife's ability to breast-feed and encourage her.
- If she seems to be failing, still be optimistic.

These meetings grew in number. One energetic woman obstetrician filled her car with expectant mothers and drove to the meetings of the La Leche League. Now she regularly has her prospective mothers meet in her house, while various other members who have been successful in breast-feeding lead discussions. The medical advisory board of the La Leche League has now expanded to include worldwide medical authorities.

The meetings of mothers who were successful in breast-feeding and those who wanted to breast-feed proved to be very valuable. Those seven mothers talked to several of their friends who were expecting babies. The purpose was to give the new mothers the benefit of what they had learned and experienced. The meetings were a small, informal group of mothers, with free exchanges of ideas. It seemed to be particularly helpful to realize that other women had problems, as well as for nursing mothers to find out how other nursing mothers solved their problems. It was also found that success came from being able to get encouragement when a mother thought that she was failing because her breasts seemed empty and her baby was crying. It was helpful for this mother to talk and listen in a whole roomful of nursing mothers or those who hoped to nurse. They admired her for nursing in contrast to her many friends and relatives who thought that she was crazy or old-fashioned to nurse. There was great gratitude on the part of mothers who had tried several times to breast-feed and failed and then, after the help of the La Leche League, were able to breast-feed for the first time.

To help mothers away from the Franklin Park area, the founding mothers and their friends wrote and published *The Womanly Art of Breastfeeding*. It has just gone through many printings and a second edition has sold over one million copies. This does not include the British edition, put out by the Souvenir Press in 1970, or the Spanish or French editions. It is also on tape and in braille.

In 1969, the La Leche League formulated an exhibit that has traveled to several important health meetings of the Pan American Health Organization and the World Health Organization. The President and other members of the La Leche League have attended several White House conferences on nutrition and children. At the fifteenth anniversary convention in Chicago in July,

1971, the late Princess Grace of Monaco was a featured speaker. With great poise and dignity, she told how much breast-feeding meant to her. The La Leche League News, which comes out bi-monthly, is a marvelous way to keep abreast of the different activities and developments in relation to breast-feeding. I recommend that every mother who is going to have a baby try to join her local chapter of the La Leche League. Further, I recommend that if you are nursing your baby and are having difficulty, look in the phone book and see if you can find a La Leche League group. If you cannot, then I suggest that you write the La Leche League Headquarters, 9616 Minneapolis Avenue, Franklin Park, Illinois 60131; or call, 312/455-7730 or 312/767-6015. The counseling office will advise or give you information on how you can get advice about breast-feeding.

If your pediatrician or physician who is caring for your baby, has recommended that you wean the baby, I suggest you call the La Leche League headquarters before you follow the advice. The League's advise will be sound because it reflects the experience of many nursing mothers as well as the advice of the Medical Advisory board which is made up of responsible physicians. At this writing the members of the La Leche by and large know more about breast-feeding than many male physicians whose wives did not nurse. Read ONE PHYSICIAN'S APPROACH TO BREAST-FEEDING. This does not mean that your physician, because he doesn't know all the problems of breast-feeding, is inadequate to take care of your child. In the past physicians were trained to cure illness; to handle breast-feeding has been a more recent acquisition of knowledge as training programs in the 1980's emphasize breast-feeding. If you are very much interested in breast-feeding, the La Leche League group in your town will help you find a physician who will be sympathetic and helpful. More and more physicians are working with various La Leche League groups.

As of June 1, 1983 there are 10,057 La Leche League leaders qualified, by the Franklin Park headquarters, in experience and knowledge to lead mothers in breast-feeding. There are also 4,052 groups in 44 countries. These figures mean that the mothers affected by advice of the La Leche League are in the multiples of millions around the world.

EXCESSIVE FLOW OF MILK

When you begin to nurse, you get the letdown reflex in 30 to 90 seconds or even when you hear your baby cry, the milk begins to come into your breasts and will drip or even squirt out in a stream from your nipples. Frequently when you are nursing at one breast the milk will flow from the other. You may think that you are nursing discreetly in public but, when you look down, you see that the front of your dress is soaked with milk from the other breast.

Sometimes you are taking a shower when the milk pours out and forces you to take another shower. An excessive amount of this is inconvenient. It wets your clothing and in general, is messy. One good trick is to let your baby nurse for about one or two minutes from the first breast. When the milk is flowing well from the other, pinch his nose gently to make him let go. You can pry your finger into his mouth to break the suction. Then without burping shift him to the other breast, and let him nurse there. (You make this shift after he has nursed for only one or two minutes on the first side.) Usually the milk will not flow as much from the first side, where he has nursed, so that you can nurse on the second breast for about five or ten minutes and then let him go back to the first breast, will usually stop by the time the baby is two months old.

It would seem that nature has been very wise. She had deemed it important to keep you at home without too many good clothes on until the baby is two months old. However, I do not like to have mothers feel that breast-feeding is confining. If you must go out, even though you have an excessive flow of milk, and it begins every time you hear a baby cry or every time you think of your baby, buy a loose fitting bra and put one of your husband's folded handkerchiefs over each breast.

This is better than most cotton pads or plastic shields. My mothers tell me that pushing inwards on each nipple for about two minutes will stop the flow. Even though the use of plastic shields routinely protects your clothing, it tends to soften your nipples and make them tender. They should only be worn in emergencies.

CAESARIAN AND BREAST-FEEDING

There are gas pains following the caesarian section that last a few days, just as in any major abdominal operation. Usually it is difficult for you to nurse lying down. It may be easier for you to prop yourself sitting up. Put a pillow on your lap and lay the baby on the pillow and then nurse sitting up. Sometimes the physical discomfort following the caesarian will delay the letdown reflex that you usually experience by the fourth day. There is no interference with the hormonal mechanism of breast-feeding when you have a caesarian section. Just be patient and you will be able to nurse all right.

DELAYED MILK

It is not uncommon for a mother's milk production to begin slowly. For the first two weeks or so she may not produce much milk. The baby has to nurse frequently from both breasts to stimulate the production of milk. If you are one of those mothers who have delayed milk, don't get discouraged. Just resign yourself to frequent nursing, get plenty of rest, and do not be frightened. Eventually you will be able to breast-feed your baby completely for several months. In forty years of practice, I have not seen a mother have to stop nursing because of delayed milk.

Several mothers have come to me frantic because their babies' weight at two months was the same as their birth weights. Some had been told that their babies would be mentally retarded if they did not get enough to eat in early infancy -- 'starved babies brains do not develop normally!' That may be true in a formula fed baby but I have not seen it in a breast-fed baby even when their weights are below the third percentile. See GROWTH CHART.

On examination these babies seem perfectly healthy friendly smiling happy babies who just had not grown. The mothers did not want to give formulas nor solid foods. The mothers needed encouragement in breast feeding which I gave and that was the most important part of the therapy -- to convince the mothers that they were capable of increasing their milk supply so that with plenty of rest and frequent nursing (15-20 times daily) their babies would grow 5 to 7 ounces per week.

One such mother had six children and she was a slow starter with every one. At two months their weights were the same as at birth. She brought each in for me to examine at two months. Except for weight they were normal. Their heights were normal for their ages (two-months). They all passed the Gesell developmental tests with flying colors. With encouragement, although I think she encouraged me more than I encouraged her, nursing frequently and resting she nursed each for over two years some three years. Most of her children are grown now. They have better than ordinary health and are overachieving in high school and college.

It is wonderful to watch these determined mothers, who are slow starters, make it with breast alone. Also it is helpful in preventing allergies.

For some of the slow starters I have recommended the Marshall-Kamesson breast pump and asked them to pump each breast for 10 minutes about 1 hour after the first two or three morning feedings. save the pumped milk and give it to their babies in the evening from a dish with a spoon. They can water it half in half to make it go farther. Read the HUMAN MILK BANK.

OVERFEEDING OF BREAST MILK

Overfeeding is almost impossible in the breast-fed baby. It is not uncommon in the artificially fed. If you produce more than one or two quarts a day, you may be overfeeding your baby. If a small baby is getting more than a quart a day, he is probably taking all he can hold. He will have about fifteen bowel movements per day and sometimes will spit up. He will gain well. The baby will control over-production of milk by not taking it all. Then the milk glands will not produce as much. Some very vigorous babies take more than they can hold, and some mothers expel a large amount of breast milk quickly. The baby then spits out what he doesn't need or vomits all of it. then he nurses again because he is still hungry. The result is that such babies will grow in the ninetieth and ninety-ninth percentile, but the baby will not, in any real sense, be overfed. There has been no correlation with obesity later on. This is not so with the formula fed babies. The overweight bottle fed often become overweight adolescents.

HOW TO INCREASE YOUR BREAST MILK (UNDER FEEDING)

An underfed breast-fed baby may weigh at one month just about what he weighed at birth. He seems perfectly happy nursing five or six times a day. His skin is clear and his eyes are bright but slightly sunken. His mother thinks he is getting enough to eat because while the baby nurses at one breast, milk flows out of the other. But weighing before and after feeding shows that the baby gets less than fourteen ounces a day. In this instance the breast milk fits the baby so well that it satisfies all his desires to eat but he just doesn't get enough to grow.

If your baby fits this description, continue to breast-feed without any schedule. After the third time of nursing in rapid succession, say every hour, offer four to six ounces of formula. Feed from a dish with a spoon, from a small measuring glass, with an eye dropper or from a bottle with a fast flowing nipple, but don't offer this formula until you have nursed your baby three times in rapid succession. Wake the baby if necessary to get these extra breast feedings into him. If the baby has been underfed, he will rapidly begin to grow. You will now be encouraged and in turn will produce more milk. You can help the milk production by hand expression into a cup after you finish nursing. Put the expressed milk into the refrigerator. You can give your milk, instead of the formula at the end of the day when the baby is not satisfied with just the breast.

Some underfed babies will now change and want to be nursed frequently. In this case put your baby to breast every hour and nurse from both breasts each time for about ten minutes. It can be twice that long on the second breast. Then he gets a breast milk that is high in fat. If he cries, do what ever is necessary to get the letdown reflex. go to bed and take your baby with you. Calm the baby and nurse him again. You should do this at least three times before giving a formula. If you persist for two or three weeks, your baby again will be completely breast-fed. Your milk will rise to the baby's demand. See DELAYED MILK.

Some of my colleagues, who are good leaders in breast-feeding, use ripe banana three times daily when mothers do not have enough milk. I do that when the babies are allergic to milk. See ADVANTAGES OF BREAST-FEEDING.

I prefer that mothers try to increase their milk supplies without using formulas or solid food. She can pump her breasts with a Marshall-Kanesson pump about an hour after the first two morning feedings. Then nurse when ever the baby wants to. As evening comes, if the baby is nursing more frequently, she can give the baby pumped breast milk from a dish with a spoon.

COLIC

Colic is usually the period of irritable crying from the hours of six to ten at night and usually the baby's abdomen is distended. He folds up or stiffens his legs, he screams piercingly. This condition usually begins at about two weeks and may continue on for three months. It usually occurs with a baby who is very placid and quiet in the hospital and very lively and crying at night when he gets home. It is more common in the formula-fed but it also occurs in the breast-fed. The cause of this colic is really not known. It is probably some form of indigestion. It is estimated that twenty five per cent of the babies have severe colic and another twenty five per cent have mild or intermittent colic. It is probably some type of indigestion in a nervous system and a gastrointestinal system which is immature.

Colic is made worse if the mother is upset. Colic seems to occur more often from six o'clock to ten o'clock or from ten o'clock at night until two o'clock in the morning just when the mother is very tired and wants to get some rest. It is amazing how some babies will sleep all day, awaken and take breast-feeding or bottle feeding regularly every three or four hours all day, and then cry all night. It usually occurs in babies who are gaining faster than the ordinary weight and are very healthy in every other way except that they cry all the time and are colicky.

You may take some comfort in the fact that the colic occurs in the healthiest of babies from parents who are rather high-strung. The colicky baby will outgrow his colic usually at three months, although occasionally I've seen it go on as long as six or ten or even eleven months. However, more than six months is extremely rare. Your baby who is colicky will probably be a very aggressive grown-up who will "collect a lot of salt". She won't be content to go home after the movie, but will have to go dancing afterwards. She will be a leader with better-than-average ability.

THE TREATMENT OF COLIC

If you are breast-feeding and your child is crying from six to ten, you will have to be sure you are getting the let down reflex at the early evening feeding or six o'clock feeding. Many mothers who are nursing their babies have a beautiful let down reflex in the morning but at six o'clock, when the father comes home, they may have to get supper and take care of other children, and, when they nurse the baby, there is no let down reflex. That baby is going to cry. If the mother puts him to the breast again, he will nurse for a moment or two and then arch his back and pull himself off and cry.

This didn't happen with our first child because I was a hero overseas in the army and my wife was developing character and nursing beautifully. But when we had our second and third, I had come back from overseas and was trying to build a practice. Oftentimes my wife would be very upset because the baby cried around suppertime and in the early morning. Mothers of my patients would scold my wife because I was not available and I had forgotten to tell her that I was going to another hospital. I can remember her giving me the baby after she had nursed and he was crying, saying, "You are a pediatrician; figure out why this baby cries."

What worked very well for me is that I would carry the baby around and sing several football songs (off-key which he didn't seem to mind). Before I got started on the songs, I mixed up a strong bourbon and water and I gave it to my wife and told her to go lie down. She was allergic to beer and wine. I continued to walk around carrying the baby and he was amused at my off-key songs. After about twenty minutes, I put my finger in the baby's mouth and saw that he grabbed hold and would suck. By making that profound diagnosis, I told my wife that the baby was hungry. She took the baby and nursed him and we didn't hear from him the rest of the night.

This worked so well with my baby that I recommended it to many of my patients. Over the past forty years, I have had many mothers who have been successful in nursing their babies by using this technique, or a reasonable facsimile, where they had been unsuccessful before. After the first successful results from this method, I talked to an obstetrician about it. He was unfamiliar with the phenomenon. He thought we ought to conduct an experiment to see if some of the whiskey came through the breast milk and anesthetized the baby and made the baby sleep so well. However, when I talked with the late Dr. Clifford Grulee, who was a great advocate of breast-feeding, he referred me to his first book on infant feeding which quoted work that was done in Germany early in the twentieth century. They found that no measurable amount of alcohol came into the breast milk unless the mother had drunk so much that she could not stand..

One drink gave the mother a sense of well being -- dulled her anxiety and feelings of fatigue so that her brain no longer suppressed the pituitary gland which is responsible for the letdown reflex.

Recently Ruth Lawrence has reported in her excellent book on breast feeding that too much alcohol (drunkenness) will suppress the excretion of oxytocin and have the opposite effect. Just enough to give a sense of well being, if it is within your culture. Some mothers get the letdown reflex by sitting in a rocking chair and drinking a soft drink or an auto ride, boat ride or taking the baby to the movies.

Some breast-feeding babies cry so much that they get their stomaches full of air. They nurse about one or two minutes, and then suddenly arch their backs and then pull away. Or they may just stop nursing. If the mother puts them down, they will cry. You should, in this instance, hold the baby in a sitting position by his head and gently squeeze his abdomen. Don't break his liver. You'll get a bubble up and then he'll nurse again. If a baby cried a great deal before nursing and swallowed a lot of air, you may have to shift him every two minutes from one breast to the other in order to get the whole feeding into him. After you succeed in doing that, he may sleep.

You may try all those things and still cannot quiet your breast-fed baby in the early evening feedings even though you may have nursed him two or three times. In this instance the best thing to do is for mother to go to bed and lie flat on her back and put the baby across-ways across her abdomen. Then she should roll and knead him like dough. If he will accept a pacifier, he should be given a pacifier. If you nurse him on a big bed, almost invariably he will go to sleep. Very gently, you can crawl out from under and leave him on the big bed. Do not leave him on a big bed if he is over three months of age, however, because he might roll off it.

If these procedures don't work and your baby seems to get red in the face, his abdomen gets distended, his legs draw up and then stiffen; take a bulb syringe which holds one or two ounces (an ear syringe is all right), lubricate it well and gently insert it into his rectum. Instill into his rectum about one or two ounces of warm tap water. Following this he will have an explosive bowel movement but with it he will pass a lot of gas and will usually relax and go to sleep. Read the section PULLING AWAY FROM THE BREAST. If this doesn't work, then you should take about a teaspoonful of whisky, two teaspoonfuls of water, and a pinch of sugar and put it into a glass. With a medicine dropper, give him two or three squirts of diluted whiskey and nurse him again. If that does not work, you should call your doctor for some colic drops.

Another good trick is to wrap a hot water bottle in a diaper, put it in his crib and lay him stomach-down on the hot water bottle. This warm protrusion into his abdomen seems to help him get rid of gas. You can also try the pacifier on the bottle-fed baby. Usually, bottle-fed babies accept pacifiers better than breast-fed babies. If your baby is screaming, walking with him seems to be very helpful. You can put him in a sling pack on your back or have a sling so that he is in front of you but keep your arms free to do other things. If none of these tricks work, it may be necessary to change his formula.

It could be that the colic is due to a mild allergy to the cow's milk protein. In this instance, shift him to a soybean milk based formula. It is easy to prepare. Use one can of the soybean milk, which is about thirteen ounces. Make it into a quart by adding nineteen ounces of water. Depending on the size of your baby, make five bottles of six and one fourth ounces or four bottles of eight ounces. Shifting the formula in this way works dramatically when it works. You suddenly have a very quiet baby. However, two or three days later he's back in his old pattern again. You should then shift back to the original formula. I have carried some babies by having them shift back and forth between two formulas every three days. It keeps the baby quiet until he is three months old when he can take any kind of formula. Some observers may think that if you carry a baby around all the time either in your arms or in a pack, or if you run and pick him up when he cries, that you are spoiling this baby. I do not believe so. Spoiling comes later, sometime after they are six months of age.

NURSING AWAY FROM HOME

One of the advantages of breast-feeding is that you don't have to haul along a lot of equipment on trips. On car trips you can nurse the baby while your husband drives. (Bottle-feeding mothers have to stop and find a restaurant where they can warm the bottle.) If you are traveling by airplane ask the stewardess to put you in a seat where you can nurse inconspicuously. On a train or bus you can pull up one side of your sweater to nurse discreetly.

Visit people with whom you are comfortable. If you aren't at ease with the people you will see, don't go. It could spoil the weekend if you weren't able to get the letdown reflex. Read the section the DANGER WEEKS.

It is better for you to be a guest than a hostess. When you are a guest your letdown reflex works well because you don't have household responsibilities. Being a hostess can inhibit the letdown reflex because you have to worry about entertaining and feeding your guests; even when you have plenty of help, you have the responsibility. Travel around the world while you are nursing. Visit all your relatives and show off the baby while you are still nursing. Your letdown will work perfectly even at funerals. After the baby is a year old, if you are not nursing, visit your relatives without your children. When your children are between one and six, grandparents should come to you to see the children unless they understand compartmentation. There is nothing that makes mothers lose control faster than visiting with children aged one to six.

NURSING DURING MENSTRUATION

Most women do not menstruate while nursing, at least for the first six months. However, there are a few who do. Your baby may not like to nurse during your menstrual periods. She will nurse for a shorter period of time, less vigorously, and will seem less satisfied. I have often thought that the letdown reflex did not work as well during menstruation. But mothers have told me they felt the letdown reflex during their menstrual periods just as much as when they were not menstruating. One of my very successful nursing mothers suggested that the menstruating woman has a different bodily odor which the babies do not like. While she was menstruating her babies nursed better after she took a shower. A complete dedication to breast-feeding, that is, nothing but breast milk for the first six months, will tend to suppress menstruation. The addition of solids or complementary or supplementary formulas decreases lactation and ovulation and menstruation tend to recur. Menstruation is no contra-indication to breast-feeding.

REFUSAL OF ONE BREAST

Some babies prefer one breast but will nurse on both, while some actually refuse one breast. It is possible for a mother to nurse just on one breast. But most mothers don't like this lopsided production or the difference in size in the two breasts. It does no harm to the baby. The way to handle this problem is for you to start the baby on the breast that he prefers. When he has nursed well for one or two minutes, put him on the refused breast while he is at the height of his appetite. Then he will nurse a little at the refused breast. When he refuses it again, put him back on the good side. Then hand express all you can from the poorer side or use the Marshall-Kanesson pump. You may never get your production equal in both breasts, but you will eventually have him nursing from both breasts and you will become less lopsided.

PULLING AWAY FROM THE BREAST

Some nursing mothers have told me their baby nurses well until the milk begins to flow. They get the letdown reflex and the milk squirts into the baby's mouth, and suddenly he arches his back, screams, and won't nurse anymore. He acts as though the breast milk gives him cramps when it hits his stomach. If there is allergy in the family I ask the mother to stop eggs, milk and wheat in her diet. Fifty percent of the allergic babies are allergic to one of those three. The other fifty percent are allergic to something else or they outgrow it before the cause can be found. My wife states that our oldest son got cramps whenever she ate pea soup. Another mother said that a salad would always upset her completely breast-fed daughter. Cabbage, chocolate, pizza and high seasoning have been accused culprits.

If two weeks of no eggs, milk, or wheat for the mother did not stop the cramps dramatically then look for something else. Keep a food diary to see if you can get a hunch. Under no circumstances should you wean the baby. Read the section on the VALUE OF BREAST-FEEDING.

Fortunately this situation is rather rare, but it is of great concern to a mother when it happens. If you can not prove allergy to something in your breast milk, then I am not completely sure just what the answer is. Dr. Charlotte Naish has said that this is a cross baby and it is his temperament. She recommends sedation. Sometimes I have used this course. Usually it is associated with a baby who has had more than the usual amount of trouble being born, but this situation does not occur often enough to make a positive correlation. I have had good luck in these situations by telling the mother to immediately put the baby to the other breast and often he will suckle at the second breast. Another course of action is a little whiskey for the baby. Mix one teaspoon of whisky with two teaspoons of water and a pinch of sugar, and with a medicine dropper give your baby a few squirts when he pulls away. Wait five or ten minutes and try to nurse again. Unless the baby is allergic to something the mother eats it disappears when he or she is three months old. Do not get disturbed and do not wean. Read the section on COLIC.

SABOTAGE

It used to be common practice, when a mother did not have enough milk, to offer 2 to 4 ounces of formula after nursing. When the baby was not allergic to cow's milk, he or she liked the bottle. This worked very well for several weeks and the mother said: "Ha!, I have solved my breast-feeding problem."

Unfortunately the baby was not lowering the intralobular pressure in the breast enough to stimulate the pituitary gland to produce enough prolactin, thus the decrease in the circulating prolactin in the blood told the cells in the breast to produce less milk. The formula satisfied the baby's hunger so that he suckled less which further failed to lower the intralobular pressure which made less prolactin and less breast milk. Finally there was not enough breast milk to interest the baby so he preferred the bottle except maybe at night. Gradually the mother lost her milk and the baby became entirely bottle fed.

This practice has been going on since formulas were invented. It was the most common way to sabotage breast-feeding and in some quarters still is. When I lectured to medical students I said that it was a mild form of malpractice. Those in the group, whose wives were bottle feeding, didn't like it much. But, when prescribed in the countries where there was poor sanitation, it was a death sentence to the child because the mother did not have the facilities, nor the know how to mix a proper formula, nor the money to buy it. Read the section HOW TO INCREASE YOUR BREAST MILK.

The "gad about bottle" prescribed for the baby when mother and baby were leaving the hospital was another form of sabotage. True, mother should never feel trapped and she should return to work as soon as she wants or needs to, but if she can not take her baby with her to work or play, she should pump her breasts and have her sitter feed the baby breast milk, plain, or diluted, from a dish with a spoon. Or the sitter can use a medicine dropper or a small shot glass to feed the baby. These are preferable to bottles. Read the sections: BREAST-FEEDING AND WORKING also

THE HUMAN MILK BANK.
PUMPING AND STORAGE OF MILK

Pumping your breasts after nursing your baby will enable you to leave your baby with a sitter occasionally during a feeding time. Pump your breasts about an hour after the morning feedings and put the milk in a sterile jar in your freezer. Then you can thaw it for the sitter to give when you want to be away from your baby for one or two feedings. It can thaw at room temperature or under the hot water tap. You can use this extra human milk if something happens to prevent you from letting down you milk. Some large hospitals have human milk banks, to which you can donate your milk if you have a lot. It is used for sick babies who cannot tolerate formula and whose mothers can't nurse them. Read the section THE HUMAN MILK BANK.

Pumping will stimulate your breasts to produce more milk. Here's how it works. Suppose you give your baby six ounces at 6 a.m. You will probably be able to give him five ounces at 10 a.m.; at 2 p.m. four ounces; at 6 p.m. two ounces; at 8 p.m. one or one-half ounce. Your baby will want to nurse frequently in the evening because you can only produce a half to one ounce at a time. You must increase your milk production. This is how you do it. Nurse your baby in the early morning; give your husband and other children their breakfasts and get them off to work and school. Then get another cup of coffee and sit down and pump each breast for about ten minutes on each side. Or you can hand express into a cup. Pour the milk into a sterilized bottle and store it in the freezer. You can put new milk on top of frozen milk. Store the milk in four-ounce quantities. Fresh milk can be kept for three days; frozen milk, for two years.

Pumping of your breasts in the morning and early afternoon will stimulate your breasts to produce more milk. It is as though you had a twin; the breast pump or hand expression is your twin. After about two weeks your production will have increased enough, so that you will be able to satisfy your baby in the evening as well as in the morning.

When you want to use the frozen milk, put the bottle under cold running water. Gradually turn on warm water until the milk has liquified. Then heat it in a pan of water on the stove. You may let the milk stand at room temperature to thaw, or put it in the microwave for a half minute. You can add water to the milk if you want. The mixture can be one-third milk, two-thirds water. Spoon feed this milk to your baby or give it to him in a bottle with a fast-flowing nipple. You can use a large medicine dropper and squirt it into his mouth.

Pumping and storage of milk frees you so that you can socialize or work and still nurse your baby successfully.

THE HUMAN MILK BANK

Many maternity services in hospitals in this country and abroad maintain human milk banks for babies who need it and who cannot obtain their own mother's milk. The milk is hand expressed or pumped with electric breast pumps and kept frozen until needed. The electric breast pumps are expensive about $800.00 each. The Egnell Pump (developed in Sweden) can be purchased through Air Shields Company in Chicago. Recently two fathers of the La Leche League developed a very effective and inexpensive hand breast pump that consists of two cylinders one inside the other like a piston in a cylinder. It works by hand and is very effective because it is capable of considerable negative pressure which can get the milk out. Mothers like it. It is known as the Marshall-Kanesson pump and is available in most large drug stores for about $25.00. If not carried in your community write: La Leche League International, 9616 Minneapolis Ave, Franklin Park, Ill. 60131, Telephone: (312) 455-7730.

For several years the large formula companies have been supplying hospitals in large cities with prepared sterilized formulas without cost to the patient or hospital. this has resulted in less routine feeding of human milk to premature and sick babies unless a baby demonstrates a special need such as an allergy to formula. Unfortunately, allergy is usually not demonstrable until after the baby is home from the hospital and many different formulas have been tried.

Fortunately in many communities there are many mothers who are successfully breast-feeding their babies. Many women now are having formula trouble and need human milk to save their baby's life can call the LA LECHE LEAGUE. (They have a telephone number in every large city.) In this way lactating mothers can be found to wet nurse the allergic baby, to pump or hand express human milk for the baby who cannot tolerate formula. The La Leche League also has been eminently successful in helping mothers to re-establish their own lactating ability. They have in their files the case histories of many women who were able to re-establish lactation in about four weeks when they had never breast fed before.

As more women breast-feed, the establishment of human milk banks will be easier. The demand for human milk is not frequent but urgent in a few instances. How a human milk bank was established at the Evanston Hospital in Evanston, Illinois is described below:

In 1952, one of my mothers had a premature baby boy. During his early life in the incubator, he had mostly human milk. He could not tolerate any of the usual formulas. When fed a formula, he got red in the face, had diarrhea, vomited, and broke out in a rash. He was too small to suckle directly from his mother. His mother pumped her breasts but could only produce a few drops with each pumping; she tried for several weeks but could not increase her production. The baby's reactions to formula became more violent. He had convulsions. The human milk agreed with him so much better that it was obvious human milk was the only food this baby could tolerate. Since his mother could not produce enough herself, she decided to get the milk from other mothers. I gave her a list of nursing mothers. She rented six electric breast pumps and put one pump in the home of each nursing mother. These mothers nursed their own babies and usually about an hour or two after nursing, they pumped their breasts for the premature baby. This devoted mother of this allergic baby visited the homes of the nursing mothers each day and collected their gifts of lifesaving human milk. She usually made six stops a day. Sometimes she drove thirty-five miles a day to make all the stops. In this way her allergic son was fed human milk completely until he was six months old. Then he started on solid food. Soon he was able to drink cow's milk. Today he has no allergies.

Shortly afterwards there was another very small baby who could not tolerate formula. He was also fed pumped human milk for six months and this mother also had a "milk route" everyday. From these two infants the Junior League of Evanston saw the need for a Human Milk Bank. They met with the late Dr. Newcomb, chief of pediatrics, and myself, on Thanksgiving Day in 1956 and the first free Human Milk Bank was established at the Evanston Hospital. From then on these elegant ladies became known as "milk maids". They bought or rented twelve electric pumps and placed them in the homes of nursing mothers. They received the names of the nursing mothers from the pediatricians who practiced at the Evanston Hospital. They collected the milk donated by the nursing mothers and took it to the hospital. There the milk was melted again and stored in twelve-ounce bottles, frozen, dated, and kept in the deep freeze. Frequent spot check bacteriological examinations were made. If a donor was sick, the breast milk was marked contaminated and used for research. This operation grew. The ladies purchased 35 breast pumps through the help of some generous citizens and the Women's Auxiliary of the Evanston Hospital. These pumps were kept circulating among the nursing mothers.

It was found that the Human Milk made convenient charity for young women. The volunteer collectors of the human milk were able to get out of the house without having to go to the trouble and expense of hiring a baby sitter. They took their preschool children with them. They drove in pairs. One young mother stayed in the car and watched her partner's and her own children while the other volunteer visited and collected the milk from the donating mothers. When possible they stopped for coffee and told a contributing mother of the progress of a particular baby who was receiving her milk. These wonderful nursing women looked forward to the regular visits from the volunteers. They also anxiously awaited the progress reports on the little ones who were receiving their breast milk.

Most of the babies receiving the human milk were getting it because they were allergic to every other kind of milk. Some had had extensive abdominal surgery and human milk agreed with them better than anything else. Recently human milk has been given to babies who lost their hair and fingernails and had much bleeding from the gastrointestinal tract and extreme loss of weight. As soon as they received human milk their hair and fingernails began to grow again. Their bloody diarrhea stopped and they gained weight. The Human Milk bank at the Evanston Hospital to date has responded to eight calls for milk for this dreadful disease. It was found that it was not necessary to completely replace other milk and foods with human milk. A few ounces of human milk daily was enough. It is as though there is some unknown factor in human milk that some babies cannot live without.

Human milk from the Evanston Hospital Milk Bank has been flown to most of the large cities in America; one shipment was flown to the Belgian Congo.

The philosophy of the human milk bank is to feed a baby during an emergency period or until local sources of human milk can be established. When a pediatrician from Brooklyn called me about little Karen, four months old, he sounded desperate. Every time she took formula she vomited, had diarrhea, wheezed, developed an allergic rash, and then seemed to collapse into shock. Whenever she took human milk, she smiled and was very happy. We shipped 48 12-ounce bottles of frozen human milk to Karen. Her father, who was a cab driver, put a notice in the paper about the need for human milk for Karen. Seventy-five women in Brooklyn answered the call. They hand expressed their milk for Karen. In the meantime her mother put Karen to breast even though she had not nursed before. In about four weeks, Karen's mother was producing milk and she was able to breast-feed Karen completely. Her mother breast-fed her for about a year. Karen is now in school. She no longer has allergies. She has the usual good health of breast-fed babies.

The Evanston Hospital Human Milk Bank does not pay for the milk it receives nor does it make any charge to the recipients. Requests for human milk must come directly from the doctor. The milk bank accepts donations and asks the physician, who requests the milk, to write up the history and diagnosis and his opinion on whether or not the human milk helped. In the case of Karen the volunteers for several months received one or two crumpled dollar bills accompanied by a note of thanks scribbled on a scrap of paper always in the same handwriting. One could just picture the cab driver telling about Karen and the human milk bank in Evanston. His fare in turn responded and left an extra tip for the "milk maids" in the middle west. These humble notes with one or two dollars meant more to the girls on the "milk route" than the hundred dollar donations they usually received.

The human milk bank can be operated on a low budget. One need a place to collect the milk, nursing mothers, pumps, a doctor who is enthusiastic, and enthusiastic helpers to encourage mothers to donate the milk. Mothers who donate the milk do not deprive their own children of milk. The pumping stimulates the breasts to produce as much milk as needed. The mother usually has to nurse her own baby less often. The breast pump acts as a twin. While the mother's production rises to meet the need of the pump, her own baby gets more milk than he would if she were not pumping. By pumping and donating, the breast-feeding of her own baby becomes better organized. She produces more at the end of the day hence there is less getting up at night. The mothers find that by giving to others they give more to their own.

Within a few months after the establishment of the human milk bank at the Evanston Hospital the number of babies breast-feeding when leaving the hospital increased from one-third to two-thirds. This was considerably above the national average of ten percent (10%). In 1983, when I check the number of nursing mothers on the maternity floor, it averages eighty (80%)

due to the increasing number of smart young mothers who insist upon breast-feeding. The establishment of the human milk bank in a hospital seems to be a positive influence towards helping mothers to breast-feed.

THE PREMATURE BABY

The majority of my premature babies are completely breast-fed. The mothers pump their milk and bring it to their babies. When the baby gets up to five and one-half pounds, usually at two months of age, he suckles at the breast directly. About half of the premature babies under my care have been breast-fed for nine months. As for the other half, one or more of a number of difficulties made complete breast-feeding impossible and the mothers lost their milk.

Human milk is the best food for premature babies. Some authorities, who favor breast-feeding, believe that a little richer formula will make premature babies grow faster. Human milk is low in salt content. It agrees nicely with the immature kidneys of the premature baby. Ordinary formula which is made from cow's milk contains about twice as much salt as there is in breast milk. This will not be excreted properly by the immature kidneys and may make the premature baby retain water. That may explain why the formula-fed premature babies gain a little faster than the breast-fed. I see no reason not to feed breast milk to premature babies even if they do not gain as fast.

Recently the formula companies have made a formula with salt content that is similar to that of breast milk. That is a step in the right direction when breast milk is not attainable. There is some evidence that the mother of a premature secretes a milk that is more adaptable to the needs of her own premature baby and is better for prematures than the milk of the mothers of full term babies who supply the milk banks. Modern intensive care units are making great efforts to obtain breast milk from each mother of the premature.

BURPING

As your baby gets older, it is very important to get the air bubble out, especially in a bottle-fed baby. Your baby will swallow a lot of air when he cries. Some babies will seem to have a lot of air in their stomachs even when they haven't been crying much. Air and milk, of course, cannot occupy the same space. The air has to give way to make room for the milk.

The way to tell if your baby needs to be burped is that he suddenly stops eating. If he is taking the breast, he will pull away. Some babies have a wide-eyed look when they are full of air. If you are breast-feeding, sometimes you can get the bubble up if you hold the baby in a sitting position and gently massage or squeeze his tummy. Give it a few rhythmic squeezes. Usually the bubble will come up. Sometimes milk will come with it. If this method doesn't work, put a diaper or washable blanket over your shoulder to protect your clothing and put the baby on your shoulder so the point of your shoulder is in his abdomen and his head is looking backwards over your shoulder. With the free hand, rub his back and pat him gently between the shoulder blades and a little lower. If the baby still doesn't burp and is wide awake after he eats or has an anxious or searching expression, try walking with him resting against your shoulder in the burping position. Play gently with him. Try this mild activity to bring the bubble up; then put him down. If he just goes limp and sleepy after eating, don't bother to get the bubble up. This occurs quite frequently with breast-fed babies.

Refusal to eat and still being wide awake usually means a bubble. Sometimes your baby will vomit a large amount of milk as a result of having too much air in his stomach. This is usually a result of feeding too fast. Take about 20 minutes to give the baby his bottle.

If you have a fast nipple, you should stop every few seconds in order to let him exchange air for formula. Like drinking coke out of a bottle. Occasionally, a breast-fed baby will vomit for the same reason. There are mothers who give a lot of breast milk quickly, perhaps six or eight ounces in 45 seconds. The milk runs out in streams with a powerful let down reflex. If the baby has an air bubble at the bottom of his stomach, he will nurse for one or two minutes and then suddenly stop. He will look wide-eyed and will toss up a large quantity of milk. Often he is still hungry, and then you should nurse him again.

Some babies will grow perfectly well but they seem to take two feedings, one they throw up and the second one they keep. You can improve this annoying situation by stopping the baby from nursing after he has nursed for about two minutes. Sit him on your lap; hold him by the head and squeeze his abdomen gently. Don't rupture his liver. Do not spend too much time, no more than thirty seconds or he will cry. Then put him to the other breast for two minutes. Stop! Again hold his head and gently squeeze his abdomen. Put him back to the first breast for two minutes. Shifting him and burping him at regular intervals helps.

After your baby can stand and walk the air comes to the top of the stomach and comes up spontaneously when he eats and drinks. The air is no longer trapped as when he was lying down.

HOW MUCH SHOULD A BABY SLEEP?

Most babies will sleep as much as they need to. Most breast-fed babies just sleep and eat. But there are some babies who sleep very little. they don't cry; they just lie awake and look around. They often turn out to be assertive adults. In the early months most babies sleep from feeding to feeding unless they have indigestion. If your nursing baby is waking up during the night, be sure to take a nap or two during the day so that your let down reflex works properly in the evening. Your baby will then get enough to eat at the evening feedings, so he doesn't change night into day.

DIARRHEA

Infectious diarrhea in the breast-fed baby is extremely rare. In fact, breast milk is used to treat infectious diarrhea in some newborn nurseries. A breast-fed baby may have 15 to 20 green, watery stools per day, but if there is no blood in the stools, the diarrhea probably is not infectious even if there is mucus. It is usually the result of too much human milk. The mother is so productive that the baby just cannot handle it all. Babies do not get diarrhea because their mothers have eaten chocolate. Sometimes an overfed baby relieves himself by vomiting. The late Dr. Joseph Brenneman, who was a great advocate of breast-feeding, once scolded a young resident physician vehemently because he weaned a baby from the breast and gave her weak tea when she had 15 green, watery stools per day. The baby was gaining perfectly. It was just that the mother was giving the baby too much breast milk. This was the baby's way of getting rid of the milk that she couldn't use. If you are breast-feeding your baby, do not let 15 stools a day upset you. If your baby is gaining well and there is no blood or mucus in the bowel movements, he will be all right. He will control your overproduction by nursing less. Read section in NO SCHEDULE PLEASE.

CONSTIPATION IN THE BREAST-FED

Constipation or lack of bowel movements, in the completely breast-fed baby, is usually the result of no excess of breast milk. There is none left over to make a bowel movement. I have seen many completely breast-fed babies who have a normal, soft, mustard-colored bowel movement once every two weeks. They are perfectly happy and are growing well. If a baby gets 16 ounces of breast milk a day, he will grow well. Occasionally a baby who is completely breast-fed will strain, get red in the face, and pass a bowel movement with difficulty. An insertion of a thermometer or a glycerin suppository, which can be purchased at a drugstore, will help the baby pass the stool more easily. If your baby is completely breast-fed, and seems to strain every two or three days, it is wise to insert a suppository every day. It is not habit-forming. If your baby is passing soft, almost liquid, stools and the opening of the anus seems small, tell your physician about it. He will insert his little finger and stretch the anus slightly so that the bowel movement will be easier. If you have any difficulty inserting a small glycerin suppository, tell your doctor.

A baby who gets any formula or solid foods should have a bowel movement at least every other day. If he does not, he will be uncomfortable.

DIET OF THE MOTHER

If you are nursing your baby, you can eat an extra 1000 calories per day. Those calories go for the baby. If you are overweight, you can reduce while nursing provided that you eat properly. The kind of food that you need to produce a large quantity of milk rich in fat is lots of protein: eggs, meat, cheese, fish, grains, and vegetables including potatoes (without the butter or sour cream). Excessive amounts of bread, cake, cookies, cabbage, spices and starchy food should be avoided. Think protein, then salads and fruits. Drink three quarts of liquid per day. Take the same vitamins, iron, and minerals that you took during your pregnancy. Continue this for as long as you nurse.

BREAST-FEEDING TWINS AND TRIPLETS

It is much easier to breast-feed twins than to give them formula. In my study there were 42 sets of twins completely breast-fed for several months. The normal woman is able to nurse twins and triplets. She has to make a little more effort., rest more, and nurse a little more frequently to get her total milk production up. A woman can increase her lactating capacity to nurse twins or triplets. Ten of my mothers of twins had single births after the twins. They had to work just as hard to get the milk production up for the single one as they did for the twins.

If you have twins, you should nurse each twin every feeding in the hospital. When you get home and have had your three days in bed, you should nurse your twins simultaneously. This will probably seem awkward at fist, but it is a good way to do it so that the let down reflex occurs for each baby at the same time. This keeps you in good balance. It tends to increase your milk production because the interlobular pressure is reduced in each breast at each feeding. The wet nurses in the old days always nursed their own and the other baby at the same time. You can tuck one twin under each arm with the feet pointing toward your back. Support your arms on the arms of the chair or on pillows. Hold one head in each hand while the babies nurse. Or you can put the twins on top of each other on your lap.

Usually you will have to nurse every two or three hours during the day and once or twice at night. You must get plenty of rest so that your breasts will make enough milk for two. Several of my mothers of twins donated milk to the Milk Bank while they were nursing their babies. So don't believe anyone who tells you it's impossible to nurse twins. There is no reason why a mother cannot nurse twins completely until they are six months old. Then the solids and vitamins can be added. It is a good idea to rotate the babies so one baby doesn't nurse at the same breast each time. That way the breasts will receive equal stimulation if one baby is a stronger sucker than the other.

Usually a mother nursing triplets, will nurse two at a time and the third one has to wait until the other two finish. Then the third one will nurse both breasts, just like a single baby. Triplets must be rotated so the some one doesn't always get the leftovers. I know of three sets of triplets who were completely breast-fed for six months. Mothers nursing twins and triplets should make sure they get enough calories, which should consist mainly of proteins. These mothers should also take multiple vitamins with minerals similar to those they took while pregnant.

NIPPLES BURN AND BREASTS ACHE

A few mothers have told me that their breast feeding had been going very well for one or two months when suddenly their nipples began to burn. Sometimes this has been so severe that they could not stand any clothing on their nipples. Occasionally it will occur with the second and third babies, when I question these mothers very carefully, I usually find that they are overdoing and their lactating abilities are being over strained. When I am successful in getting the mothers to relax -- take 2 one hour naps, or one 2 hour nap or nurse lying down and take a cocktail before lying down; their burning nipples and the ache in their breasts, after nursing, goes away. Also shifting from one breast to the other every two to five minutes helps.

LUMPS IN THE BREAST

Lumps occur frequently in the lactating breast. They are due to the plugging of the tiny ductules, tributaries of the larger ductules which are tributaries of one of the 18 ducts that carry milk from the cells through the nipple into the baby's mouth. When they are all working there are eighteen sprays of milk going into the baby's mouth.

There are several factors that cause the plugging of the tiny ductules that are tributaries of the larger ductules. There are hourly variations of the level of oxytocin in the blood which controls the ejection reflex (let down reflex). Also the prolactin blood level, the intralobular pressure, and the production of breast milk are all interdependent. One has observed in humans as well as in cows the coagulation of milk (cheesy particles) that plug small and larger ductules from time to time. Local injury has been suggested as a factor but that is immediately confused with the failure of the letdown reflex because of anger, fear, anxiety and pain from such injury which lowers the oxytocin which prevents the ejection of milk and causes the milk to dam up in the ductules. Some have suggested that some of the ductules large and small have anatomical narrowings which would explain why the lumps recur in the same locations.

Lumps are frequently associated with lymph node swelling in the arm pits which also vary daily or weekly in the lactating breasts and from month to month in the non lactating breasts. As long as the lumps vary in size before and after nursing and in the menstrual cycles in the non lactating breasts there is no real danger of cancer.

Most of the lumps are associated with a plugged duct in a small or large tributary. If you feel that it does not change with lactation or the menstrual cycle and it is small, hard and worrisome, you can have it removed surgically under local anesthesia without disturbing breast feeding nor cutting one of the eighteen ducts that conduct the breast milk from the inner breast through the nipple to the baby. Microscopic study will tell you whether or not it is malignant. Larger lumps the size of a golf ball in a lactating mother can be aspirated with a needle and the contents can be examined microscopically. I have seen no cancer in the breast of a woman who has breast fed for a year or in a woman who has breast fed several months and then expressed a few drops of milk daily until her baby was one year old. However that does not mean that a nursing mother should ignore persistent or growing lumps because there is always a first. Cancer of the breast, treated early can be cured.

BREAST ABSCESS AND PLUGGED DUCT

"You doctors should figure out what causes these abscesses!" said one charming professor of physics shaking her finger at me after the fifth abscess in the same location.

Almost always the breast abscess and plugged duct is associated with some *lactating indiscretion*. The nursing mother has been doing too much. One mother raked leaves all day. Another stayed up until 3:00 a.m. with her husband papering the living room. Another had her husband's boss and wife for dinner and the boss' wife didn't breast-feed. Another had her in-laws visiting and one got sick. With such a *lactating indiscretion*, fatigue or worry and she doesn't get the let down reflex. Then the baby cries because he doesn't get enough to eat and this adds to the mother's dismay.

In the case of the professor of physics married to the professor of mathematics, I was never able to get a definite history of a *lactating indiscretion* from this brilliant lady, except that her house was always very neat and she was writing a text book on physics. Another young mother had five recurrences in the same location while nursing her second child. Her two and one-half year old was not compartmentized.

By nursing frequently and trying to relax, perhaps with a cocktail or two, the mother finally gets the let down reflex. She and the baby get to sleep, but the next day she notices a hardness, swelling, and tenderness in a portion of her breast. The ducts in a small portion of her breast remain plugged which causes swelling and hardness. It is as though in subsequent nursings, after the *lactating indiscretion*, she didn't get the let down reflex in every part of each breast. It seems as though one part definitely didn't let loose the milk. Perhaps there is a narrowing in the ducts in one part of the breast that make the ducts susceptible to getting plugged?

When the area of swelling and hardness becomes red and tender and the mother has fever and chills, then the plugged duct has become infected and the lactating mother has a breast abscess. This phenomenon is more frequent during the epidemics or respiratory infections in both adults and children. The germs causing the breast abscess (usually staphylococcus) probably came from the nose of the suckling baby, who in turn got it from his mother's nose and throat transmitted by her hands, or some other older child or adult who kissed and handled the baby without washing his/her hands. The plugged duct sets the stage for the develpment of the abscess. The virulent germs get into the milk ducts that are plugged with precipitated milk and from there the infection spreads to the tissue between the ducts. The lack of flow of the breast milk, because of the stasis of the milk, helps the germs get a foothold in the breast tissue.

The treatment for the breast abscess is first bed rest, second hot wet compresses continuously and third frequent nursing from both breasts. One of my colleagues, Dr. Caroline Lawler, a great promoter of breast-feeding, said that she wished that bed rest were a prescription that would cost the patient a thousand dollars; then it would be carried out.

The hot wet towel is usually easy to apply. Turn the hot water faucet on until the water is very hot; then take a large heavy bath towel roll or fold it long ways, by holding each dry end, wet the middle in the stream of hot water. Then twist each end until the wet middle is wrung out. Place this on your sore breast and climb back into bed. When you place the wet towel on your breast, lift your breast a little so that the wet towel props up your sore breast. You will be more comfortable.

This is particularly useful if the abscess is in the lower, outer portion of the breast. (5 or 7 o'clock). Some mothers like to put waterproof plastic over the hot wet towel and then apply an electric heating pad. This helps the wet towel stay hot and frees you from having to jump out of bed every 30 to 60 minutes to put the bath towel under the hot water spigot again. Sometimes your infected breast may be so painful that you can not bear anything, even the hot wet towel, to touch your breast. Ice cubes in a plastic bag could be applied for 12-24 hours and then you can shift back to the hot wet towel.

Wet heat seems to penetrate better than dry heat. Also you can ask your physician for a pain pill. Your breast may be so painful that it hurts to nurse. You can position your baby while nursing so that it doesn't hurt so much. Feet over the shoulder or twisting the breast so that your baby's upper jaw does not come down hard on the hot tender reddened area in your breast. By avoiding that tender area you can keep yourself comfortable enough so you get the let-down reflex.

It is extremely important for both you and your baby to nurse as often as the baby will nurse; 18 times a day if the baby will suckle that often. Frequent nursing for the plugged duct or the breast abscess makes your breast get well much faster than weaning because the suckling keeps the milk moving and relieves the stasis within the infected breast. If you have fever of chills or really feel sick; your plugged duct has probably become infected and you will also need an antibiotic. Call your doctor, but tell him or her you wish to keep right on breast-feeding.

There are some leaders in breast-feeding who believe that the germs from the suckling infants nose and throat get into the cracks and fissures in the nursing mother's nipples and from there spread into the breast tissue to make the abscess. I have treated hundreds of cracked nipples, some very severe where the nipple had deep fissure and in only a few instances have I seen any real evidence of a breast abscess developing from a cracked nipple.

When infection does occur as a complication of the cracked nipple it is usually limited to the brown area surrounding the nipple (areola) and the immediate surrounding breast tissue. Almost always the breast abscess develops deep within the breast and remote from the nipple. In fact in some instances it is difficult to palpate the plugged ducts coming to a point at the nipple like a piece of pie. In such instances the plugged duct, the precursor to the abscess, must literally have occurred deep within the breast. Read the section SORE NIPPLE.

THE CONTROVERSY IN THE TREATMENT OF THE BREAST ABSCESS

The treatment of the breast abscess has undergone an interesting development and explains why the patient may still find herself caught in a therapeutic controversy. In the thirties at Yale, the department of surgery asked the department of pediatrics; if a mother could nurse her baby after a breast abscess had been cut open and an ounce of pus had been let out. Dr. Powers, the chairman of pediatrics, said he saw no reason why not, so she breast-fed.

However Christopher's textbook of surgery recommended immediate weaning from both breasts and binding the breasts and packing them with ice. In 1949, Charlotte Naish wrote a thoughtful monograph in which she recommended continuing breast-feeding to relieve the stasis of sudden weaning. She quoted the research work of several English physicians. Meanwhile, Christopher's textbook of surgery which was used in almost every medical school went through five editions (20 years) recommending immediate weaning from both breasts if a breast abscess developed in one breast.

Therefore most of the doctors in America were taught to wean immediately when a woman developed a breast abscess because Christopher's textbook was used in most medical centers. Of course there was some justification for that position because the breast abscess was exquisitely tender even to touch -- let alone letting a baby nurse. One of my mothers became hysterical and had to wean.

In the forties and fifties, whenever one of my mothers developed a breast abscess, she either called me or her obstetrician. I made a house call on every mother and examined each breast, as well as drawing a picture of it for her baby's record. If she called the obstetrician first and was told to wean and pack her breasts in ice I agreed, encouraged her and wrote a formula for her baby. If she called me first, I made a house call and drawings of the abscess. I told her family that she must stay in bed, showed her how to use hot wet Turkish towels on her breasts, and prop them with pillows or folded towels so that she was comfortable. Read PLUGGED DUCT AND BREAST ABSCESS.

She either kept her baby in bed with her or in a bassinet next to her bed. She was allowed out of bed only to go to the bathroom. She nursed her baby whenever he squeaked 18 to 20 times a day. She was given an antibiotic -- penicillin at first and then newer ones as they became available.

There were 32 mothers with breast abscesses who were weaned suddenly and their breasts were bound. The abscesses began in the following locations:

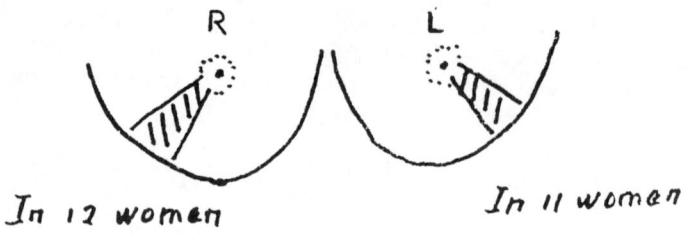

In 12 women   *In 11 women*

In 9, randomly elsewhere

Two-thirds (12 o'clock in the right and eleven in the left) in the lower outer portions of each breast. The other third (9) began randomly in other parts of the breast. In 24 (3/4) the abscess spread to other areas of the breast, in a few the whole half of the breast was involved in hardness. Sixteen (1/2) required surgery (incision and drainage under anesthesia.) Six required surgery twice, one: three times and one: five times over a five month period. The hardness in breasts of six, who were given stilbesterol (dry up pills), lasted three weeks. But the over-all average of those who weaned suddenly was two months before the breast returned to normal.

There were 122 mothers who called me first and all but one continued to breast-feed. Among the 121 who continued to breast-feed, two required surgery, but continued to breast-feed like the patient did at Yale in my medical school days. The average duration of palpable hardness in the breast was one-week in those who continued to breast-feed; it was two-months in those who weaned suddenly. Bacteriologically, the staphylococcus was found.

Concerning the 32 mothers who were weaned suddenly, I called each respective obstetrician and told him or her of the difference in duration of the breast abscess between those who were weaned and those who continued to breast-feed. Each thanked me and recommended continued breast-feeding with the next abscess that he or she encountered.

The breast abscess has not been a great problem in the past ten years. There have been plenty of plugged ducts but we have learned to put the mothers to bed, immediately with hot compresses and frequent nursing and they were over it within three days. The antibiotics are better now and are used if we suspect infection.

ILLNESS IN THE MOTHER AND BABY THAT REQUIRES WEANING

When I began practice (1940) mothers with active tuberculosis were not allowed to nurse because the live tubercle bacilli came into the milk. But now almost every mother has a chest X-ray early in her pregnancy, so that, if tuberculosis is discovered, she can take the proper medication and be able to nurse by the time her baby is born.

If a mother is delirious or unconscious she will not be able to nurse because she will not get the let-down reflex. Even if her milk does dry up because nursing has had to be discontinued, she can resume nursing when she is well. I've seen mothers resume nursing after stopping for several months. I've also seen mothers continue to nurse through appendicitis, gall bladder surgery, bronchitis, and pneumonia.

A mother with an upper respiratory infection should wash her hands right before she nurses her baby. The antibiotics she takes will prevent any live organisms from going into the milk.

Most hospitals take a dim view of the baby going to the hospital with the sick mother. Whenever I am involved in this situation, I make a big fuss and the baby is allowed to stay with the mother in a private room. Now that breast-feeding has become popular again, hospitals will be able to make this kind of arrangement more easily. If you cannot find a hospital that will take you and your baby, pump your breast four times a day while you are in the hospital. You will be able to keep your milk going and resume breast-feeding when you get home.

It is rare for a breast-fed baby to be so sick that he/she cannot nurse.

But like for a premature, or a baby with a cleft palate, the mother can pump her breasts and give her milk to the baby by dropper, dish with a spoon, or slowly with a fast nipple. Babies with pyloric stenosis (an overgrowth of muscle between the stomach and small intestine) vomit everything they take in. But these babies can be operated on and miss only one or two nursings.

IF YOU DON'T GIVE SOLIDS AT SIX MONTHS HE WILL STEAL THEM

The reason that a six-month old baby can reach out and grab an object and put it in his mouth is because the nerve fibers that connect the various parts of the brain for hand and eye coordination has become insulated at six months so that the nervous impulse (a measurable electric charge) can go to where it is supposed to go for the first time. Nature had decided when he should be fed solid food no sooner and no later. The young baby is not ready for anything except milk until he is six months old.

Babies like food from your plate that you mash up so that it is soupy -- mashed ripe banana (black speckled). Buy some every few days so that you have ripe ones all the time. Use canned baby food that you buy, *but no mixtures please*, only pure beef, lamb, peas, squash, etc.; no soups until you have introduced each ingredient separately. Take one week to introduce each new food. You might nurse at one breast for five or ten minutes then shovel in the solids, about one tablespoonful the first day. In a week's time increase to a baby can or jar. To understand what he might be allergic to, don't introduce mixtures until you have introduced each ingredient separately. If he doesn't like a particular food for three consecutive days, say spinach, cross it off your list for two months before trying it again. Never give him something he dislikes mixed with something he likes.

For the past 40 years I have been assembling information about as many babies as I can who have had nothing but breast milk for six months. The weight curves for these babies are the same as for those who started solids earlier. The completely breast-fed babies had no anemia and considerably fewer allergies. There is no value in starting solids early and there is a disadvantage. It increases the tendency for the baby to become allergic. Read the section THE VALUE OF BREAST-FEEDING.

You should start giving solids one at a time, over a two-month period. Start with ripe banana as described before. After banana, start cereal, one tablespoonful mixed with water, cow's milk, or breast milk until it is soupy or of a consistency that your baby likes. Start this at six pm or at two pm and six pm.

Next your baby should get some egg yolk. A taste of daddy's soft boiled egg at breakfast is enough at first. From this taste, work up to the whole yolk in about a week. You can give a hard boiled egg yolk. After it is cooked hard, mash it with a fork and mix it with a little water until it is mushy. Give it in that form with a spoon. After you are sure that the baby takes egg yolk well and develops no rash, you can mix raw egg yolk with the cereal. do not give the white of the egg until the baby is a year old. Egg whites can be saved for the family to add to scrambled eggs or to angel food cake. Some food experts have observed that the raw egg yolk is not as digestible as the cooked egg yolk. This is correct, but the difference to the baby after six months of age is so slight that it is not worth the inconvenience to have to cook the egg yolk.

Orange juice should be given at breakfast diluted one to one with water. Start with one or two tablespoonfuls and work up to two ounces. It can be spoon fed or given in a small glass. It can also be put into a bottle.

Next add a vegetable. It can be a green vegetable, such as peas, or a yellow vegetable, such as squash or carrots. They should be pureed or ground so fine that the baby cannot choke on the little chunks. Canned vegetables are acceptable, however, home-cooked vegetables are better. In this day and age, it is not necessary for a mother to knock herself out to cook her own vegetables. Leftover vegetables from the table or canned vegetables, whichever are more convenient, can be used. After your baby has been taking strained food for a few months, he will be able to chew and swallow, even if he does not have teeth. Mash the large chunks into small bits. It is quite common for mothers to shift from the strained food to the chopped or junior foods. This is particularly convenient because if the baby does not finish the jar of chopped food, you can eat it yourself. You do not have to cook lunch especially for yourself.

The majority of my patients stay on the strained foods until the child is eleven months to a year old and then shift to the food from the table. The foods should consist of peas, carrots, beets, baked potato, mashed potato, bread, rice, and foods that do not have large fibers that are difficult for your baby to swallow. Often a baby will not shift to the foods from the table, but will persist in liking a strained food. He might prefer the strained spinach until he is over four years of age. There is nothing wrong with going along with this preference, provided the child gets enough other foods to chew on.

Some babies love to sit in a high chair next to the table and steal the grown-up food. This is an interesting and enjoyable experience, provided that you don't try to teach your baby manners or reprimand him for spitting out the food. Table manner come later by example.

OCCASIONAL BOTTLE?

SHOULD I GIVE MY NURSING BABY A BOTTLE OCCASIONALLY TO FAMILIARIZE HIM WITH IT IN CASE I HAVE TO MISS A FEEDING BECAUSE OF AN EMERGENCY?

Absolutely not. A breast-fed baby might balk at taking a bottle from his mother, but he will accept it from someone else. It is ridiculous to think you should accustom your baby to a bottle in case of emergency. That is like asking your two-year old to steer the car so he will be a good driver when he is sixteen.

Formula is likely to make a baby under six months of age allergic. My study and that of some allergists show that babies who are fed things other than human milk before they are six months old are more apt to have asthma and hay fever in later life than babies who get nothing but mother for six months. If a mother has to miss a feeding, she will probably know about the event a few days in advance so that she can pump a little milk each day and freeze it so the baby can have human milk when she is away. Read SABOTAGE.

ORAL CONTRACEPTIVES & BREAST-FEEDING

It is rare for a woman to conceive if she is nursing her baby completely and not giving him any solid food or formula. In my 42 years of practice, I have seen only two women conceive while they were nursing babies under six months. One woman conceived very easily. She did not menstruate for the first six years of her marriage and had five children. But she gave solid food early to her first several babies. In her later pregnancies she didn't give any solids until the babies were six months old, and she didn't conceive as quickly. Another woman got pregnant twice while she was completely breast-feeding a four-month old baby. Her menstrual periods resumed soon after her babies were born. This is very unusual under six months or so when the mother is giving the baby nothing but breast milk.

If your menstrual periods resume before your baby is six-months old, and if you don't want another baby yet, it would be wise to use some other form of contraception. But don't start the Pill until your baby is six- or eight-months old. The oral contraceptives tend to dry up the milk.

BREAST-FEEDING WHILE TAKING MEDICINE

You can take any medicine your doctor prescribes while nursing unless the baby is allergic to the medicine like he might be allergic to eggs that you eat or cow's milk that you drink. The amount of medicine that your baby gets, by the way of breast milk, is so small that if it doesn't disagree with you, it usually will not disagree with your baby. Be sure to contact your doctor for the sudden appearance of a rash, crying, or vomiting

There are a few drugs that are controversial, like propylthiuracial which shrivels the thyroid; then the baby should be monitored by taking blood samples for thyroxine levels. One of my hyperthyroid mothers was so treated while breast-feeding. Her daughter was monitored by taking periodic bone ages. This attractive young lady is now on the dean's list in college. If in doubt consult your doctor and the LaLeche League. Now periodic blood monitoring for thyroxine (T4) excreted by the thyroid gland of your baby is a simple and inexpensive way to monitor your baby's thyroid function.

PREGNANCY & BREAST-FEEDING

CAN I CONTINUE TO NURSE MY BABY IF I BECOME PREGNANT?

Yes. Your unborn baby will not be shortchanged on calcium or anything else. Be sure to tell your obstetrician what you are doing. He will probably give you extra calcium to take. If you didn't take extra calcium, the calcium for your milk and your unborn baby would come from your bones. The late Dr. Henry Gerstenberger, chief of pediatrics at the University Hospitals in Cleveland, Ohio, once deprived a cow of calcium to the point where her bones broke. But the calcium in her milk did not vary.

All pregnant women, especially those who are still nursing a baby, should get plenty of protein, vitamins, calcium and iron.

SHOULD I WEAN WHEN PREGNANT?

I AM PREGNANT WITH MY SECOND CHILD AND STILL NURSING MY FIRST. WHEN SHOULD I WEAN HIM?

Many La Leche mothers nurse their toddlers right up until their next child is born. They often continue to nurse a toddler and a small baby. There is no harm in doing this. It is good mothering.

Nursing for a toddler is mainly for solace. The mother is usually not giving the child much milk, but it makes him feel good to be able to run to his mother and nurse for a moment or two when he bumps himself or the world gets to be too much for him.

ALLERGIC TO BREAST MILK?

IS IT POSSIBLE FOR A BABY TO BE ALLERGIC TO HIS MOTHER'S MILK?

No. But the baby could be allergic to something his mother eats which is transmitted in very slight quantities to him through his mother's milk. I have had five mothers whose babies showed allergic reactions when their mothers ate eggs. One baby's lips blistered if they were touched with egg yolk. When the mothers stopped eating eggs, their babies' rashes cleared up. Under no circumstance should you wean your baby if this happens. He will outgrow the allergy sooner if you stop eating the offending food and continue to nurse him. He will probably outgrow it by the time he is between 10 and 14 months old if you continue to nurse him. Sometimes it is impossible to figure out what the baby is allergic to in his mother's milk, but he should not be weaned. Read: HOW PROLONGED NURSING HELPS ALLERGY.

BREAST MILK TOO RICH OR TOO WEAK?

IS MOTHER'S MILK EVER TOO RICH OR TOO WEAK FOR A BABY?

Never. Your milk was made specifically for your baby and there is no substitute of as good a quality. The fat content of breast milk does vary between the first portion of milk that is let down and the later milk. The first part of the milk the baby gets is low in fat, while the hind milk is rich in fat. This is nature's way of regulating a baby's diet. If his mother has a lot of milk, the baby gets a lot of lower calorie milk. If the mother is not producing too much, the baby gets mostly high caloric milk.

BREAST-FEEDING AN ADOPTED BABY

MY HUSBAND AND I ARE PLANNING TO ADOPT A BABY. CAN I BREAST-FEED THIS BABY?

Yes, even if you have had no natural children. If you have had children of your own, it is easy to get your milk going again, even years after you have stopped nursing your baby. I recently taught three mothers who have never been pregnant how to nurse their adopted babies. A month or so before you get the baby you should start hand-expressing colostrum from your breasts. (Read HAND EXPRESSION section.) Do this four or five times a day to get your milk flowing. Then when the baby arrives he will increase the milk supply. He will probably nurse 16 or 17 times a day. Give him a bottle after nursing three times in rapid succession. Frequent nursing and a strong desire to nurse your adopted baby will enable you to do it even if you have never been pregnant. (Read: THE LACTATOR.)

ADOPTION AGENCIES & BREAST-FEEDING

HOW DO ADOPTION AGENCIES REACT WHEN A PROSPECTIVE MOTHER SAYS SHE WANTS TO NURSE HER ADOPTED BABY?

In my experience, they are alarmed and appalled and think the mother is a little unbalanced. If you are adopting a baby through an agency, I suggest you do not volunteer your intention to breast-feed the baby. One mother came to me after she had heard the don't-call-us-we'll-call-you routine from an agency because she told them she wanted to breast-feed.

I was able to recommend an obstetrician who was sympathetic about breast-feeding. He had an unmarried mother who was about to deliver and put her baby up for adoption. He was able to arrange a private adoption for my patient. The way to go about making a private adoption is to make your wish known to a few obstetricians who are in contact with unwed mothers who want to give up their babies. When the baby is born you and your attorney are notified. You can pick up the baby when the mother signs the papers over to your attorney for the adoption. There should be no contact between the natural mother and the adoptive parents. All the work should be done by attorneys.

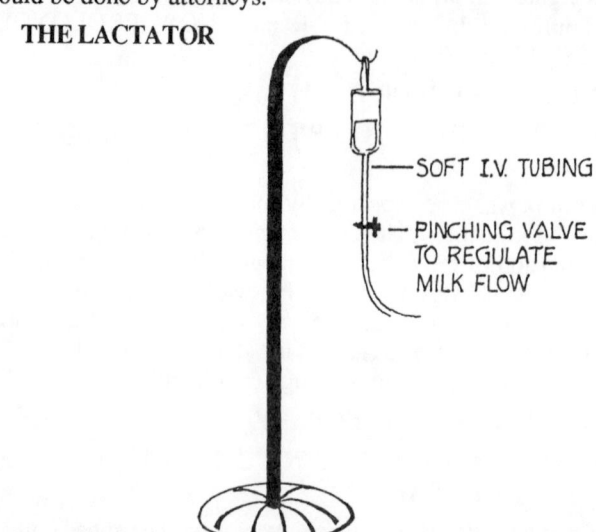

THE LACTATOR

You may buy or the hospital may give you the I.V. bottle used as a premature baby feeding tube. If you attach this premature's tube to your nipple by taping it to your breast the baby can stimulate your lactation and at the same time be getting the donated breast milk or formula. This milk flow can also be regulated by the dial which is attached to the I.V. tubing. This is a marvelous method of stimulation because the baby will not be frustrated because he is getting no milk.

One of my mothers did this every two hours during the day and whenever it was needed during the night. The bottle could also be hung on a hook on the wall or a chair directly above you. Use a comfortable chair with your feet up as high as your heart. The bottle must be hung slightly above your head.

BREAST-FEEDING AFTER SILICONE IMPLANTS

When the implants have been inserted under the breasts, a mother can nurse perfectly well. The let-down reflex works because neither the ducts nor the sensory nerves leading to the brain have been cut. I have had several mothers nurse successfully after such implants.

MOVING WHILE NURSING

Moving while nursing is terrible. Nursing while traveling is wonderful.

But a nursing mother who has to pick up and move into a new home is usually in for trouble. It is not the big things that create tension, it is the little things, like the curtains that don't fit or don't match the rugs. Then the mother doesn't get the let-down reflex. My wife lost her milk completely when we moved, but we got it back again. If you have to move, consult your physician and get a tranquilizer so that everything looks rosy. Don't wean because of moving. One of my patients just told me that she has moved seven times while nursing a baby. I admire her greatly.

HOW TO PREVENT SPOILING

"If you baby a baby when he's a baby you won't have to baby him all the rest of his life." La Leche League

It is hard to spoil the baby before he is six months old. It is equally hard to keep him on schedule. If you are breast-feeding, you cannot always let down your milk on schedule. If you are bottle feeding or breast-feeding, he may have so much colic that his spoiled cry and the pain cry from the colic are so mixed together that you cannot tell which is which. If you pick him up, he smiles. When you put him down, he cries. Then you pick him up, he smiles again. Repeating this several times you can convince yourself and your baby that he is crying only to be picked up. He is not in pain. If you don't want to keep picking him up, you can convince him that he will not get anywhere by these sudden spells of crying which change to laughing when he gets picked up. Let him cry for five minutes, then go and pat him. Turn him over; do the minimum necessary just to stop him from crying and then leave. Go to him every five minutes to break his crying spell. Be sweet. Make believe that you do not understand his crying.

Although it is impossible to spoil babies, as a grandparent, I believe that all grandchildren were made for the purpose of being spoiled. That does not mean parents can't spoil their children if they handle them the way grandparents do. My definition of a spoiled child: "is one who has learned to turn-off all grown-ups and who doesn't listen even for his own good. The turning-off habit began when he was a toddler and it occurs primarily in those children who were not breast-fed for many months or were not compartmentized. their techniques of resistance and habits of disobedience have persisted into childhood." Read COMPARTMENTATION.

A baby becomes spoiled after he learns to crawl because he has not learned to play by himself in a playpen, crib or gated room for two to four hours a day. This is not to say you should not hold, cuddle, and play with the toddler. He needs to be fondled all his life. But he should be spending two to four hours a day playing by himself in a playpen or gated room. The rest of the day he can be cuddled and played with.

Once I was called to see a year-old baby who would cry all night long if he wasn't held. He was an only child in a house with his parents and both sets of grandparents, whose lives revolved around this child. He wouldn't sleep at night except in the arms of one of the six grown-ups. On examination he was one of the healthiest, brightest eyed, happiest baby's I have ever seen while in an adult's arms. He watched my every move with shining dark eyes, but when he was put to bed he cried until he vomited. He stopped immediately when picked up. He could turn it on and off at will.

From the time he was very young, the adults would sit up with him all night. Each adult took a two-hour shift. This child had been spoiled after he learned to crawl. If I had seen this baby at an earlier age, I would have gone along with the sitting-up procedure until six months of age. After that I would have put a stop to it by insisting that he spend two to four hours in a playpen during the day and going to him to break his crying spell every five minutes before he could work himself up so much that he vomited. By the time I saw the baby he was so firmly entrenched in his routine that it was very difficult to stop but not impossible. Read RECOMPARTMENTATION.

"Four kids and two dogs are too much even in a king-sized bed!" exclaimed one father - a trial lawyer whose income was in the six figures. "After three nights of no sleep, I found myself arguing on the wrong side of a case."

I have always tried to teach my mothers and fathers, that in psycho-emotional situations, the woman is biologically stronger than the man. The double XX chromosome in every cell gives her more deoxyribonucleic acid (DNA). In the male there is less DNA because of the smaller XY chromosome. Statistically she lives seven years longer than her male partner. She can take it better. When mother is breast-feeding, there is no point in waking father. If the infant is not yet walking have a cot bed in the nursery so that mother can nurse frequently without waking a more brittle husband. When the baby is fed formula, neither father, mother nor baby are so lucky.

You may be over doing so that you are not giving him enough at the bedtime feeding. If you think this is happening, get off your feet for at least two one-hour periods during the day. A mother's work is never done, so part of your duty, is to get off your feet for two hours a day. Nursing while lying down helps. Some mothers can relax in a rocking chair. Relax you must.

You might also augment the over nine-months old's diet during the day. Give him solids -- meat, cottage cheese, and other high protein foods -- at least twice daily.

Some babies awaken during the night because they do not get enough calcium. A lack of calcium could cause a slight cramp which awakens him. Discuss this with your doctor.

When children wake up at night many family adjustments may have to be made. Great grandmother used to say: "Men are charmed by beauty, women by kindness, children by love -- they see it in your eyes."

The way the La Leche League fathers praise their breast-feeding wives has helped me to help children -- as a husband, father and physician.

After you, with the help of your doctor, have exhausted all causes for his changing night into day, then think and practice compartmentation.

Preschool children, of working mothers and fathers, in day care centers, sleep well at night. When mothers work and fathers look after the toddlers at home, they sleep well when fathers compartmentize.

IS THE ENJOYMENT OF BREAST-FEEDING SEXUAL?

Psychiatrists, obstetricians, pediatricians, generalists and laymen, mostly men, have asked me this question. For an answer I defer to the ladies. Dr. Niles Newton, scientist, breast-feeding mother of four and very much a woman observes: Coitus and breast-feeding are both fundamentally pleasurable enough to have sustained the race for thousands of years. The physiology of the letdown reflex (ejection reflex) have several scientifically observed features that are similar to the orgasm of the woman in sexual intercourse: the body temperature rises one and one-half degrees and skin erythema occurs about the face, neck and torso; the uterus contracts and the cervix opens; the nipples become erect and breast milk squirts out several inches, wetting the husband; and the pituitary glands excretes an oxytocin hormone that makes the woman sleepy after the letdown reflex as after the sexual orgasm.

Many mothers have told me that the letdown reflex had made them more content and have less need for sex. Others have said that their husbands touching their breasts has sent lightning through them and their demand for sex became quicker and stronger than it was before breast-feeding.

Many toddlers get erections while nursing; it should not bother anyone because they also get erections in sleep.

Some other random observations; "For man each incident of intercourse is complete in itself. It progresses from foreplay to the climax of ejaculation and ends with complete relaxation and sleep. A woman's true orgasm begins with intercourse, quickens with each ensuing incident, progresses through pregnancy, reaches climax with the ejection of her baby and ends with the relaxation of nursing."

"A woman who nurses her baby enjoys her body more than the one who is opposed to nursing."

"Breast-feeding got me over a fear of my body in fact I became so confident in all of the functions of my body that I became conceited."

"I have always fit myself into roles to satisfy somebody. I was a tomboy because I suspected that dad wanted a son; I was a good student to compete with my sisters, I acted mature and interested in family affairs to win extra time with my mom; but being a mother is the most natural role for me, indeed it is no role at all. For the first time, I am completely at ease, I am doing what comes naturally."

"The few times I have been bitten by a nursing baby, the pain transferred from my nipple to somewhere below my diaphragm and then straight down to my vagina. It definitely is not a heterosexual stimulation, though; it is strictly a maternal feeling."

Babette Francis observes that "a mother derives great pleasure in breast-feeding an infant over six months of age. Such an infant responds positively to her by patting her body, caressing her face, touching her lips and generally showing delight not only in the milk she provides, but in the close contact with her". The breast-feeding painting by Mary Casat hanging in the Art Institute of Chicago shows the baby feeding, smiling and trying to pat its mother's face all at the same time.

Ms. Francis goes on to say "women are sensual creatures who have a tremendous capacity for enjoying caresses and skin to skin contact with a loved one. The possibility that some of the frustration, discontent and hostility many women feel today is not because they are unliberated but because their production of the hormone prolactin has been suppressed and a vital expression of their sexuality has remained unfulfilled."

WORKING AND BREAST-FEEDING

With a little planning, mothers can work and breast-feed. In many instances they can take their babies to work with them. One research chemist took her baby to work with her when one-month old and kept her in the ladies lounge adjacent to the lavatory of a big chemistry room where the mother supervised a distilling process. She could hear the baby if she cried and go to her to nurse without a schedule. The presence of the baby at work made all the other workers want to have a baby to bring to work.

Another mother was a university librarian. There was no facility to keep the baby in the library so the mother kept her baby in a rooming house across the campus lawn with a student sitter who called the mother when the baby was hungry. The mother walked across the lawn, nursed her baby, and walked back to the library. She completely breast-fed this baby for several months. He is now grown and eminently successful at sales.

Another mother kept her baby in the back of her husband's jewelry store. Between frequent nursings she helped her husband with the customers.

It was heartening to read, a few years ago, that a judge ruled that a woman fireman could bring her baby to work and breast-feed on the job. Eventually the private and public sectors of employment will use "breast-feeding on the job" as a fringe benefit of employment that will be cost effective in the wage scale competition.

School teachers will keep their nursing babies in a corner of the classroom. Executives, bankers, lawyers, doctors, secretaries and all workers in the public and private sectors will do what the chemist did and what Madame Curie did.

One of my mothers, a physician, had her first baby early in her first year of residency. She wanted to breast-feed completely because she had allergies. She rented an apartment across the street form the hospital and hired a sitter to live with her and her husband who was a stock broker. She went back and forth from her apartment to the hospital. She did both jobs well while competing with the male residents. She pumped her breasts and stored her milk in the deep freeze to be melted and given to the baby when she was tied up helping in a long neuro-surgical operation or had to stay up all night with a critical patient. This physician was so good at her job, she was asked to stay on in the residency training program for four years. A second baby was nursed for a year while she completed her training.

Her children are now honor students in high school and extremely well adjusted. The mother is a board certified internist and working full time in research. Her husband is a successful stockbroker. Now, there are no allergies.

In the eighties most of the female pediatricians having children while in their residency training are nursing. When they cannot actually bring their children to work, they pump and freeze their milk so the babies get nothing but breast milk for six months.

The Marshall-Kanesson breast pump can be carried in a lady's large purse. The nursing mother can go into seclusion, pump her breasts to relieve herself, freeze her milk, and add it to her store at home.

Nursing mothers can go back to work when they feel ready, but I would not urge it until after the DANGER WEEKS have passed. Read that section as well as the LETDOWN REFLEX and the PUMPING STORAGE OF HUMAN MILK.

WEANING

"HOW LONG SHOULD I BREAST-FEED?

Lucy, a young mother of two, did not compartmentize. She breast-fed Suzanne, her oldest until she was two. then Suzanne weaned herself. When Lucy's son, Michael, came along, she breast-fed him even longer. There were no gates or playpens. When he bumped himself, he ran to his mother to nurse a moment or two, then ran off to play with his older sister. Both children were very friendly and extremely adaptable and passed the Gesell tests with flying colors. At three Michael adapted beautifully to nursery school -- just like the compartmentized toddlers. At three and one-half his mother was concerned about his frequent nursing before and after nursery school. He chased her all over the house to breast-feed after every argument he had with his older sister. This went on several times a day. Lucy was tired of it. Her husband thought Michael was old enough to quit. I suggested that mother go to the movies and let father put Michael to bed. It worked beautifully. Michael didn't miss nursing that night.

Although he was very adaptable, Michael wanted to nurse whenever he had a problem. Like most children he had lots of little problems. Finally, mother had had enough. She wanted to stop nursing altogether. I sent her to Palm Beach to visit her mother.

During the week she was gone, Michael did not seem to miss his mother or his breast-feeding at all. "Nanny" took care of him and he loved it.

When mother got back home she and Michael took one look at each other and he was breast-feeding again. Lucy felt her milk come back. Again Michael nursed several times each day. I told her to stay away this time for two weeks. Again, when she returned, it was the same all over again. One look at his mother and Michael began nursing again.

One day when Michael was nearly four, he brought a friend home from nursery school. His mother graciously greeted them both. Pointing to his mother's breasts, he asked his friend if he would like some "num num". That did it. His mother ran to the other end of the house, slightly mortified. She refused. Michael was weaned at last.

Both Michael and his sister are now honor students in high school and very adaptable.

There is no rule of thumb in months or years as to how long a child should breast-feed. After urging nothing but mother for six months, I introduced solids one at a time until nine months of age. After cow's milk from a cup was established, breast milk production decreased and the toddler's eagerness to suckle diminished. They parted by mutual consent.

When mothers were emotionally upset or were allergic, they nursed longer. Those pre-school children, who were not compartmentized, ran to mother when the "No" was too much for them. They suckled for a moment sometimes to the point of embarrassing their well groomed mothers.

Some mothers used prolonged breast-feeding as a means of child spacing -- effective but not totally reliable. Some La Leche mothers nursed toddlers at the same time as a younger infant. It helped jealousy they said.

Most babies will wean themselves when they are ready. Some mothers are happier weaning after nine months when their baby can drink from a cup. Many babies just stop nursing suddenly. Probably the mother's letdown reflex is not working as well or she isn't as productive as before. It is upsetting to mother not to be wanted, but child led weaning as recommended by the La Leche League is the best way to go.

I usually encourage allergic mothers to nurse until the toddlers are three years old. They usually don't bite except at the beginning of the feeding or at the end. Mother should end that feeding when she gets bitten. They are usually telling mother they're not hungry. The animals briefly and quickly punish their young when they bite.

When mother wants to wean the three year old and the child wants to continue breast-feeding; it is best for mother to take a night or week off. Out of sight, out of mind; the child adapts to some one else taking care of him very well at three and younger, especially if he has been compartmentized.

Two of my most allergic babies I recommended their mothers nurse until after their fourth birthday. Both are teenagers, honor students, and without allergies. I recommend prolonged nursing for my allergic patients. Read: VALUE OF BREAST-FEEDING.

Recently a dentist, who specialized in the care of children's teeth, told me of a three year old who developed extensive dental caries. The child slept with his mother and suckled off and on all night while they both slept. The American Dental Association describes "Nursing Bottle Mouth", which is caused by the frequent exposure of a child's teeth to liquids containing sugar (milk, formula, fruit juice and other sweetened liquids). The sugars in these liquids are used as an energy source by the bacteria in plaque. The bacteria produce acids that attack tooth enamel.

I have always encouraged prolonged breast-feeding and prolonged bottle feeding without causing dental caries. I have found that it helped the pre-school children psychologically especially when they were not compartmentized. One four-year girl had to have many of her deciduous teeth capped because of caries. She had developed caries long after she was weaned from both breast and bottle. The family all drank well water without fluoridation.

Because of the dilemma between the psychological help form suckling versus dental caries, you should look for caries behind the upper incisors. That is where it usually starts. Discuss the controversy with your child's physician.

The toddler doesn't need to nurse all night while both he and his mother sleep. Mother should just nurse him to sleep and then be careful not to awaken him. Bottles should have plain water in them. The water doesn't need to be sweetened.

PROLONGED BREAST-FEEDING FOR ALLERGIC FAMILIES

A.H. was seen by his mother one-half hour after delivery. He was red and wrinkled and in an isolette. He weighed six pounds eight-ounces and measured nineteen and one-half inches. He nursed well for the first time when he was fifteen hours old. He had some mucus in his stools during the newborn period.

When A.H. was two weeks old he was given rice cereal. Following this, considerable mucus formed and he had to be aspirated and then mucus again appeared in his bowel movements. At six weeks Similac was used to dilute the rice cereal. Also carrots were started and one week later the mucus in his nose became worse. He was given cortisone which seemed to help. At two months he received his first DPT shot without reaction.

When A.H. was three months old the mother developed a breast infection with a 104 degree temperature. She attempted to wean him and gave a bottle of Similac following which there was a convulsion followed by more diarrhea. I was consulted by phone and recommended the continuation of breast-feeding and proper antibiotics for the mother. Mother was put to bed; she nursed the baby frequently from both breasts and hot wet towels were applied to the breasts. She was well within a few days.

At three and one-half months, he was admitted to a distant University Medical Center where he received an upper G.I. series, barium enema, sweat tests, blood counts and many skin tests to all of which there were negative reactions. In the hospital it was found that, when he was given Similac, a rash developed immediately. He also experienced severe colic. It was therefore recommended he remain on nothing but breast milk until he was six months old.

At four and one-half months he received his third DPT without reaction.

At six months strained lamb was started without reaction. Three weeks later green beans were started following which there was colic and mucus in the stools. His development was normal and he was sitting alone at six and a half months and at seven months, he pulled himself up to standing in the playpen. By phone I recommended stopping all solids and nothing but breast milk and iron.

I examined him when he was eleven months old and found him in excellent health. His height was in the tenth percentile and his weight was in the fifth. He was ahead of schedule in the developmental tests. I recommended continued breast-feeding, iron drops and try to desensitize him against cow's milk. It was found he could tolerate one-half teaspoonful of milk, but one-teaspoonful made him vomit. I saw him from time to time and recommended compartmentation. He received nothing but breast milk and iron until he was 19 months old.

At nineteen months he was given a little applesauce without reaction. Two weeks later he drank some cow's milk following which were severe cramps, diarrhea with mucus and hives. His temperature rose to 104 degrees. At twenty and a half months milk was tried again with the same reaction.

At twenty-one months rice cereal cooked with water was taken without reaction.

However, by my urging, breast-feeding was continued and again solids were discontinued. He was given nothing else except a half teaspoonful of milk to desensitize him and five drops of iron daily. He was talking intelligently, toilet trained, and growing in the tenth percentile.

Breast-feeding, 5 drops of iron, 1/2 teaspoonful of cow's milk continued without exception. At two years and four months he ate a dish of ice cream and didn't vomit. The next day he drank a glass of milk and felt all right. Overnight he seemed to have "out grown" his great sensitivity to cow's milk. His mother said it was a miracle because he suddenly began to drink a pint of milk a day when a few days before he could not drink even a teaspoonful without vomiting.

Gradually his diet broadened. He took cereal with milk and enjoyed pancakes with syrup. Over the next few months he began to eat small amounts of chicken, steak from the table and his pint of milk without trouble. He gradually stopped nursing.

A.H. is now on the dean's list in college. He has no food allergies. He received immunizations against ragweed while in high school and one year had three brief attacks of asthma -- none since. In short his allergies are now less troublesome to him than those of the other members of his family. He is above average in intelligence, health, and adaptability. He's on his way to a brilliant career.

Another case where prolonged nursing helped allergy is that of P.H. born January 24, 1968. He was brought in at three weeks of age because he was a nursing problem. He had colic; was allergic to his mother's milk, and weaning had been recommended. The father, thirty-three years old, over six feet tall and well built, was a writer. He was allergic to wheat and corn and had not been breast-fed. The mother, thirty-seven, five feet ten inches, and medium weight, had two years of college. She has many food allergies and does not know her breast-feeding history.

P.H. was the first and only pregnancy. It took the mother two years to conceive; she conceived in May 1967, shortly after her fallopian tubes had been inflated. A missed period without nausea was the first symptom of pregnancy. The pregnancy was uneventful and she gained thirty pounds. She went one week over the due date and then went into labor spontaneously. The baby was born by caesarian section after twenty hours of labor in which not enough progress had been made. The section was performed under a general anaesthetic and the mother was not awake. She first saw the baby eleven hours after birth and in her own room. The Apgar was said to be 10. Birth weight was 10 pounds and 2-1/4 ounces. He was 21-1/4 inches in length.

He had no mucus or spells of blueness and suckled well the first try when twenty-four hours old. At home after ten days in the hospital he weighed 9 pounds and three ounces. The baby dropped to eight pounds 12 ounces, and then in three weeks was up to birth weight. The baby was crying a lot and seemed to be colicky. I saw the baby for the first time at three weeks of age. I told the mother to go to bed and nurse frequently. In one week the baby gained one pound. Next month the baby gained a pound and a half. The weight gain went along on the ninetieth percentile, the same as his parents. The child's development was normal.

When six months old, the family moved to Italy and they lived there a little over a year. While in Italy it was found that the child was allergic to several foods. She wrote me complaining that the Italian doctors were trying to get her to wean her baby. I wrote her I thought she should continue to breast-feed if the baby was allergic to any food. She did this.

They came back to the United States when P.H. was twenty months old and still nursing. She went to an allergist and the baby was tested and found to be allergic to apples and corn. The tests were negative to more than thirty other substances. She alone was allergic to about thirty foods. I recommended to continue breast-feeding because the child was flourishing. He was still gaining at the ninety-fifth percentile and performing above normal in the Gesell tests. When the child was four years old he stopped nursing and had no allergies. Now in high school, he is the picture of health and adaptability.

Since A.H. and P.H., I have had a few other dramatic improvements in children with severe allergies who were breast-fed into their second year, as well as a few who were breast-fed as long as four years. One had such severe eczema from head to toe that he looked as though he had been burned all over and his "burns" had become secondarily infected. He was hospitalized several times and fed intravenously until it was decided that he could tolerate only breast milk, when his mother eliminated eggs, wheat, and milk from her diet. He was allergic to those and almost all other foods. He was breast-fed fours years and is now an honor student in high school, athletic and non-allergic.

Several other children were nursed for four years and have completely "out grown" their allergies. Many others became non-allergic while breast-feeding in their second year of life.

I have in my files more than a dozen cases in which I have urged the mothers to nurse many months because the children were allergic. In every instance the prolonged nursing seemed to make the allergy better than the allergy in either of the parents. In a few the allergic states were eliminated altogether. There is something about human milk that is extremely beneficial for allergies. If someone wants to study this more thoroughly, I recommend reading: "The Uniqueness of Human Milk" by D. B. Jelliffe, Vol. 24, *The American Journal of Clinical Nutrition.* In this symposium one gets a glimpse of the enormous number of little differences in the milks of various animals. There are more than 300 scientific papers published during the past decade that describe these very interesting bio-chemical differences.

CHAPTER XV

VARIATIONS ON A THEME: COMPARTMENTATION

NURSERIES

A substitute for compartmentation is for you and your spouse to live in a nursery. You can put away your books, wedding presents and build shelves near the ceiling for your records. But it is virtually impossible for adults to live in a nursery for very long. You are bound to leave your purse within reach of your toddlers some day, and then you will be angry with them for smearing your lipstick on the carpet.

Unfortunately, most of the child care books recommend that you put your valuables away and make your whole house childproof. They condone taking your child out of the playpen at one year so he or she can explore. Many families do just that, and everything seems all right at first. But a few months later the child learns to climb and trouble begins. Not everything can be locked up.

But, even if you could make your whole house absolutely childproof, compartmentation is still necessary. Small children who roam all over four or five rooms all day long are tired and irritable by the end of the day. Children of eighteen months and two and a half years get especially whiney.

When our grandson was two and a half years old, he usually spent three or four hours a day in a gated room or fenced yard. When his mother went to the hospital for an operation, he spent a week with us. Our house was no longer compartmentized because our children were grown and gone. Like all grandparents, we believed our grandson could do no wrong. When he visited us we let him do anything he wanted, and we never said "no". He was delightful and so were his visits. During the week he was with us, he had the run of the house, inside and out. He played with the dog and was good. By the end of the week, however, he was tired and irritable. He said "no" frequently and was not as amenable to suggestions as he was at the beginning of his visit.

His mother noticed the same irritability, which lasted two days after he got home. It did not disappear until he was back in his old routine of the gated room and fenced yard for three or four hours a day. I believe that the expanded world for all his waking hours at our house was more than his two and one half year-old mind could take.

NO-MAN'S LAND

Another group of noncompartmentized children who have overachieved are those who have grown up in families that were physically or socially isolated. The non-mechanized remote farm or ranch where there was a shortage of money. Where parents and children were forced to work closely together to make a living, they combined forces to combat poverty. Distances were so great that they were isolated socially. When there were strong mothers and smart children they overachieved.

Ann Roe, a pupil of Dr. Benjamin Bloom from the School of

Education at the University of Chicago, studied the lives of scientists who had made outstanding contributions in their respective fields. In these biographical studies she detected one common finding: Between 5 and 9-1/2 years of age, each scientist had an illness requiring a lengthy convalescence causing him to be alone without radio or television for many months. Each seemed to develop a particular way of thinking which motivated each to a greater than ordinary accomplishment.[1]

In these instances illness forced intelligent youths to overcome techniques of resistance and habits of disobedience that might have been acquired by "free running" in the pre-school years.

NANNIES

Another substitution for compartmentation is to raise your children on a tropical beach. A calm relaxed mother, or a nanny specially chosen for her loving gentleness, can protect the child from drowning and sunburn. There are few "no, nos" for these pre-school children. It is reminiscent of the European aristocracy. Wealthy parents turn their children over to dedicated nannies, the tutors, the boarding school and finally the university.

Sir Winston Churchill loved his nanny. In the 19th and early 20th centuries, the world was run by about 200 overachievers who had simple beginnings from loving nannies. In the eighties, compartmentation helps mothers of average strength and wealth to raise children who overachieve.

---

[1] *Personal Communication*, Dr Benjamin Bloom. University of Chicago

CHAPTER XVI
TOYS

Placing the playpen or crib in front of a full length mirror helps. Looking at another baby will make her laugh.

The fewer toys an 18-month old has the better. Parents and grandparents buy too many toys for small children. A colleague of mine sent his first born daughter one new toy a week -- expensive dolls and clothing, etc. Finally his wife, a pediatrician, wrote that this daughter enjoyed the wrapping paper. Paper, cardboard boxes, blocks, telephones, an old pocketbook, old hats and pots and pans continually fascinate the pre-school child. They like to play with things that they see adults use. Expensive store toys are almost always second best. Lets look at how Stephanie coped with toys.

Stephanie was a former teacher who had been given an advance to write a history book for eighth graders. She decided to work mornings while her eighteen-month old Joshua was in the playpen or gated room. She did not want to send Josh to a day care center. She wanted to save that money.

She acquired five card board boxes from a retail store. She marked each for a working day: Monday, Tuesday, Wednesday, Thursday, and Friday. She put a few toys in each box and put them in a closet with a hook high on the door, that Josh could not reach, when he was running loose about the house -- about one-half his waking hours.

On Monday morning after breakfast, Stephanie washed the food off Josh's hands and face while he was in the playpen. Then gave him the Monday Box and after cleaning up the kitchen, she sat down to write.

After a few days of giving Josh the appropriate box each day, she found that it worked better if she kept the "Monday Box" near her typewriter and handed him just one toy at a time; when he became restless. After five or ten minutes, she handed him the second toy. She let him cry for five minutes before she gave him the third toy. While she was giving him the third toy, she took away the first and put in in the box. By rotating three toys she could extend Josh's time in the playpen or gated room to two or three hours at one session. After a brief walk outside (after his nap), Josh spent another two hours compartmentized. When father got home, he played running free.

As your child gets older, the rotation of toys becomes more important than the number or quality of the toys. A playpen or a chest full of toys, to which a toddler has free access, is not as interesting as being without a toy in a gated room or playpen and having one toy handed to him. With toys it is important to develop the "want."

Super saturation turns the child off. Salespersons have discovered that bringing out "something special" from the back room will make the customer buy when the full display will not. So it is with the toddler. He/she enjoys being handed a toy when he/she has none. Going to a large supply and being able to pick what he wants, only makes him disinterested in all toys. Parents who do not understand this seem to be frustrated about their pre-schoolers' blase attitudes toward toys.

WHAT KIND OF TOYS DO THREE- AND FOUR-YEAR OLDS NEED?

Toys that allow the use of the pre-schooler's imagination are the best. Packing cartons or large wooden boxes made into large blocks as described in the chapter THE DAY CARE CENTER are simple, inexpensive toys that allow the pre-schooler to imagine that he or she is in an elevator, a boat, an auto, or some very secret place. The make believe changes every few minutes. Such simple toys have lasting effects on the pre-schoolers which extend into the school years.

In your choice of toys, do not try to imitate at home the toys that your pre-school child may be exposed to in a well equipped nursery school or day care center. Do something different.

A single rope attached to a strong limb with a large knot or a rubber tire at the bottom makes a more intriguing swing than the usual park variety. It's also less expensive. Be sure to drill several holes in the bottom of the tire so it won't hold rain water.

A dump truck load of sand is more inviting than a sand box full of sand for children to play in. Although the pile may not please the neighbors in the manicured suburb.

At a day care center that I visited about one-half of the three- and four-year olds spent their time in the play yard with the live caterpillars that were crawling on the leaves of the bushes in the play yard. The caterpillars were favored over the swings, jungle gyms, and the wooden boxes that were piled like blocks.

More than toys the three- and four-year olds enjoy nature walks, where they can collect stones, sticks, frogs, toads, injured or dead birds and mice and moles. The four-year old becomes absorbed in the phenomenon of death. He or she is ready for an explanation. It becomes preparation for learning about eggs, hatching, birth and lactation. All this precedes explicit sexual education which should begin in the early school years and describe the habits of animals. Living with animals, or frequent visits to farms or farm zoos are interesting and educational for all ages.

Life at the seashore where the pre-school children can observe minnows, crabs, starfish, shells, birds, etc. is continually fascinating. On a windward shore or on an inland lake or quiet creek with a beach, the flat-bottomed row boat is excellent for the pre-school child. The row boat is attached to a long line so that it can be pushed out to float, but not over the child's head before he/she has learned to swim. The getting in and out, the pushing and pulling develops the knowledge of balance in a boat. Then the pre-school child learns to paddle and then to row. The flat-bottomed boat is still staked out (tethered) on a 30-foot line. After they have learned to row and swim, you will find them holding up oars with their jackets attached to catch the wind -- sailing before the wind. Most cannot master the art of sailing, however, before the age of eleven.

Fishing should be introduced with a hand line rolled up on a piece of wood. Rods and reels are too complicated for the pre-schooler. They are always getting tangled so that they become over dependent on adults to get them untangled. Simplistic ways to compete with nature, getting into trouble and out of it on their own have more lasting value. Catching crabs with a piece of string tied to an uncooked chicken neck will fascinate the preschool child for hours. The long line with a hook and worm attached to a long twig, as a pole, is poetic and adequate for the young child.

It is better when the parents give their children animals to take care of instead of expensive toys. But it is easier for the parents to give toys. Animals require work by the parents because the children cannot take full care of animals until after their tenth birthday. Dogs have saved pre-school children's lives many times, but parents must supervise their care. Small animals die when parents fail to supervise. Pre-school children helping in their care learn at a young age to face responsibility, success or failure, life or death.

Near where I practiced, there is a "boys club" that has been operating at a profit for over 60 years (three generations). It specializes in "hyperactive pre-school boys and girls" that ordinary nursery schools can not handle. They always have a sway back lazy horse and a tame cow, sometimes with a calf, that the children help take care of. It always amazes me how successful this nursery school is in calming the hyperactive pre-school children when the ordinary nursery schools fail.

When I have been able to convince families to acquire large animals: a donkey, cow and calf, a horse for the children to care for (over ten); both the parents and children have thanked me for the rehabilitation it has given them.

When you feel compelled to buy an expensive toy for your pre-school child, buy an animal instead, one that is different from your neighbors. Then help him/her take care of it. Also if you feel like taking a motor boat ride with your pre-school child, hire a row boat. Let your child participate helping you row while exercising your large muscles. Such motorized toys as go carts, motorbikes, motorscooters, outboard motors run by children often make them "smart aleck" when it doesn't kill them. Tragedy can happen in an instant, even with supervision.

CHAPTER XVII
JEALOUSY

It is wrong to try to punish or verbally chastise your two-year old for jumping into the playpen and stomping on the baby. If you do, it will only drive his jealousy underground. He will be sneaky about what he does to his younger brother or sister when your back is turned. He won't understand until he is four that he isn't allowed to hit with a stick or any object.

The two-year old will normally dump his truck into the small baby's crib either from "love" or "jealousy". The four- or five-year old, who has not been compartmentized, will also bother the baby out of jealousy or to get his parents attention. Neither a scolding nor a spanking will cool jealous behavior. The older child feels that a spanking is better than being ignored. Jealousy is a reaction to a pain of separation, and obeys a kind of equal-and-opposite law that is familiar to physical forces. The pain of separation is felt by the older child because the parents must now divide their time and devote a lot of time to the baby. Jealousy gives a person a kind of power and strength; they can "get even".

So jealousy is a fact of life. You cannot spend less time with your baby or try to reason a suitable compromise with the older but under four-year old child, and spanking him just increases the pain and forces a reaction of more and greater jealousy. Try kindness, understanding, protection, and some creative theatrics.

Rather than spanking the older sibling, it is better to pre-empt jealous behavior by using a hook on the door, where the baby naps or sleeps. Or replace the solid door of the nursery with a screen door. You can also keep the little baby in a playpen with a protective cover. Try a crib net as used in hospitals.

Several ingenious fathers bought two playpens and placed one upside down on top of the other. They tied them together in two or three places. The babies spent half of their waking hours protected this way.

I have observed that boys are more overt in their feelings of jealousy: "We don't need the baby." Girls and women, on the other hand, will just watch or hold a baby for hours. My beloved by all, office nurse Blanche Watt, now of 94 years, used to tell me after a busy day: "Well I did get to hold two babies." A few school girls would stop in to see the new babies. Sometimes they didn't get home for supper and had to be scolded. Many girls seem to have latent built-in "mother instinct." They want to help, and they get pleasure from helping, but their ways of helping may be inappropriate.

The pre-school girl is taught to love the new baby. She follows the examples of the other grown-ups visiting the baby. She hugs and kisses and wants to hold the baby. She plays with the baby's hands. Suddenly with great excitement, she pushes the baby's fingers backwards. She wants to see the baby cry. Love turns to experiment. Jealousy forces her to "get even", perhaps for all the pain the baby's pleasure and attention causes her. She is fascinated. She trembles. Her excitement is confusing. She states vehemently, "Send the baby back to the hospital."

If she is punished for abusing the baby, her love turns to hate. Understanding the confusion the child feels helps, because the toddler has conflicting emotions and the impossible problem of sharing of "Mine and Thine". The under four-year old can't understand sharing as well as being shared. The parent is forced by the reality to share their love between the baby and the child, especially if measured in time spent with each. If there are increased hugs and kisses all around, the sharing is a little less distinguishable, and so is the jealousy.

Mothers who are nursing the toddler as well as the new baby don't witness this love-hate emotional conflict. The toddler just goes to his mother and nurses for a few moments. That solves everything. There is enough all the time. Sharing is indistinguishable.

When you bring your new baby home, grab your older child and hold him or her. Hug him in the rocking chair. Kissing and cuddling helps. Explain that as the older child, he came first and nothing in the world can replace him in your heart. The day that he was born was the happiest day of your life. Nothing can ever change that. A younger brother or sister can never replace an older brother or sister.

Try to do all this before the older child hits his little brother or sister. Repeat this performance many times even when the older child isn't thinking of hitting the baby. The older child can never have too many hugs and kisses. These help him with the confusion of being divided, feeling the frustration of Mine and Thine, of sharing; all painfully frightening feelings until after he is four years old. After four, they may still be frightening, but they can at least be thought about and discussed.

When you are too late and the older sibling has already made baby brother or sister cry; then reverse your behavior. Cuddle the baby and turn your back on the culprit. Explain to the little baby, when he or she stops crying, in a language that the "big brother" (the culprit) can understand. But don't look at the perpetrator.

"He didn't mean it."

"Your big brother loves you."

"When he is older, he will protect you."

"He'll outgrow his animal instincts."

"Gerbils fight."

"Puppies fight."

"Cats fight."

"Horses kick and bite each other and then whinny

pathetically for three days when they are separated."

"He has to grow more so that he won't hit."

"He can't help himself at his age."

"He really loves you."

"He will learn to control his jealous impulses."

Go on and on in a soothing voice, cuddling your youngest but never once glancing at your oldest for whose benefit you are talking. Ham it up, but never catch his eye. The more you practice the better actor/actress you will become. Remember, by ignoring the oldest who is over four years old, you are encouraging him to reflect, or think about the past. It must be as recent as possible, for active short term memory, is powerful, but newly acquired. This is where he sorts out the feelings into a way of feeling, which is an idea, or a thought with some sort of pattern.

Some would argue that you are just making the oldest feel guilty. Not really. A tiny fraction of the experience would evoke guilt in the toddler. We must first convince the toddler that there is a crime, because he is acting out of jealousy which bypasses guilt. Jealousy is getting even, a fantasy with the irrational pain that one feels with separation, with rejection, or of sharing. Talking soothingly and rationally to the infant, the victim, and letting the culprit hear is exposing the irrationality of this jealous act. Thus magically making it rational. The culprit is also soothed in a way by being able to listen and by not directly being confronted.

The greater the intelligence of the older brother or sister, the more intense are the feelings of jealousy. Pity him. In my 42 years of practice, I have never seen an older brother or sister seriously hurt a younger brother or sister when he or she used only the weapons that he or she was born with: teeth, hands and feet. The child cannot concentrate long enough to inflict a serious injury; for the same reason that he has trouble controlling his jealous impulses -- the nerve fibers are still in the process of being covered (myelinated) with insulating cells that prevent them from shorting out before the message is sent.

All the important injuries from children fighting are from instrument: sticks, stones, knives, and guns, etc. "He hit me with an instrument, " -- my children always got my attention by saying that.

"An ounce of prevention....." Keep your baby away from the sibling by physical barriers when you are unable to monitor all activity. Horse trainers never let a multi-million dollar racehorse run in the same pasture with other horses. The risk is too great.

CHAPTER XVIII

SOME COMMON QUESTIONS AND OBJECTIONS CONCERNING COMPARTMENTATION

"I feel guilty about compartmentation"

You should not feel guilty about separating yourself from your preschool children. You will find your are not as tired when you compartmentize and so you will be more energetic and relaxed with your children. The time you spend with your pre-school children will become "quality time".

Don't let your friends talk you out of compartmentizing.

"I want my child to develop initiative and not be stifled by being confined in a playpen."

This is an objection that I have heard for many years. The advice that a child's initiative is stifled by being in a playpen for four hours daily is a myth of the worst sort. The facts point towards the opposite. The development of initiative is enhanced by compartmentation.

In my study it was always interesting when the teachers could tell who had been compartmentized and who had not. In many cases, the differences in initiative persisted into adult life.

It is unfortunate that the bad behavior of the two year old does not manifest itself until several months after compartmentation has been discontinued. If the majority of young mothers understood this cause and effect relationship, they would never give up keeping their children in the playpen., gated room, or fenced yard for part of their waking hours.

"How can I deal with my anger?"

Even children who have been compartmentized will bug their parents. Rob, his brother, his mother and father all had spring colds. Mother got it first, then Rob caught it, and then little brother caught it. Rob was four, and couldn't go to nursery school. He wasn't very sick and he didn't need the doctor, but he had to stay in. There was no good place to play, at least not big enough for Rob, so he would run and jump in the living room. His mother would ask him to play in his own room, but that was not big enough for running and jumping. This didn't bother mother very much until the end of the day. Then they really seemed to get on each other's nerves. Mother knew she should let him run in the living room so that he could let off more steam, but she was trying to sell the house and buyers were coming two or three times a day. She had to keep the house neat. At the end of the day, Rob started asking a lot of questions. What is this for? What is that for? When you press the button the light goes on, right? His mother was tired and Rob himself was tired. He seemed to deliberately ask these questions to see if he could get her to lose her temper. Being a good mother, she would try to restrain herself and answer his questions. Finally, at one very legitimate question, she just blew her stack. She said, " I'm very tired and I have been trying to show this house; your father isn't home yet; you've asked me many questions that you know the answer to, and if you don't stop questioning me, I'm going to spank you and you go to bed."

Well, she felt better after the air was cleared. Rob, of course, cried. Then she fed and hugged him and kissed him and told him that she loved him and they made up.

Repeated questioning is a common way that children bug their mothers. It should be a general rule for mothers not to hold themselves in. They should try to figure out why the child is asking these multiple questions. If the mother thinks her child is just trying to get her goat, she should tell him so. A very frank confrontation without anger is the best way. She should say, "Rob, I know you want to learn and you learn a lot by asking questions. I like to answer your questions because I want you to learn a lot, but right now I am tired. I am trying to sell this house; your father isn't home yet; you're tired because you haven't been outdoors; you're getting over your cold; and I think it would be good if you didn't ask me quite so many questions at this time." You will feel better and your child will probably stop pestering you because he'll realize he can't make you explode. If you make an open confrontation with all the cards face up, you will be better off in the long run.

There is a lot of hard work and deprivation involved in being a parent; Doing laundry, cleaning up messes, cooking, stopping fights, drying tears, reading, strolling around zoos and museums, trying to save money for college and trying to make enough time to sit down and just enjoy your children. Certain problems are created by trying to deny your fatigue and crossness. The child too, will hide his feelings of anger toward you, but they will show up as fears of insects, of going to school, of being separated from his parents. Don't ever feel that your antagonistic feelings are too horrible to admit. A child is happier around a parent who is not afraid to admit that he or she gets angry. Justified anger clears the air.

It is no disgrace to work so hard that you are tired. So, don't be ashamed to admit it. Mothers who try to be noble when they have a legitimate reason for being angry are likely to overdo the punishment when they finally explode.

I don't think that directing anger toward a child under four is justified. The things he does that make you angry are probably the result of natural exploring urges. Rather than waste time getting angry at the child, you should remove the objects that he is touching. Stop expecting him to share his toys in general. Don't expect more of him than he can give, according to his developmental level. This is compartmentation, and if you practice it your life will be more relaxed and happier.

Rob's mother was caught unprepared. She didn't have an alternative plan to distract Rob from bugging her -- like a picture book, or watching T.V., or the presentation of a different toy. Any one of these positive efforts would have precluded the threat of a spanking. A mother who plays martyr and finally explodes usually feels guilty afterward, and overcompensates by giving her child gifts or letting him walk all over her. This is confusing to a child and can make him materialistic. Then he will deliberately provoke his mother to the point of anger so he will get something nice afterwards.

"What do I do if the baby cries whenever he or she sees me?"

Be very jolly and make believe that you don't understand that he or she wants to be let out. Break the crying spell by getting on your knees and kissing him. Don't hide from him and don't be afraid to be seen. He will get used to seeing you and staying in the playpen. Don't let him cry more than five minutes without breaking his crying spell. When you do go to him, do the minimum that will stop his crying. The moment he stops, withdraw.

When one of my mothers brought her 15-month old in for a check up, I praised her for keeping her daughter in a playpen. (She passed the 15-month Gesell test with flying colors).

"It wasn't easy. I had my daughter in a playpen in the back yard. She began to cry. I decided to let her out. As I was walking toward the playpen, my mother-in-law called from the upstairs window. She had been watching her. 'If I can stand her crying at my age, then you can too!' She had hit where it hurt -- my pride. I kissed my daughter. She stopped crying. I gave her a new toy which interested her. She remained in the playpen another hour."

If you are really having a rough time, re-read the advantages of compartmentation every time you are tempted to let the baby out. That will take your mind off the toddler's crying a little longer.

"When does a child understand mine and thine?"

About four years of age -- some bright girls seem to understand it at a younger age.

"Some believe a child can run free out-of-doors at two."

I believe that parents should fence them in or tether them outside until they are four years old.

"When both parents are very relaxed and both have the temperament to live in a nursery, do you still recommend compartmentation?"

Yes, for another reason. When an eighteen-month old runs loose all day long in five rooms, even when they have been made childproof, he becomes more tired and more irritable than the eighteen-month-old who has been compartmentized for four of her waking hours.

"Why four hours?"

Four hours is usually about half her waking hours. She is given the free run before lunch, and after her nap before she goes out-of-doors, and then after dinner until bedtime. This usually adds up to about four hours in which she is exposed to the adult "no" and four hours in which she is free from it. I have observed more overachievers reared in this way than when the whole house was made childproof and the toddlers had the run of it all their waking hours.

"Since my son is eighteen months old, isn't he too old for the playpen?"

Not unless he can climb out. But to get ready for that event, it would be wise to childproof a room. Put a gate in the doorway so that you give him relief from the boredom of the playpen.

"How can the crib be used as a playpen?"

Clarence was 18 months old when his mother brought him for a check up. She was in tears. "My husband's grades are not good enough to get his PhD this year. I'm so mad that he didn't say anything about it a few months ago while I was nursing Clarence.

He's very sweet with the baby, but Clarence is becoming a little devil. He flushed my husband's term paper down the toilet. I had spent hours typing it.

I can't keep Clarence quiet at night so that my husband can study. He has to go to the library. He is in the laboratory and classes all day. He doesn't sleep well. The baby gets him up every night. I wish we had never come to this university."

After doing some tests, I found that Clarence had developed several techniques of resistance and habits of disobedience.

"Why have you given up the playpen?" I inquired.

"We live in one room; there is no room for a playpen. There is barely room for my husband's desk, the baby's crib and our bed. It's called an efficiency apartment.

"Use your child's crib as a playpen and keep him in it for four hours a day."

"I've read that if you keep your child in his bed during the day, he won't want to nap or sleep in it at night."

"The crib can be used as a playpen, if the child is not kept in the crib more than four of his waking hours. He should be taken out and allowed to run indoors and outdoors for four hours a day. Toddlers thrive in both extremes. Compartmentation in the crib and free run -- equal time for each."

Clarence was brought back for a follow-up examination three months later. He passed the developmental tests ahead of his chronological age. He was sleeping better. He was friendly, assertive and cooperative. Father was doing better academically. Mother was able to type themes and earn an income.

Father won his PhD and got a job on the faculty. They bought a small old house. Later Clarence overachieved in school.

More than a hundred young families had similar experiences. They were students or Infant Welfare mothers residing in crowded living facilities, usually one-room efficiency apartments or boarding houses with kitchen facilities down the hall.

With mother's books and father's books there was no room for the playpen. They used the crib with the BEAR CAGE as a playpen and it worked. Their children were much more adaptable than those who ran loose all the time and were chastised continuously for tearing up their parents books.

"Do younger siblings always need to be compartmentized?"

I have a few scores of families where the older children were compartmentized and overachieved. The younger brothers and sisters were not because they wanted to run with their older brothers and sisters. Some of these also overachieved because the older siblings helped the younger ones understand the adult "no". When it was the other way around, the older child was not compartmentized, but the younger ones were, the eldest almost invariably underachieved and the younger siblings became very adaptable and overachieved -- other things being equal.

I have records of several families with ten or more children. In one, all were compartmentized and all overachieved; in another, none were compartmentized and none overachieved. In a few other families with ten or more, compartmentation was mixed, but adaptability and achievement seemed to have a positive correlation with compartmentation when the intelligence and temperament of each were comparable.

I have a hundred files of parents and children of mixed intelligence and nervousness which introduce other hereditary and environmental factors that affect adaptability and achievement.

"How can I teach my child to share?"

You shouldn't. The pre-school child does not understand what you are talking about. Direct orders will make children share and many (especially girls) will serve (which is a form of sharing) because they have watched their parents serving guests and family.

When children want the same toy in the nursery school, their attention is quickly diverted to another toy on a nearby shelf. There is no discussion of sharing. Experienced teachers and aides have learned that it is counterproductive to waste their prestige as teachers on such unteachable concepts.

In the home the child who owns the toy has priority. An older child should not be expected to share a toy with a younger sibling unless the older one wants to . Parents have to make sure that the younger child becomes reasonably enchanted with a substitute.

When an older child wants to play with a younger child's toy and the younger child doesn't want him to, the owner of the toy is again the boss. In this case also, the parents need to make sure the older child finds an appropriate substitute. Then usually the younger child reverses himself and wants the older child to play with his toy.

"What about T.V."

"Mom won't let us look at T.V. on school nights!" said this student coming out of a depression due to his parents' bitter divorce. It took his mother two weeks to enforce this rule (not hearing the T.V. while talking to him from work). Now he is proud of his mother's rule, and he is getting A's again.

Recently I read about " the boat children" from Vietnam who are now in prestigious universities. Their parents did not let them look at television during school nights.

Each family has to set its own guidelines for television watching. No more than one hour per day per child is a rough guide. It is still debatable whether murders, thefts, kidnappings, seductions, abandonments, tortures and romantic love stories hurt the well balanced child. Yet, we do know too much television makes the child dull and lethargic. They need action. Try to get the child out of the house and involved in walking, playing and other types of physical activity. If parents have the problem of watching too much television themselves, they should review their habits to see if they can partake in other activities with their child -- like reading to each other.

Radio stations devote most of their time to news broadcasts, sports and music. Classical music on the F.M. band is excellent for children especially when they are sick and it is too tiring for them to watch television. Watching television takes more energy than listening to the radio.

Parents can help children decide which movies to see. A child under seven doesn't need to go to the movies at all. Some great men and women leaders have never been to the movies.

For the most part, cartoons on TV are geared toward selling toys and food through children. Cartoons, like comic books for the preschooler, should be free from violence.

One father who sent his children to me told me he never had a TV in the house. His five children watched TV only when they visited their friends in the neighborhood. This father thought that none of the programs were worthwhile. Not everyone will go to that extreme. But the importance of reading and interacting with children cannot be overemphasized. The purpose of compartmentation is to give the child time to grow in his own world at a comfortable pace. He or she should never be left alone in the playpen to watch TV for hours; to be bombarded by sights and sounds. Any TV watching should be supervised and controlled, but most importantly, limited to a very short portion of the child's day.

It has been estimated that children spend more time watching TV than they do in school. And verbal SAT scores of high school students have been going down. I feel there is a correlation.

CHAPTER XIX
TOILET TRAINING

"I want tinkle", said two-year old Skip pointing to the toilet. The baby sitter, a loving spinster, had been putting him on the toilet daily for the past week. His mother took off his diapers and put him on the toiler. He urinated and climbed off.

"Why you little man!" exclaimed his mother, pleased and surprised.

Skip, 100% compartmentized had suddenly begun to imitate his father in various little ways. The way he squatted in front of the fireplace. The way he watched the fire.

Buzzie, same age, had never been compartmentized; fought his mother when she tried to put him on the toilet. On the advice of her pediatrician, she gave up toilet training.

If a parent did nothing about toilet training, a child would eventually imitate his parents in this function -- at two to three years of age. If the parents use a knife, fork and spoon to eat with, the child will do likewise.

If the parents use the woods as a toilet, the children will do the same. If they use an outhouse, the children will follow suit. Children will imitate their parents on the flush toilet although sometimes they have to sit on it backwards. They can hold on better and it fits better when they straddle it, sitting backwards. They don't think they are going to fall in.

Compartmentation helps the child in toilet training. He is not frustrated with the adult world because half his waking hours he has been separated from it.

If you change the diapers every two hours, so that he or she does not stay in soiled or wet diapers for long periods; then he or she will appreciate dryness. She doesn't want to wet. She will tell you. Then you leave the diapers off and she will imitate you on the toilet or go in a pottie of her own in the gated room. No fuss. When she tells you that she doesn't need the diapers at nap time, and then later at bedtime, then let her try napping without diapers. No rush. If this doesn't happen by three, let you doctor examine her. Children, like adults, like to be dry. They learn quickly that diapers are only temporary expedients. They are glad to be rid of them.

Barry's mother says: "My son has been compartmentized since he was six-months old. Barry is very friendly because adults aren't always at him with 'no, no's.' His life is organized; he knows what to expect. He eats very well and feeds himself completely. He has been toilet trained since fifteen months of age. Both of these accomplishments, I believe, have been helped by confined play. He is toilet trained because he is so regular. He doesn't tell me when he has to go; but nine out of ten times he holds it until I put him on the toilet because he knows when I am going to come to get him. He has learned to enjoy his own company, an asset which he'll have all his life. He is so conditioned to his room that when I tell him to go into this room to play, he often goes right in and about his business. I have a lot of time to myself, and I am easily able to finish all my work."

CHAPTER XX
THE SINGLE PARENT AND COMPARTMENTATION

In several instances, mothers and fathers are forced to raise their children alone.

In the few instances that fathers have been allowed custody of their children, I have urged compartmentation either in the home with a baby sitter or by using a day care center.

In my study, the children reared by single parents who breast-fed, and left their babies at the day care centers did as well, other factors being equal, as the children reared by both parents with 100% compartmentation and breast-feeding. It was the good "quality of time" that the working mothers or fathers spent with their children that helped prevent the techniques of resistance and habits of disobedience observed in the non-compartmentized children. The children, who ran free all their waking hours, wore their parents out. Mothers and children became so tired and irritable that all they could do was argue and fight. Compartmentation allowed mothers and toddlers to rest so that the "quality of time" remained.

EPISODE I

Priscilla was 17 when she dropped out of high school due to a lack of interest in studying because she had an unrecognized reading problem. On Saturday, she worked as a waitress at a restaurant near her house. She thought this was much more exciting than going to school. Priscilla was pretty with a quick smile and received generous tips. After several weeks a well dressed sales person asked her out. They fell in love and married after three months. Priscilla moved into her husband's single bedroom apartment. She continued working in the restaurant because they needed the money.

In the middle of her pregnancy, Priscilla found a note saying "I'm not the family type. I'm leaving." She could not face going back home. She was afraid and filled with grief and bitterness. But when she felt the baby move, her parental instincts forced her to react to her situation. The rent was due and she had to eat and take care of herself. She went back to work at the restaurant and was able to eat her meals there. Then she registered at a free prenatal clinic. When the resident in obstetrics examined her, he was concerned about the depth of her bitterness about her husband and referred her to the resident in psychiatry. From then on she saw both physicians at each prenatal visit. Under their supervision, she worked as a waitress up until the day she delivered her seven pound baby girl. She chose me as her private pediatrician and wanted to breast-feed her baby.

The resident psychiatrist suggested that a volunteer from a local civic organization call on her at her apartment to help her cope with the problems of being a single parent. The Junior League was running the Premature Baby's Milk Bank. Priscilla had lots of milk and she could donate. The

League helped get her settled in her apartment, left an electric pump with her and showed her how to collect and freeze the breast milk. She found a day care center and returned to work.

Priscilla nursed her baby in the morning. Then she left the baby off at the day care center with a bottle of frozen breast milk. She reported to work at seven. She got time off to nurse her baby several times during the day.

Priscilla brought her baby to me regularly and her child performed well. The volunteers visited her from time to time. Sometimes a volunteer would accompany Priscilla when she brought her baby to me for a check up. The baby was almost two years old and still breast-feeding.

One day the volunteer wanted to speak to me privately. She said that Priscilla is still very angry about her husband, the father of her baby, walking out on her. She thought that Priscilla was using breast-feeding to assuage her anger. Sometimes she woke the child to breast-feed. Whenever the volunteers confronted Priscilla with a decision, she would grab the baby, nurse her, and then answer the questions. They were all talking about this '"nervous nursing."

This confrontation surprised me. I knew that this particular volunteer employed a pediatrician who believed that a baby should not nurse more than one year. I had heard his say so at meetings. This was in the 1950's before many women began to take up breast-feeding and the LaLeche League recommended letting the child nurse as long as she wants to. There are still those who disagree.

Thinking of the breast-feeding practices in the pre-industrial societies, I found myself defending Priscilla. All my Gesell testing showed that Priscilla's baby was well adjusted and on schedule. Politely as I could, I told this bright very well organized volunteer that I thought , in Priscilla's case, we should let nature take its course. I must have convinced her because she employed me for her second baby whom she breast-fed completely. She had not been as successful breast-feeding before.

Priscilla continued to work in the restaurant six days a week. She went in later on Saturdays and left her baby with a friend. She was asked out on dates frequently, but was not interested in dating -- her baby was her life. Being on her feet all day, she was tired at night and she slept well. Her baby weaned herself and Priscilla gradually got over her hate and mistrust of men.

Eventually Joe began to eat lunch at the restaurant. He was single, quiet, unsophisticated and uncomplicated -- quite different from Priscilla's husband. They went on dates after the baby was asleep for the night.

Priscilla decided that her daughter should have a father. Her love-hate feelings about her ex-husband had cooled down enough that she could handle this uncomplicated steady relationship. Joe put a down payment on a lot and was planning to build a house on it.

Joe and Priscilla married and moved into Priscilla's small apartment.

Joe got a G.I. loan and started to build a small house, on weekends. It took two years to complete the house so that it was adequate enough to move in.

Priscilla had two more children: a boy and a girl. She dropped off her children in a day care center each day and continued to work. When they moved into their new home, she worked from five to midnight in a plush fish and steak house. Her husband looked after the children in the evening. Finally Joe added another wing for his mother. Priscilla now had a built in baby-sitter. Priscilla and her mother-in-law had always gotten along well; so the adjustment was minimal.

The children adapted well in school. The boy began clowning around in second grade. He made Donald Duck noises when it was time to read. Under my direction Priscilla gave her children some reading tests.[1]

The eldest, 12 years old passed both the eight year old and the sophomore reading test.

The boy, eight, failed the eight years old reading test. His younger sister six, almost passed. She read better than her older brother.

With my direction, the grandmother taught her grandson to read. The boy read to his grandmother right after supper for five days a week all through high school. When he went to college, he majored in law enforcement.

The oldest daughter became a beautician and eventually acquired her own shop. The younger daughter became a registered nurse. Each had successful marriages.

In Priscilla's case, compartmentation centered mainly in the day care center.

EPISODE 2

Madge was the only child of a widowed mother who lived and worked in another city. Madge was bright, attractive, efficient and 28. She managed a six person office. Her boss, Bill, was 38, dynamic and married. Bill and his wife had three non-compartmentized children under five. His home was in such a turmoil that he dreaded going there. He preferred to talk to Madge. After several months of seeing each other, Madge became pregnant.

Bill wanted to pay for her abortion and keep everything the same, but Madge wanted to have their child.

She got a job in another city with an insurance company. Bill insisted on paying for her apartment rent in the new city. She checked in with an out-patient obstetrical clinic of a teaching hospital. This university hospital

---

[1] The eight year old reading test which I give routinely to every school child consists of the words: go, stop, jump, happy, birthday, butter, believe, and receive. If they can read those words correctly at eight years of age, they usually have no trouble with reading.

maintained a boarding house for out of town unwed mothers. The pregnant women worked in homes with small children as mothers' helpers for pay until their due date. Madge gave up her job and moved into the boarding house.

After examining her eight pound baby boy, I told Madge how healthy he was.

Madge was different from many other unmarried mothers in that she wanted to keep her baby and breast-feed. My enthusiasm for breast-feeding made her choose me for her pediatrician. She did not want to go to the free clinic.

Madge named her son William. She told everyone that her husband was killed in Korea.

Madge became an ideal nursing mother. She followed orders beautifully. She took three one-hour naps the first month and two one-hour naps after that. There was no schedule. She nursed on demand. By four weeks, he was sleeping through the night.

When William was two months old, she wanted to go back to work. She thought she would return to the insurance company where she worked before. I recommended a day care center nearby. I told her how to judge its quality as described in the section: THE DAY CARE CENTER. When she visited, she found two small babies crying for twenty minutes before anyone went to see why they were crying. She would not subject William to that. A mother nursing her six-month old daughter lived in the same apartment building. She consented to take care of William and to breast-feed him when he became restless. Since the apartment was within walking distance from her job, Madge was able to go there at noon and at coffee breaks to nurse William. Madge threw herself into her work and did well.

Like other completely breast-fed babies, William did the Gesell tests with friendly assertiveness a little above his developmental level. She was devoting herself completely to her job and breast-feeding her child. Whenever she got a letter from William's natural father asking her to return to New York, she felt the need to nurse William more often. She was still breast-feeding when he was three years old. Sometimes he would bite: "It was a sharp pain that passed from my breast down to my vagina."

Madge's friend, who looked after William while Madge worked, wanted to get a job. She needed the money. Madge got her a job with the insurance company. The mothers put their children in the day care center nearby. Both mothers felt their children could now handle the day care center.'

Throughout her life, Madge raised William as a single parent. She read to him and he to her almost every evening. On her days off, she took him to all the parks, museums and libraries. Eventually, William won a scholarship.

EPISODE 3

Jean was adopted as an infant by a wealthy older couple who lived in the country. At the graduation dance from an exclusive girls school, she met a first-year law student. It was love at first sight. After several dates, they were married.

The newly weds set up housekeeping in a one bedroom flat at the law school. It was partly paid for from the bride's allowance. Their first son was born within a year and three more were born 18 months apart. She breast-fed them all for a few months.

Jean thought marriage would be parties -- not studying every night in law school. After her husband graduated, she expected more from him than preparing briefs every night as a young lawyer. She did not understand why her children were so mischievous. She shouted and slapped and tied their bedroom doors to keep them in their bed. The father thought that they should have "due process", but he did not understand what one should expect from a child at a given age. Both parents rejected compartmentation. Both were ineffective. Jean, who stayed at home with the " little devils", lost her self-esteem and became depressed.

I recommended psychiatric counseling for Jean. It immediately lessened the stress. The psychiatrist suggested that she volunteer her services at a nearby army base: to talk to soldiers coming home from the war. She hired sitters and volunteered two days a week. This was Jean's way of practicing compartmentation.

Suddenly the psychiatrist, whom she had known for over two years, died of a heart attack.

While doing her volunteer work, she met a sergeant. He had developed a reputation about camp. He had beaten a soldier with his fists almost to the point of death. The soldier was hospitalized. A court martial cleared the sergeant of criminal charges.

Jean told her husband that she wanted a divorce and he could keep the four children. She ran away with the sergeant.

After the father got over the shock of his wife's leaving him, he put his children in a day care center and began to learn how to raise four boys as a single parent. With the help of sympathetic neighbors, he was able to set up a household routine.

He learned to cook, clean, make beds, dust, wash, dry, mend and sort clothing.

He was faithful about their check-ups. They performed better than they ever had. They went to the day care center after school until the age of 12 years.

EPISODE 4

At 2:30 one morning, I got a call. "Come quick, my wife died after nursing the baby."

When I got there, the distraught young father and both sets of grandparents were in semi-shock. They were taking turns walking with a healthy four-month old baby boy who smiled at me.

The fire department had taken the mother's body to the hospital for an autopsy. It seems that the baby had awakened in the middle of the night. He usually slept through. His mother nursed him back to sleep. Then she complained of a terrible headache and went unconscious. Her husband gave her artificial respiration as did the fire department. Her doctor said that she had died of a cerebral hemorrhage. They wanted me to show them how to feed the baby a bottle. He had never had one. He had been completely breast-fed.

We found bottles, nipples, and powdered milk that were advertising samples. We boiled water and sterilized the bottles and the nipples (in a closed jar) and gave the baby his first bottle. He took it as though he had been doing it all his life. It showed how foolish it used to be to prescribe a freedom bottle so that a breast-feeding baby would get used to a bottle. Sometimes called a "gad about bottle."

The father's mother stayed for two weeks. Then they all had to get back to work. A middle aged widow was hired as a housekeeper. Before the baby became mobile, I taught her the art of compartmentation. This housekeeper liked the concept. It made her job easier. She told me that she wished that she had known about compartmentation when her own children were toddlers.

When the father brought the baby to me, he always tested well, free from techniques of resistance. His adaptability was as good as that of the other toddlers who were 100% compartmentized and living at home with a mother and father.

Fathers can rear children as single parents as well as mothers if they practice compartmentation or a facsimile.

CHAPTER XXI
DAY CARE CENTERS

"I would go on relief before I would put my baby in a day care center," said one mother of a year old daughter. Divorced, she had gone back to work in the store that her father had founded. Her baby was a few weeks old when she returned to work. Her neighbors had a four year old daughter and took care of her infant as well.

"They don't pick up the babies when they cry. I won't subject my daughter to such neglect."

This young mother had more confidence in her neighbor than she had in the licensed day care center in her neighborhood. Many young mothers feel like this mother. Especially if they are breast-feeding and the day care center is not enthusiastic about her coming in to breast-feed at her lunch hour.

Many of the "experts " say that mothers should stay at home and take care fo their babies while they are babies. But many mothers have to work. They may be single parents, fathers have deserted the mothers, are alcoholic, or have sea duty. Or mothers need to work to supplement the family incomes. Mothers may have spent several years preparing themselves to be self supporting. Before they are too old, they want to have babies and breast-feed. They feel that they can not indulge themselves in the luxury of staying at home and breast-feeding. Their careers are too demanding. They must finish their internships or go for the vice presidency. Nursing a baby is not going to stop them. In fact they have become more competitive since having a baby and breast-feeding. Sixty percent (60%) of the young American mothers want to continue in their careers and still breast-feed their babies. They should be encouraged. The urge will not go away.

How long should a baby cry before someone goes to the baby to see why he or she is crying? Five minutes? Ten minutes? 20, 30 or should you risk breaking your leg jumping over the furniture to get to him the moment he cries?

I asked this question to one of the founding mothers of the LaLeche League. Such information is helpful, when advising mothers about how long to let a child cry in the playpen; before going to him or her to break the crying spell.

"In our house, a baby doesn't cry more than five minutes" the veteran mother replied. This is a good rule of thumb that can be applied to the modern day care center as well as in the home.

I visited several licensed plush day care centers that did not measure up to that standard. It reminds me of the days when I began to practice; when 30 babies, in a central nursery, all began to cry at once about a half hour before feeding time. It became a loud chorus. Rooming in and going home early quieted this cyclic crying in the old fashioned central nursery.

There were three small babies crying at once in one scrubbed day care center I visited. It had attendants one to four, as recommended. Neither of the attendants, one was feeding and one was changing, went to either of the babies to rub her back or turn her over. The body was there, but not the spirit.

In another fancy day care center a year old stood at his crib and cried for 20 minutes. No one came to break his crying spell. The well dressed manager, who was showing me around, explained that this was the baby's first day. He is not "adjusted to the routine yet." Her attitude turned me off. I felt like hugging him.

Your child must not cry more than five minutes without someone trying to find out why he is crying. Check to see if the day care center that you are contemplating can indeed soothe a child's crying. If anyone objects to your snooping, find someone else to look after your baby. You do not want to use a facility that lets a baby cry to the point of exhaustion.

The physical plants of the day care centers vary greatly. It could be one room in an apartment that has been made childproof. It might be a small or large house. It might be a mobile home, part of a church or synagogue or a college campus. Those day care centers that belong to a chain, and are run from a far away city are housed in modern brick structures with many rooms, have child sized toilets, back yards, sandboxes, swimming pools, slides, swings and jungle gyms. They usually have the best equipment and the prettiest brochures. But they have much staff turn over.

If you choose one of these "deluxe" centers, I suggest that you ask your child's teacher how long she has worked at that particular center and how long she intends to remain.

The staffs at the church, synagogue, university and the independent day care centers are more permanent. Unfortunately those day care centers associated with the larger institutions usually have long waiting lists and do not take the children until they are toilet trained. They do not serve the single parent or the working mother.

I liked the independently owned and operated day care centers the best. Three in particular had the most friendly, assertive, and dedicated teachers. The high schools sent their students there for their child development laboratories. Two were arranged with corridors between windowed class rooms so that the visitors could observe without being seen. (Gesell had one way vision windows so that classes of 30 could observe.)

The equipment was simple and inexpensive. Besides the usual swings with soft seats, piles of sand, jungle gyms and slides. There were about 20 wooden blocks similar to what my children and patients used in the 40's and 50's. They measured 15" x 15" x 15". The edges and corners were sanded so that there were no sharp edges. Some of my patients' parents added boards that measured 10' x 8" x 1". From these basics the children made houses, forts, elevators, boats and bridges. You name it. Such toys can stimulate the imagination have more lasting interest than the expensive trucks, cranes, and trains in the toy shops.

When your child suddenly objects to going to a day care center--*INVESTIGATE*.

Julie was the mother of two: a girl of six and a son of three. Julie dropped off her son at the day care center every morning on her way to work. Her daughter walked to the neighborhood school. A bus from the day care center picked up her daughter and other children of working parents and delivered them to the day care center. Then the parents picked them up after work.

Suddenly the three year old son cried and didn't want to go to the center which he had been enjoying. Julie left him crying as she pulled away from the center. That evening his sister, aged six told the story: On the play ground an aggressive two and a half year old took a ball away from Julie's physical three year old. Julie's son got it back. Where upon he was attacked. Julie's son retaliated by dirtying him, scratching his face, and pulling out chunks of hair. For punishment, Julie's son was put in a dark room by himself for an hour.

Julie immediately withdrew both children. "I will save money on food rather than send them to that day care center. If it hadn't been for my daughter I would never have known what happened."

I think Julie should have known that something was wrong! Her son gave her the signal by suddenly "not wanting to go to school." In similar situations, where such detail cannot be obtained because the children are too young to tell; the "not wanting to go to school" will disappear after a heart to heart talk with the teacher; or a change in the day care. Remember, Julie's day care center was modern, licensed, and had a good reputation. It is still serving the working mothers needs; but not Julie's.

Before long, Julie got another job. Across the street in an old house, there was a day care center. Julie could wave to her children when they were in the play yard, have lunch with her son and observe him during her coffee breaks.

When they became "latch key" children they always called her at work. They were making A's. The son wants to be a doctor.

One good day care center asked for "swat permission: from the parents. Although it is better for the child's inner security for the parent and the teacher to win, when the child misbehaves; neither punishment, nor shouting, nor whistles would be necessary if the programming were geared to the growth of the child.

"What is best for the child must be the basis of every decision," said Bishop Hamilton West, founder of the Episcopal Day Care Center in Jacksonville, Florida. It was designated by the Bush Foundation of Yale University as one of the five best in the country relative to reducing family stress and building family strengths.

By describing in detail the program of this facility, I hope to help you find what to look for, and to demand, in the day care center that is convenient for your use.

When I visited recently there were 435 infants and children ranging in age from a few days to 5 1/2 years located at 5 sites. There were 26 groups housed in ten old but newly painted buildings. In every group the children were smiling or laughing. All day long I heard only one child cry. He was a three year old who bumped his head on the slide. The aide examined his head and kissed the hurt. Immediately he climbed the slide and with a twisted smile slid down again.

The room containing 15 babies, ranging in age from a few days to a few months, was supervised by a registered nurse. About half of the infants were on the floor with two aids who were also sitting on the floor helping the cruisers wash their toys in large shallow pans of warm soapy water. Many were smiling and squealing with glee. Some were sleeping in their cribs. A few were being fed. None were crying.

The one year olds were equally happy. One gray haired grandfather was sitting on the floor helping the toddlers wash their toys. All volunteers, if they are physically able, were encouraged to sit on the floor with the infants and one year olds. There was much giggling as the children helped wash the toys in warm soapy water. It reminded me how my small children, and now my grandchildren, were fascinated by the garden hose -- permissible in warm weather and the subtropics.

The smiles and laughter among the two year olds were also a revelation. Again both the teacher and her aide were sitting on the floor playing with the two year olds. Some were finger painting on large posters. Others were washing their toys in another large pan of warm water. If one child grabbed a toy from another, the loser's attention was quickly diverted to the many toys on the low shelves all around the room. Like experienced mothers, these teachers and aides did not waste time teaching the two year olds "to share". Also they did not teach "mine and thine" until four. A concept that is not well understood until they develop an ethical sense at eight years of age. In this center, I saw no "terrible twos". Everyone was happy.

Observing the structured education of the three, four, and five year olds was a unique experience. After breakfast and clean up, the mornings were divided into three 45 minute periods: art, discovering, housekeeping, blocks, and manipulations and language and mathematics concepts. Groups of 15 children experienced this curriculum through play. They were grouped by developmental level. The teacher remained in her class room with her teaching materials. Every 45 minutes the teacher cared for a new group.

The aide moved with the same group of 15 children all day; unless one was removed for speech therapy, developmental examination, or computer work. The aide was responsible for moving as well as toileting. With the younger children, this took 17% of her time; with the older 6%. After a hot noon meal, there was a nap period and later a afternoon snack.

Between 3:30 and 4:50 there were a variety of activities that the aide still piloted her group through, according to the children's developmental level and interest. There was music, songs, rhythm activities, dramatic plays, crafts, cooking, library films, learning games, and outdoor play. Every day was similar, but every day was different.

In observing 435 infants and children located in five centers all day, I never heard a teacher or an aide raise her voice and very little time was spent in transition. It was the same with the day care centers associated with the churches and synagogues but not with many others. The movement of children was sometimes accompanied by shouting. One teacher had a shrill whistle. At a pre-school I observed a teacher or aide would get an unacceptable grade for shouting.

The teacher taught a new group of children every 45 minutes; three, four, and five years old in developmentally based groups. This shift gave the teacher a varied experience. The shift gave the aide, who remained with the same group of children, the experience of watching her 15 children's responses to the different activities and teachers. The aide was responsible for maintaining the class lists and the roll book changes. Also the individual learning packets for each child was carried by the aide from room to room.

The system of grading the staff is an incentive for excellence. The executive director or a child development specialist spends at least half a day with each teacher and aide at work at least every three months.

The way the child development specialist records his/her findings is unique in this wonderful day care center. There is a grid of small squares. Each square represents two minutes of time. The name of each child in the 15 pupil group is recorded opposite a square along the ordinate. The time of day is recorded horizontally (abscissa). A code of performance is filled in for each child for every two minutes of the 45-minute session: on task = 1; off task = 2; wandering = 3; disruptive = 4.

If every member of the group has ones (1) for every two-minute period, then all the pupils are on track. If there are a lot of higher numbers for many, then the teacher must adjust her program to fit the children's needs. If one child gets many 3's and 4's, then that child has to be examined developmentally to find why he/she doesn't fit. Is it the teacher? The aide? The program? Or the child? The Reddy F.I.T. chart named in honor of its inventor, Dr. Nancy Reddy (past director of the Episcopal Day Care Center and now a consultant), has proved to be a non-threatening way to train teachers. As a part of the child's permanent record, it becomes a practical way to match the curriculum to the needs of each individual child.

When a child sits and stares off in space, looks out the window, wanders around the room without purpose, punches another child, or is disruptive; the teacher and aide are graded downwards. Even if a child has to repeat her question to an aide or a teacher, both are marked down. When a teacher gets an A, she gets a $200 government bond and every other teacher and aide in the building gets an additional $50 bond. Thus the staff shares their expertise with each other in their system that rewards teamwork.

The grade "D" is unacceptable. Everyone helps the teacher or the aide to improve her grade. If, after a month, she cannot get her grade up, she is replaced. *"The good of the child is the basis of every decision."*

During the free choice activities, the aide with the help of the teachers, reviewed each child's progress. Each child took home some of his/her creation every night. The level of the child's development determined whether or not the child belonged in the group to which he was originally assigned. Or should he or she be moved up with more developmentally advanced children or down to be more comfortable with children of the same level. The abilities within each group became fairly homogeneous in this very ideal day care center.

A few mothers have told me that children graduating from the highly structured pre-school programs have trouble adjusting to first grade in public school. They had been taught to cross the capital "J". The public school wanted the "J" uncrossed.

In my Gesell testing of the first, second, and third graders; I could not tell whether the child had attended a highly structured day care center or had been watched by a mother (not structured at all) in her own home in a childproofed room or play yard.

Although my Gesell testing could not determine whether the child had attended a structured or a non structured day care center; it could easily spot the child who ran free at home without spending part of his waking hours in a playpen, behind gates or in a fenced yard. The techniques of resistance that developed in the non compartmentized persisted into grammar school.

As a mother, it is more important that you send your child to a day care center, that is less than perfect, than to keep him at home non compartmentized.

The day care center, or the unlicensed mother, who looks after her neighbor's children as well as her own, while she does the family washing or mending, usually creates a better environment for the pre-school child; than the natural mother who lets her children run free all day long. The latter confuses children because she gets tired, angry and feels abused. It jeopardizes marriages as described in **"The Golf Widow."**

The techniques of resistance and habits of disobedience, developed in the non-compartmentized, persisted into adult life as lack of ambition as described in THE EPILOGUE.

In the eighties one out of two American marriages end in divorce. The children of divorce are being reared by single parents, as was described in that section. One parent is taking care of them between marriages or both parents are working. The day care center is becoming an increasingly more important way of rearing children as we approach the 21st century.

I have found fault with almost all day care centers but only to try to make them better. In the same way the quality of life with the pre-school child at home is better with compartmentation.

Child abuse is as old as recorded history. Almost all child abuse occurs in the home where there are non-compartmentized children and sick parents. Abuse is lubricated by the parental use of drugs, usually alcohol. And by those parents who were abused themselves as children. To blame the day care centers is inaccurate, unfair and a step backwards.

Smart working mothers demand good quality day care centers. They know that the staff is more important than the physical plant. Eye ball to eyeball they will confront the center they are about to hire. " will this person take good care of my baby?" " Do I get good vibes?" If you don' t, look further. Check your observations repeatedly as Julie did. You will improve the quality of care most significantly; not by passing laws (passive expectation), but by choosing carefully (active participation). Supply and demand in the market place really is an important factor. The "bond of mother love" gives you better judgement than you may think you have.

CHAPTER XXII

CAN COMPARTMENTATION BE OVERDONE ?

"He's a dummy."

"He is not dumb; he's my baby," replied another enthusiastic young worker in a crowded orphanage. These two teenage workers were spoon feeding eighteen month old babies in their beds.

This by-play occurred frequently among the young ebullient workers in this over crowded orphanage. The feeding crews fed a group of infants and toddlers and then moved on to the next group. The diaper changing crews followed. When all were fed and changed, it was time to start all over again. There was no time for these warm hearted young ladies to play with the individual children. All they could do was feed and change.

These irrepressible young people would play games. One would accuse; the other would defend. Every time the defender passed the baby, who had been called "dumb", she would speak to, pat or hug "her little baby". Within a few days the little toddler would smile and laugh looking for the attention. No longer could anyone call him a "dummy".

I witnessed this scenario when I was invited to perform my modified Gesell tests in this large orphanage which was contemplating closing. The management was considering placing the children, who were awaiting adoption, in individually selected foster homes rather than in the present over crowded institution. Many of the infants were received by the institution soon after birth where they awaited adoption. Most were adopted by the age of two years.

All the infants and children were well nourished. They were kept in crib beds all day and all night. They were picked up only when fed a bottle and solid food and when they needed a diaper change. The crib sides were 24 inches high or 20-inches above the mattress. After one and one-half years, the crib sides were 48 inches high -- like the cribs in the children's hospitals. The orphanage staff knew that aggressive two-year olds can climb out of the cribs with 20-inch sides and fracture skulls and break arms. As in the hospitals, the nets covered the tops of the cribs to keep the climbers in, as described in YOUR CHILD'S CRIB.

The results of my Gesell testing of the children under one year of age were similar to those obtained in my office testing the compartmentized children living at home. There were no techniques of resistance or habits of disobedience evident as in those children who crawled around the house all their waking hours (non-compartmentized).

In those tested in their second year of life, there was a distinct difference from those toddlers who lived at home.

Those who spent 24 hours a day in their cribs during their second year of life, showed a definite lack of enthusiasm in performing the Gesell tests: they put the pill in the bottle at 15 months, made a tower of three blocks at

18 months and six at two years. They performed normally, but with indifference. Their eyes seemed dull and heavy-lidded. There was no sparkle of joy. No smiles, but no fear. No techniques of resistance as seen in the non-compartmentized two year olds living at home. They reminded me of Homer's description of Ulysses meeting with "the mild eyed lotus eaters."

When I reported my findings to the administration, they told me that they didn't have enough help to play with the children. They could only feed and diaper.

The supervisor went on to say that some times an infant would not gain well. Then the attending pediatrician recommended immediate placement in a foster home to keep him from "languishing to death." The baby was suffering from "institutional amentia." [1]

After placement in a foster home he immediately began to gain weight and performed the Gesell tests normally.

In my private practice, there was one mother whom the nurses said "acted crazy". She made unpleasant remarks to the girls in the office. Nothing pleased her. Everything was bad. Her sons were exceedingly polite and cooperative. They obeyed her instantly. The three and one-half was kept in a gated room eight hours a day. The 18-month old was in the playpen eight hours a day. I recommended four.

This over compartmentation made no detectable difference in the Gesell testing at the time that it was practiced nor in their over all achievement as adults. One became a lawyer; the other an executive after the Harvard Business School.

Did the excessive compartmentation in their formative years protect the boys from their "crazy acting" mother?

When I began the 40 year experiment, I chose four hours of running loose and being hugged and taught the adult "no, no"; four hours of compartmentation and four hours of being fed, washed and changed. The rest of the time the pre-school children slept.

All of my observations indicate this is an adequate time for the child to enjoy his or her own world and offer some time for parents to pursue their endeavors. I continue to recommend 4-hours a day with excellent success.

---

[1] Dr. Arnold Gesell, who began his work in 1911 in an orphanage, was one of the first physicians to describe "institutional amentia." Babies in an institutional routine did not get enough individual handling; when just their physical needs were being handled and there was no one to play with them. When such children were sent home or to a foster home, within a month they were normal again. There was no permanent damage. Within another month they shared the same techniques of resistance and habits of disobedience that their peers shared after running free all day without compartmentation. (In 1950 only 10% of American mothers practiced compartmentation or a reasonable facsimile of it.)

CHAPTER XXIII
FURTHER OBSERVATIONS OF MOTHERS

During the course of my 40-plus year experiment, I met many well educated mothers whose various ideas about compartmentation were completely opposed to mine. They did not want their children to be "confined" in a playpen at all. They thought it was cruel. If they could breast-feed for three or four years and "live in a nursery", they had adaptable children. Most could not. They seemed to have misjudged their abilities to "live in nurseries".

They left too many valuables around that became fair game for the pre-schoolers. Then they got too many "no's"; while running all over -- indoors and out -- all their waking hours. They developed techniques of resistance against teaching and became non-competitive.

Another group of older mothers had been self supporting for ten or so years before having children. Some held advanced degrees. These mothers became completely absorbed in motherhood. They wanted no part of compartmentation. Their latent maternal feelings had become so strong that they seemed to believe that they had to make up for lost time. They cuddled their toddlers all their waking hours. They gave them what they wanted when they wanted it.

A few were able to breast-feed for three or four years. Then their children remained adaptable. Those who were not breast-fed as toddlers, became "spoiled brats". They were called "menopause babies." They achieved even less than the non-compartmentized and non breast-fed children of the mothers who were half their ages.

When these older career mothers went back to work, their toddlers care was turned over to the relaxed care of those who were not so involved emotionally. Then the preschoolers became adaptable. The time that the mother spent with her children became "quality time." It usually took a month to turn them around -- so that the non-adaptable preschooler became adaptable.

Mothers in my experiment were usually attractive, happy and fulfilled in being mothers. Especially if they were breast-feeding. Some changed from childhood to womanhood over night. They seemed to be strong physically, carried their toddlers on their hips, in Gerry packs, or in slings. When they let their toddlers nurse as long as they wanted to, the preschoolers remained adaptable. When they weaned their toddlers, and did not compartmentize, they became non-adaptable. But there were fewer techniques of resistance than developed in the pre-schoolers of mothers who were twice the teenagers age -- if they had stopped breast-feeding and did not compartmentize.

Young mothers could quickly swoop and rescue their toddlers from dangers without saying a word. The older mothers tried to control their toddlers by voice commands which were ineffective and in the long run, harmful because of their ineffectiveness.

Teenage mothers usually did not accept the concept of compartmentation. Many did not try hard enough. Their sexuality and newly acquired chemistry of mother love dominated their thinking and anticipatory abilities. Some had not finished high school.

The teenage mothers, who did practice compartmentation, after stopping breast-feeding, produced children with unusual adaptability. They overachieved. It was beautiful to watch.

The teenage mothers, who went to work and put their children into the care of others (usually day care centers); those children also did well -- other things being equal.

CHAPTER XXIV
AFFECTION, AUTHORITY AND APPROVAL

To regain lost control you must live in such a way that your growing child receives AFFECTION, AUTHORITY, and APPROVAL every day. Most parents are nice, law abiding and are trying to rear their children properly. Their offspring get enough AFFECTION and AUTHORITY. It is APPROVAL that is hard to come by, even when their children are compartmentized in the pre-school years.

It takes more effort to undo the habits of disobedience than to prevent them. Yet this is the job of 90% of modern parents. Even the 10% who practiced compartmentation must work to maintain their control.

When toddlers have developed techniques of resistance and habits of disobedience, parents can get their pre-schoolers in control within a few days after establishing compartmentation. When older children resist learning, it takes longer. Parents have to do everything "just right" for months before their children begin to overachieve. Doing everything "just right" means that parents must learn in detail what their child is capable of doing at the appropriate age. Parents can get this information from old but worthy books: *Infant and Child in the Culture of Today, The Child Five to Ten, and Youth the Years from Ten to Sixteen,* by Dr.Arnold Gesell. Publishers.

By reading parents can learn in detail what their child is capable of understanding at six, at seven, eight, nine, ten and so on.

To expect the child of six to understand the "forced out" in a baseball game would be a mistake. Fathers should wait until their sons are eight before teaching baseball rules.

Your child begins an ethical sense at seven -- not at six. At six he or she is more awkward than at five. "He stumbles over a piece of string."

Children can work side by side with a parent at eight, but the parent should wait until ten before letting their children do chores by themselves. When you are so unwise, as to expect a solo performance at eight, you set the stage for the development of techniques of resistance. To expect too much too soon puts you in the position of NOT being able to give honestly the necessary daily APPROVAL. This lack leads to inappropriate AUTHORITY, and finally results in too little AFFECTION. Then the child goes to the peer group for all the needs. The peer group becomes the control.

To maintain communication and dilute peer group influence, cover your criticism with nine praises before you criticize again. Praise even when you have to hunt for a reason.

In two parent homes, whenever possible, fathers should avoid disciplining daughters who are over ten years old. Mothers should teach their daughters appropriate guidelines. Likewise mothers should avoid punishing sons when fathers can. Both parents should praise sons and daughters whenever it is deserved. Praise is a kind of celebration, so don't hesitate to praise in public; but please, punish in private. It works better that way.

After reading all you can about your eight year old, and after you think that you understand your child's level of development, then read about the nine and ten year old so that you are ready for the next stages of normal growth. Try hard to demand nothing above your child's age level for two years.

With the right combination of affection, authority, and approval most young children will overcome techniques of resistance or habits of disobedience. Yet changing your child's habits will take a lot of work and about two years of your time as parents. If you don't want to set the stage for a lot of work when your child is no longer a pre-schooler then begin practicing compartmentation when your child is still an infant. You will find yourself a parent in control before the week is out.

EPILOGUE

"If all my pupils were as good as those three, I'd be without a job, " exclaimed the principal of a grade school, referring to three of my patients who had been 100% compartmentized. As my little patients grew enough to go to school, I noticed and published a paper concluding that those who had been compartmentized as toddlers, were more adaptable in school and in the neighborhood.[1]

During the routine yearly physical examinations, after the age of ten, I asked each patient about his/her plans for life's work. Every serious decision was recorded and the age at which each choice was made. Any change was recorded when, either the original decision or the change, was not frivolous.

When these patients became high school students, their grades were recorded and adjusted as to whether or not they were accelerated (college preparatory).

Many more variables were recorded concerning the health, career, and earnings of the father; the health, education, career, and earnings of the mother; ease of conception, gestation, birth, and the infant's adjustment to extra uterine life including the landmarks of development. The collection of prospective longitudinal developmental data became my research career while I made my living practicing pediatrics.

The student's reading ability was tested every year. The amount of time a student spent reading: newspapers, magazines, and the number of books were recorded.

The Scholastic Aptitude Test (SAT) and the American College Testing (ACT), accidents, college grades, post graduate education, earnings, marriage, and divorce were all recorded.

The Research Department of the Evanston Hospital supplied me with a research fellow to program 294 variables on 639 patients into the computer at Northwestern University.[2] These patients had been followed prospectively from conception to adulthood. The transfer of this data was

---

[1] "The Pediatrician Examines the Mother and Child", *J.A.M.A.*, March 24, 1956, Vol. 160, pp.1033-1039.

[2] Due to the generosity of the Dee and Moody families, the Evanston Hospital was able to give research grants to premedical students to work summers under the direction of individual attending physicians, who were doing research in addition to making their livings in private practices.

Although the stipends to the students were small, the exposures to research were valuable learning experiences for them and of great help to the attending physicians.

finished after eight summers. The findings were presented to the professional staff of the Evanston Hospital June 1, 1981.

The SAT test scores were found to be a little above the national average. The boys did better in math and the girls did better in English. There were no significant correlations of the verbal SAT tests with preschool compartmentations but slight correlations with math. For good high school grades, there were significant correlations with high SAT scores and equally with high percentages of compartmentation. High SAT scores were associated with the admissions to the highly competitive colleges (Barron)[3] but not for college grades. For good college grades, there were significant correlations with the higher percentages of compartmentation. Sig=.0000: which means that there was less than a 1 in 10,000 chance for the correlation to occur by chance alone. A significance of 0.05 (5 in 100) is considered meaningful in biological work.

Similiar high correlations with compartmentation (sig=.0000) were found in the younger ages when the choices of careers were made; also for the competitive qualities of the careers (scientists, doctors, lawyers, engineers, etc.); later marriages, fewer divorces, and fewer accidents in the high school and college years.

Of the 352 whose earnings were evaluated after they had reached the age of 30 in 1970, only 12 (six men and six women) were making more than $50,000 per year -- mostly in sales. In this group there were no correlations with either compartmentation or SAT scores. The numbers were too small.

Of the 29 making $25,000 to $50,000, there were again significant correlations with compartmentation and the men earned more than the wormen.

Of the 106 making $15,000 to $25,000 annually there were significant correlations with compartmentation and the men and women were earning equally.

Of the 205 making less than $15,000, the men and women earned equally, but there were negative correlations with compartmentation. Many fewer compartmentized adults were making less than $15,000. The tables turned significantly.[4]

---

[3] *Barron's Profiles of American Colleges* published by Barron's Educational Series Inc., 113 Crossways Park Drive, Woodbury, New York 11797.

[4] These annual income figures were used as one element of worldly success by no means superior to others. Considering the limited funds and time and complication of the study, I thought this to be an easily measured and possibly verifiable unit. Since the incomes were queried in the 1970's, one might extrapolate a doubling of these income strata today in 1987.

Explaining the usefulness of these unexpected correlations, within a very complex number of factors that occur in bringing an infant to an over or under achieving adult, will have to await another book -- now being written. Also the rather bulky tables of numbers will be included. There I discuss my "homemade" ways to detect and correct a variety of difficulties. An important one is the reading difficulties "apparently developing" in high school.

My 25 years of experience in the rehabilitation of over 300 teenagers, who could not compete in the city or suburbia, is explained by case histories: how horses, cows, and donkeys were used as "therapists" in a ranch setting.[5]

My 42 years of practice have helped me in helping children overcome techniques of resistance to learning and habits of disobedience while living at home. It consists of teaching parents how to maintain control, or regain lost control, of their teenagers; especially as it concerns alcohol, drug abuse, and sexual activity.

Thus compartmentation in the preschool years, or facsimiles of it, may become a "leg up" during many good and bad experiences between infancy and adulthood. Breast feeding is associated with better than average health and gives the child important early doses of AFFECTION and APPROVAL. Compartmentation establishes a silent AUTHORITY and promotes ambition within the child. Also the father's sense of pride in his family, reenforces the infant's feeling of APPROVAL. The happy infant becomes a healthy child, this child a normal adolescent. The adult is what happens to these three.

---

[5]Dr. and Mrs. Kimball, with the help of his brother Donald and his wife Ruth, founded a residential ranch school in the foothills of the Ozarks in Zion, Arkansas in 1961. It is a public, nonprofit corporation called Easy K Foundation. Dr. Kimball is Chairman of the Board.

Glossary

abscissa — is the horizontal coordinate in a graph.

abhore, endure, embrace -- are the stages unwilling persons experience within gangs and other severe peer pressure groups. Albert Speer, an architect in prewar Germany, expressed these as the stages he went through in order to adapt. This negativity even when modified later by the two more positive feelings is devestating in its power especially for the child. As adults we may have to experience these stages in some hopefully minor way. A positive perspective, if only a memory, is important in deciding the last stage whether to embrace or reject. (see affection, ...)

affection, authority, and approval -- is an approach to others and an important way to manage emotions, opinions and appreciate ideas and personalities. It is also a way to think about yourself when it is projected upon you at a young age, or any age for that matter. It makes for a competitive, but positive attitude and perspective.

amniotic fluid — is the liquid that the unborn baby floats in inside the placenta.

barracuda — slang for a vigorous nurser.

Bilites — is a type of light therapy that reduces bilirubin (jaundice) in newborns.

compartmentation — the term is used in the navy. I remember feeling the relief behind the philosophy of the term off the coast of North Africa in WWII, when as we approached shore were signaled to hold position as we were in middle of mine field. I knew there were compartments within the hull. If we hit one we still had a chance. Later, I connected this with child raising. That safety should be in the design of child raising. To contain the problem before it becomes a crisis, while still allowing an amount of freedom according to the developmental age. It also relates to the confidence that both child and adult feel about themselves and each other.

fetologist — is an obstetrician or pediatrician specializing in the unborn child.

filly — is a young female horse.

foal — is a baby horse.

habit of disobedience — is a technique of resistance a child repeatedly uses becomes a H.O.D. The child uses this to defeat the authority who also habitually expects more from him/her than he can developmentally produce. (see technique of resistance).

meconium — is a dark green mucilaginous material in the intestines of the full term baby. It is a mixture of the secretions of the intestinal glands and the amniotic fluid.

myelination — is the process of a fat like cell structure forming an insulating sheath around transmitting nerve fibers.

neonatologist — is a pediatrician who specializes in the care of newborns and prematures.

ordinate — is the vertical coordinate in a graph.

oxytocin — is a hormone stored in the posterior lobe of the pituitary gland. It causes the ejection of milk and the contraction of the uterus.

posting — is to rise from and descend to the saddle in accordance to the rhythm of a horse at a trot.

prolactin — is the hormone that causes cells in the breast to secrete milk.

rapport — is a relationship of harmony and conformity to adult wishes.

resident physician — is a M.D. who is in a teaching hospital under professors learning to qualify as a specialist.

RhoGAM — is the trademark for a preparation of Rh (D antigen) immune globulin (a blood product) which when injected will prevent the mother from producing Rh negative jaundiced babies.

technique of resistance — is part of a child's natural over-defensive system that is designed to add to the protective mechanism especially children younger than four have. When the adult world threatens this child world, the child reacts to shield itself from all threats. He learns to categorically resist, to block out any influence from the outside. In effect the child resists learning itself. I began using this term in 1946.

Index

acne, 78-79
actress, learning to be, 31-32, 38, 163
adaptability, 192
adoption agencies and breast-feeding, 146
affection, authority, & approval, 190ff.
age when life work decided, 193
aide, in child care, 182-84
alcohol and pregnancy, 82
    facies, 82
    and breast-feeding, 124-25
allergic to breast milk, 145
allergy, 77-79, 129-33, 153-56
all in one bed, 148
alveolus, 87
American College Testing ACT, 193ff.
Amniotic fluid, 5
ampulla, 91
anaesthesia at birth, 100
anger, dealing with, 165-67
    in the child, 29-32
    sham, 38-39
animals, small, 160
    as teachers, 5-9, 160-61
aristocracy, 158

baby nurses, 109-11
barracuda, 91, 107
"bear cage", 12-15, 186
bed, putting child there, 12-15
beer, 97
bifidus factor, 77
biting & breast-feeding, 150, 153, 176
Bloom, Dr. Benjamin, 157-58
bold aggressiveness, 40
bone age, 144
boredom, overcoming, 16
bottle occasionally, 128, 143-44
brassiere, 79-80
breast, abscess & plugged duct, 137-9
    anatomy & physiology, 86-87
    emptying, 113
    lumps, 137
    pumps, 102, 112, 129-33, 151
    shape, 79-80
breast-feeding, and adoption, 145-46
    and appearance, 78-80
    and infant biting, 150, 153, 176
    and entertaining, 117, 126
    and feelings of mother, 73-77
    and marriage, 80
    and medication, 144
    and moving, 147
    and traveling, 117, 125
    and working, 150-51
    immediately after birth, 88-90
    Is it sexual?, 149-50
    prolonged, 153-56
    psychological help, 152-53
    the return to, 81
    to cure allergy, 153-56
    value of, 77-81
    when to stop, 1, 151-56
    with silicone implants, 147
breast milk, calories in, 112-13
    fat in, 112
    fluctuations of, 111
    frozen, 129
    increasing production, 112-13, 122
    too weak or rich, 145
breasts ache and nipples burn, 136
Brennemann, Dr. Joseph, 135
bridesmaid when nursing, 117-18
Buchanan, Dr. Douglas, 54-55, 102, 108
burping, 133-34
Buzzie, 34-35, 45-49, 64

Caesarian and breast-feeding, 121
calcium, 144-45, 149
cancer and breast-feeding, 79
Cassat, Mary, 150
caseinogen in breast milk, 87
change positions while nursing, 106ff.
Chart to Record Growth and Performance, 54-60
chemistry of mother love, 88
child abuse, 22, 185
child proofing the house, 46-48
children, older, 108
childbirth education, 110
child versus horse training, 5-9
chores for children, 190
Christopher, Dr. Frederick, 139-40
chromosomes, xx and xy, 148
Churchill, Sir Winston, 158
coal bin as playroom, 18
cocktails, 98, 124-25
coitus, 149
colic, 123-26, treatment of, 124-26
colds, in nursery school, 27-28
college grades, 193
compartmentation, & marriage, 66-72
    helps parents self-esteem, 64
    improves sex life, 69-72
    mother more productive, 64-65

too much of it, 186-87
what is it?, 3-4, 34-45
what it can do, 50-51
compartmentized, assertive, 52-53
　better students, 53-54, 193
　have fewer accidents, 53
　learn faster,51-52
　more self-assured, 52
concussion, 101-02
contraceptives&breast-feeding, 144
contractions of uterus, 79
controversy in treatment of the
　breast abscess, 139-41
Cooper's ligaments, 86
constipation in the breast-fed, 135
cot bed in the nursery, 148
crabbing, 160-61
crawling and reading, 62
crib accidents, 15
crib as playpen, 168
crying, length of time, 179-80
　for twenty minutes, 32
　in the playpen, 10-11, 167
　three phases of, 29-32
　when seeing mother, 167
Cunningham, Dr., 77

Dachau concentration camp, 76
danger weeks, 113-15
day care centers, 179-85
Dee Fund, 192
delayed milk, 121-22
dental caries, (breast vs. bottle), 153
deoxyribonucleic acid (DNA), 148
desire to breast-feed, 62, 74-81, 179
developmental, testing, 56-58
　age and need to know, 190-91
developing initiative, 165
diarrhea, treatment of, 77, 134-35
diet, augmenting baby's, 149
　of mother, 135
divorce, 70-72, 173-75, 177
doctors & breast-feeding, 118
dogs, 161
Don't ask your breast-feeding wife how
　she feels, 115-16
ducts, milk, 86

earnings and wages, 193-94
ejection reflex, 98-99,113-14,
　118-19, 124-25, 147, 149
entertaining & breast-feeding,117,126
Episcopal day care center, 181-85

erections while nursing, 149
Evanston Hospital - Woman's
　auxiliary, 131-32
excessive engorgement, 97-98
excessive flow of milk, 120-21
exploring, 46, 157, 165
farm, isolated, 157
failure to nurse because of asphyxia
　and concussion, 101-02
failure to suckle, 100-01
fathers and breast-feeding, 115-17
father under pressure, 109-10, 148
fenced yard, 19-20, 41-43
fences, no fence agreements, 40-44
first day of nursing, 89-93
fishing, 160-61
fluctuations in the amount of
　breast milk, 111-12
fluoridation, 153
formula feeding, 77, 143, 178
four hours of compartmentation,
　why?, 167-68, 187
fourth day of nursing, 99-100
Francis, Babette, 150
Frost, Robert, 33

"gad about bottle", 128, 178
gated porch, 18-19
gates, 16-20
Gaull, Dr. Gerald E., 77
Gerstenberger, Dr. Henry J., 144-45
Gesell, Dr. Arnold, 25
Gesell testing, 1, 54-60, 186-87
Gesell tests affected by
　compartmentation, 1, 40-41
getting even, 162-64
golf widow, 66-69
"good fences make good neighbors",33
grades in H.S. and college, 193-94
grading teachers & aides, 183-84
grandparents, 157, 159
Grulee, Dr. Clifford, 76-77,115,125
guilty feelings about
　compartmentation, 165
Gyorgy, Dr. Paul, 77

hand expression of breast milk, 82ff.
heat, dry, 104, wet, 139-40
high school grades, 193
home from hospital, 108-09,113-15
hooks, 17, 20
horse training, 5-9
hostess, on being one, 119, 126
house, type for preschoolers,18ff,42ff

198 / INDEX

household help, 109-111
hugging older child, 163-64
human milk bank, 129-133
hysteria, 27-32

illness requiring weaning, 141-42
increasing milk production, 112,122ff.
independence, loss of, 36-37
infections, resistance to, 77-78
infidelity, 72, 175-76
institutional amentia, 187
interns' children, 21-22
instructions, mothers following, 113ff.
inverted nipples, 106
iron drops, 154
irritability in toddlers, 157
isolated farm or beach, 157
isolation because of illness, 157-58

Jackson, Dr. Edith, 94
jaundice, 107-108
jealousy, boys and girls, 162-64
Jelliffe, Dr. D.B., 156
Johnnie won't sleep, 1-2
Junior League, 110, 130-33, 174

Karen from Brooklyn, 132
Kimball, family, 194

La Leche League, 69, 73, 110,
    118-20,147,149, 152
labor, losing control in, 101
    too fast, 101
Lactator, 146
lactating indiscretion, 137-39
latch key children, 68, 181
Lawler, Dr. Caroline, 119, 138
Lawrence, Dr. Ruth, 125
learning disability, 102
leash, child on , 23-24
lecithin, 87
let down reflex, 70-71, 98-99
    understanding, 85-86, 117
librarian, nursing, 150
life jackets, 50
lip twisting (horses), 6
longitudinal study, 192-94
lotus eaters, 187
love, dimension of, 79-80, 116

maternal instinct, 87
McElendon, Dr. Preston, 94
meconium, 89
medicine dropper, feeding, 104

medicine & breast-feeding, 144
menopause babies, 188
mental retardation, 102
mind of the mother, 87-88
milk ducts, 86, 91
mine and thine, understanding, 167
mirrors, 159
Montessori, Dr. Maria, 25
Montgomery, Dr. John, 94
Moody fund, 193
mother's complexion, 106
mother love, wildness of, 87-88
mothers-in-law, 109
mothers, observations of, 188-89
    teen aged, 188-89
    who are older, 188-89
    who went to college, 188
moving while nursing, 147
myelination of nerves, 167

Naish, Dr. Charlotte, 99, 128, 140
nannies, 158
natural childbirth, 101
navel, care of, 93
neighborhoods with no fence
    agreements, 42-45
nervous nursing, 174
Newcomb, Dr. Alvah, 131
Newton, Dr. Niles, 99, 149
nightmares, 1-2
nipple, bulbous, 106
    crack in, 102-07
    inverted, 106-07
    manipulation of, 102
    shield, 97
    small, 106
    soreness, 94, 102-07
    that is flat, 96
    white spots on, 107
no-man's land, 157-58
no schedule please, 112-13
nonadaptability, 1-2
nurseries, 157
nursery school, 25-28
    meeting alternate days, 28
nursing, away from home, 126
    dental caries, 153
    during menstruation, 127
    in general, 73
    lying down, 90
    sitting up, 95-96
    with feet over shoulder, 105

one physician's approach to

INDEX / 199

breast-feeding, 74-77
one way vision observation, 180
oral contraceptive & nursing, 144
orgasm, sexual, 149-150
orthodontia for the breast-fed, 79
overachievement,
    a closer look, 61-63
    and compartmentation, 61
    without compartmentation, 62
overfeeding of breast milk, 122
oxytocin, 70-71, 79, 98-99

plastishield, 106
plaque, dental, 153
playpen, as cure for sleep problem, 1ff.
    how to choose one, 10-11
    how to reinforce it, 10-11
    one on top of another, 15, 162
power without brakes, 45-51
Powers, Dr. Grover, 139-40
pottie, 171
praise, 190-191
pregnancy, & breast-feeding, 144-45
    and weaning, 145
premature baby, 133
pressure, on father, 109ff.,115ff., 148
professions, post graduate, 193
prolactin, 70
propylthiouracil, 144
pulling from the breast, 127-28
pump, Egnell, 129-30
    Marshall-Kanesson, 130
pumping and storage of milk, 129
punishment, 190-91
putting your child to bed, 12-15
pyloric stenosis, 142

Ratner, Dr. Herbert, 118-19
reading ability, 62, 192, 194
    learning to and crawling, 62
recompartmentation, how to, 29-32
Reddy, Dr. Nancy, 183
refusal of one breast, 127
rehabilitation of teenagers, 194
reinforcing floor of playpen, 10-11
relaxation, methods of, 98-99
relaxed parents need
    compartmentation, 167
Research Department of Evanston
    Hospital, 192
ritual of going to bed, 13-15, 44-45
Roe, Ann, 157-58
rooming in, 93-95
rope, bringing to mother, 21-23

row boat, 160
running free at two, 167

sabotage, 128
sand for play, 160
schedule, none, 112-13
scholastic test (SAT), 192-93
school, not wanting to go, 181
screen door instead of gate, 16
seat belts, 50
second day of nursing, 95-96
sex life, 69-72
sharing, teaching of, 164, 167, 169
shopping with children, 64-65
single parent, 173-78
skin of the breast-fed, 78-79
Skinner, Dr. Burrhas, Frederic, 14
Skip, 33-45
sleepy baby, 100-01
sleep, how much, 134
socializing & breast-feeding, 117-18
solids, stealing at 6 months, 142-43
sore nipples, 102-07
spanking,
    35ff.,47,49,69,71,162,165ff.
"spoiled brat", 188
spoiling, 147-49, 188
stay in bed when breast-feeding, 115ff.
Stevenson, Dr., 77
stifled by being in a playpen, 165
structural vs. non-structural day
    care, 184
substitutes for compartmentation, 157ff
    suckling failure, 100-02
    strength of, 102
    strong, 104

taurine, 77
teachers, grading them, 183-84
teasing, 7
technique of breast-feeding, 88-89
techniques of resistance and habits of
    disobedience, curing, 51-54
teenage mothers, 189
temper tantrum, 50, 64
terrible twos, 45-49, 182
testosterone, 72
tethering, indoors, 11, outdoors, 21ff.
thalidamide, 82
third day of nursing, 96-97
three days in bed after hospital, 108ff.

thyroid gland, 144
thyroxine, blood level, 144

toilet training, 41, 171-72
too old for playpen, 168
touching, 162-64
toys, 159-61
    dumping on baby, 162
    (Monday box), 159
traveling while nursing, 126, 146
T.V., 170
twins and triplets, breast-feeding, 135ff

underachievement, how long lasting, 61
underfeeding, 121-23
uniqueness of human milk, 77-81, 156

vagina, care of, 93
visit daycare center unannounced, 179ff.
visiting grandparents, 157

want, development of, 30, 159-60
water, need for, 93
weaning from breast, 1, 151-56
weaning, illness requiring, 141-42
weight gain during pregnancy, 82
West, Bishop Hamilton, 181-184
wet heat, 140
wine, 124-25
womanly art of breast-feeding, 73
Women's Auxiliary, 131
Wonder and Glory of Creation, 5-9
working mothers, 150-51

Yale University, 94, 139, 181
young mothers, 188-89
your child's crib, 12-15

SEND FORM BELOW TO: SEA GRAPE
PRESS
BOX 4122
BOCA RATON, FL 33429

Book Costs: 1 $10.95
              2 - 6 $9.95
              7 - 14 $8.95
              15+ $7.95

Chart of Growth and Performance cost: 100 copies @ $12.00

....cut..

Order form:
Please send to:

....
                                                                     your name
....
                                                                     your address
....
                                                                     city, state, zip

Enclosed: @ $............each (times) ___ copies = $____.____
                          There are no shipping or handling charges.

Copies of *A Chart to Record Growth and Performance* are
available in packages of one-hundred for $12.00. $____.____

                                        Total: $____.____

Also please indicate if you are interested in information about a soon to be
released 30 minute video cassette which describes the test for compliance to
the prescription of compartmentation. The more interest the lower the cost.